CHANGES
IN THE
STATE

OTHER RECENT VOLUMES IN THE
SAGE FOCUS EDITIONS

CHANGES IN THE STATE

Causes and Consequences

Edward S. Greenberg
Thomas F. Mayer
editors

SAGE PUBLICATIONS
The International Professional Publishers
Newbury Park   London   New Delhi

For information address:

> SAGE Publications, Inc.
> 2455 Teller Road
> Newbury Park, California 91320
>
> SAGE Publications Ltd.
> 6 Bonhill Street
> London EC2A 4PU
> United Kingdom
>
> SAGE Publications India Pvt. Ltd.
> M-32 Market
> Greater Kailash I
> New Delhi 110 048 India

Printed in the United States of America

Library of Congress Cataloging-in-Publication Data

Changes in the state : causes and consequences / Edward S. Greenberg
    and Thomas F. Mayer, editors.
        p.   cm. -- (Sage focus editions : v. 122)
    "A Publication of the Research Program on Political and Economic
Change, Institute of Behavioral Science, the University of Colorado,
Boulder."
    Includes bibliographical references.
    ISBN 0-8039-3877-2. -- ISBN 0-8039-3878-0 (pbk.)
    1. State, The.   I. Greenberg, Edward S., 1942-   . II. Mayer,
Thomas F. (Thomas Ferdinand), 1937-   .
JC325.C475   1990
320.1--dc20   90-8247
                                                                     CIP

FIRST PRINTING, 1990

Sage Production Editor: Susan McElroy

Contents

Acknowledgment

Special thanks to Jean Umbreit for her enthusiastic assistance in putting this volume together.

PART I

Introduction

1

State Change

Approaches and Concepts

EDWARD S. GREENBERG

There is much talk these days of "theories of the state," "bringing the state back in," and "state-centered" theory. The subject of the state has come to be, in fact, one of the principal foci of scholarly discourse in political science, sociology, economics, and geography. In part, this is a product of the intellectual challenge posed by neo-Marxism in each of these disciplines;[1] partly, this is a product of the seemingly inexorable expansion in the scale and responsibilities of modern states in the First, Second, and Third Worlds and the attempt by scholars to explain this phenomenon. Whatever the cause, debates about the nature of the state and the implications of its activities are now commonplace across several disciplines.

Despite this greater attention, less progress has been made in our overall understanding of the phenomenon of the state than might have been antici-pated. I believe that the lack of greater progress can be traced to three primary factors. First, there is as yet, strangely enough, no general agreement about the meaning of the term "state," the very object of inquiry. This is mainly traceable, in my view, to the unwillingness of proponents of the two main approaches to the subject of the state, Marxian and Weberian, to incorporate the essential aspects of the competing view for fear that with the definition must come all of the other epistemological and political baggage. Marxists

AUTHOR'S NOTE: I would like to thank especially Tom Mayer, Otto Marenin, Bob Ross, and my compatriots in the Political and Economic Change weekly "brown bag" for their incisive critiques of an earlier version of this chapter.

tend to stick to functional and relational concepts, while Weberians focus on the state as an organization and its monopoly of the means of coercion. Second, there is no consensus as yet on the proper conceptual/theoretical approach to be used in the study of the state. Given the general absence of consensus in most areas of concern in the social sciences, this is hardly surprising. Third and finally, scholars from all theoretical schools tend to examine the problematic aspects of the state in more static terms than is warranted. How and why states change, while not entirely ignored in the literature, is simply not often enough at the focus of theoretical and empirical reflection. Since social institutions have change as one of their essential characteristics, approaching them in anything but dynamic terms is of limited value. The purpose of this essay and of the chapters that follow in this book is to address these shortcomings in the theoretical and empirical literature, with particular attention to the understanding of change.

In order to make the exercise more manageable, I confine my attention in this essay to states in capitalist societies. I do so because it is only in capitalist societies where the state is "problematic" in a theoretical sense, given the separation of the political and economic in its prevailing doctrine. In "etatism," to use Branko Horvat's term (Horvat, 1982), the state is everywhere in both empirical and theoretical terms. In capitalist societies, and especially in formally democratic capitalist societies, it is not entirely self-evident why a state exists (since the market is, according to doctrine, a self-correcting institution) or on what grounds state institutions might be legitimated. I confine my attention to states in capitalist societies, moreover, because much of the interesting theoretical and empirical work on the state over the past decade and a half has taken the capitalist state as its subject.[2]

The State

There has been a tendency in the literature, and the Marxian literature in particular, to overly complicate the definition of the state. Frequently in this literature the state is described in terms of its functions, its effects, or its representations. What is all too often absent is a conceptualization of the state as a concrete object or set of concrete objects that can be observed and described.[3] I believe that the best starting point (but not the finishing point) is the Weberian one that conceptualizes the state as an institution or set of institutions that exercises supreme political authority within a geographically defined territory. This supreme political authority implies a monopoly of "legitimate" coercion, administration over a given territory, and the capacity to capture revenues for the support of state activities.[4] From a slightly different vantage point, the state may be understood as constituted by the civil and military bureaucracy (or state apparatus); the government, or those having formal control over the state apparatus (usually organized in branches of one sort or another); and the formal and informal rules of the game that structure the form and operation of both apparatus and government. In viewing the state in such concrete terms, it is still possible to raise questions about the relationship of the state to society, and its constituent classes and groups; it is still possible to ask whether or not the state serves certain essential functions in capitalist societies, and it is still possible to ask about the relative autonomy of the state. Indeed, most of the traditional questions regarding the state in the social sciences, its functions, representations, and effects, remain legitimate subjects of inquiry under the terms of the above definition. The clear advantage, however, is that the Weberian definition gives us a concrete object or set of objects toward which we can direct our inquiries.[5]

Aspects of the State

This general definition remains far too abstract for purposes of research. What remains to be specified are those aspects of the state that are open to change. What is it about the state that changes? Where should one direct one's attention? I would suggest that four aspects of the state ought to be highlighted: its property rules, its regime form, the nature of its apparatus, and its policies. I think about these aspects of the state in terms of the following set of questions:

(1) *What property rules are defined by, articulated in, and protected by the state?* The answer to this question helps us to classify states as capitalist, classical, feudal, or socialist. I use here the classic Marxian approach to the understanding of property rules. That is, if the prevailing forms of property to be protected are those of private property in which individuals and enterprises are free to decide the use of property and enjoy a monopoly on the fruits of its productive use, we are in the presence of a capitalist state. If the main property forms protected by the state involve public control of the uses of property and the collective enjoyment of their fruits, then we may consider the state socialist.[6]

The assumption here is that societies can be described in terms of their basic economic organization; that states in any society tend to articulate, represent, and protect the essentials of the economic organization of society; and that this articulation, representation, and protection takes the form of a set of rules, guidelines, and strictures, whether formal or informal. In Marxian terms, the mode of production that prevails in any society takes concrete form in the state. It follows that the nature of the state cannot be comprehended without taking into account that underlying structure. This suggests that all capitalist states are fundamentally alike, no matter what differences may exist between them in terms of their mode of governance, the organization of their bureaucracies, or the policies they promulgate. The same would be true of all feudal states, or of all socialist states.

Political debate and struggle in most places and at most times simply takes these rules for granted; they are not the stuff of everyday politics. Fundamental economic structures and the rules by which they are guaranteed are not subjected to continuous and contentious challenge in "normal" times. When the economic organization of a society and the rules that protect and nurture that economic organization are up for grabs, such a society is in a revolutionary situation. When the economic organization of a society and the state rules consistent with that economic organization are fundamentally transformed, a revolution has occurred. Normal politics is about choices made within a prevailing mode of production and not about the mode of production itself. A politics of choice between modes of production is the politics of revolution.

(2) *What is the nature of the political regime?* By regime I mean the formal ways in which political power is organized and exercised in any society. In the research literature, there is no consensus on how states ought to be classified in terms of the formal organization of power. Traditional ways of looking at this issue include the distinction between democracy and authoritarianism. Within democracy and authoritarianism, other kinds of distinctions have been made. As to the former, it is possible to talk about direct, face-to-face democracy; representative democracy; majoritarian democracy; plebiscitary democracy; and the like. As to the latter, totalitarianism is often (if not quite accurately) distinguished from simple autocracy in its monarchical or military clique forms. Scholars also classify regimes according to degrees of centralization of power in which unitary regimes are distinguished from federated ones. In the Weberian tradition, regimes are distinguished in terms of the prevailing forms of authority: traditional (authority based upon custom), legal-rational (authority based upon written rules and procedures), and charismatic (authority based upon the unique and nonreproducible qualities of a single leader).

When considering state change in terms of regimes, we concentrate on transformations in the forms by which formal political authority is exercised. Such transformations almost always accompany transformations in property rules, though they can and do take place without disturbing the state as an articulated set of property relations. Indeed, state regime changes are far more common than changes in property relations, even when some form of violence is involved. For example, the American Revolution brought regime change without bringing property rules change. Another way of saying the same thing is that America experienced a political revolution but not an economic/social structural one. Many other examples exist: the Glorious Revolution, which brought parliamentary supremacy in England but left property rules intact; the American imposed constitutional order in postwar Japan; the overthrow of Marcos in the Philippines which brought democratic political forms but left property relations untouched; and the like. Many have even argued that National Socialism in Germany brought fundamental change in regime form but left property rules pretty much as they were, though this remains an issue that has not yet been resolved (Mayer & Pois, this volume; Neumann, 1942).

(3) *What is the nature of the bureaucratic apparatus and its role in society?* It is by now a commonplace that all modern societies, and most not so modern ones as well, are highly bureaucratized. In modern capitalist societies, bureaucratization characterizes much of the private sector as well as the public sector. By bureaucracy, following Weber, I mean a hierarchically ordered set of offices in which full-time officials, appointed on the basis of specialized training and qualifications, work on specialized narrow tasks guided by impersonal, written rules of procedure.[7] There is a vast literature, of course, on the causes of bureaucratization; there is an equally vast literature lamenting the existence of bureaucracy as the prevailing structural form of administrative activity. Neither of them has much to say about state change.

In considering state change at this level, it is best to focus on the elements of the Weberian definition set out above. Our attention ought to be upon changes in the designation and organization of offices; on changes in the grounds for recruitment of officials; on changes in the nature of the tasks they perform; and on changes in the rules that guide the actions of officials and their agencies. Consideration of change ought to focus, as well, on the relationship of the apparatus to the other elements of the state: its property rules, its regime form, its government, and its policies. In the vast literature on the executive branch in the American system in political science, for instance, great attention is paid to the forms and degrees of control of elected officials over administrative agencies, with the potential for bureaucratic autonomy at the fulcrum. The manner in which policies formulated by elected officials are altered by agencies as they administer the law has been another subject of great interest. This notion of administrative officials as policy-makers and quasi-independent actors is now quite common in the literature. State-centric scholars (whose work will be reviewed below) have been particularly interested in the capacities of states as exemplified by the size and quality of the bureaucratic apparatus.

While state change in terms of property rules and regime form is rare (with the former being extremely rare), the change in a range of aspects concerning the apparatus is quite common, which is why such a vast literature exists about it.[8] What is generally missing, however, are systematic efforts to tie the hierarchy of offices, the nature of specializations, and the rules of operations of the state apparatus to underlying social forces and structures, though there are some important exceptions to this observation (Alford & Friedland, 1985; Clark & Dear, 1984; Therborn, 1978). These relationships, so important for understanding changes in the state apparatus, remain elusive and more work clearly is called for.

(4) *What are the general outlines of public policy?* What does the state do and why does it do what it does? This aspect of state change is the most visible, so it is hardly surprising that the literature on the state tends to be concentrated in this area. This is the stuff of everyday political life that fills the newspapers, journals of opinion, and news broadcasts. It is about the actions of presidents, prime ministers, legislators, judges, and agency officials. It is about changes in broad policy domains (e.g., defense, civil liberties, education, social welfare, labor relations, and the like) and about specific policy actions and decisions. As we shall see below, most of the theoretical and empirical material of the past several decades has been engaged in explaining how and why state policy changes. The debates between pluralists and elitists, for instance, or between structuralist and instrumentalist Marxists, are precisely over how to explain the actions and policies of governmental leaders. I will have much more to say about these matters below.

Concepts of Change in
Theories of the State

Having described the elements of the capitalist state that require attention when examining state change—property rules, regime type, bureaucratic apparatus, and policy—I now consider the three main approaches to the study of the state in the social sciences and how each of these approaches understands change. In the remainder of this essay, I will sketch how each of these

Table 1.1 Conceptual Organization of State Change Discussion

Theoretical Approaches	Elements of the State			
	Property Rules	Regime	Apparatus	Policy
Citizen-Responsive				
Capitalist State				
State-Centric				

approaches conceptualizes the state, consider how each understands change, and explore the plausibility of each in illuminating state change. I will present summary models of each tradition, simplified characterizations that I hope will capture the principal insights of each, and allow us to identify analytical strengths and weaknesses. This short essay will not be an exhaustive survey of the literature nor will it capture the many nuances, complexities, and debates within each tradition.

Przeworski (1988) observes that most of the writing on the capitalist state tends to revolve around three nodes: (1) the preferences of citizens; (2) the preferences and interests of state officials; and (3) the requirements of capitalism and the interests of the dominant economic class. A similar three-part differentiation of the state literature is suggested by Alford and Friedland in their important work *Powers of Theory* (Alford & Friedland, 1985) when they speak of capitalism, bureaucracy, and democracy as the three defining processes at work in modern society, evident, as well, in state processes and structure. My own organization of the literature divides into a similar three-part categorization: (1) the Citizen-Responsive State literature, which itself encompasses a range of approaches including pluralism, corporatism, mass movements, and voting and public opinion-centered theories of state activity; (2) the Capitalist State or Marxist and neo-Marxist literature; and (3) the State-Centric literature.[9] The discussion in the remainder of this essay focuses on state change as seen through the eyes of these three theoretical models. (See Table 1.1).

I will argue that each of the state theoretic positions has, in Alford and Friedland's terms, a "home domain" in terms of the state and in terms of change where it is most comfortable and convincing. Each focuses on only some aspects of the state, leaving others untheorized, and considers only some forms of change while ignoring others. This natural tendency to focus on only a part of the picture leaves significant lacunae in each approach that can be at least partially filled by insights from the other approaches.

What follows then is a speculative essay in which I try to characterize the essential understandings of state change in each of the three major theoretical approaches extant in the literature. In the course of this speculation, I hope to identify where each approach is most convincing and where each is least convincing; to tease out understandings of state change within each tradition that have been largely unarticulated but which seem to be implicit in the approach, and to show where insights from one approach can help fill in some of the gaps of other approaches to state change. I hope to demonstrate that none of the approaches, taken alone, can capture the richness and complexity of the capitalist state. Only by joining the insights of each is it possible to gain a handle on the subject of state change. My goal is to establish that the capitalist state can be constrained, autonomous, and responsive at the same.

The Citizen-Responsive State Model

I use the designation "citizen-responsive state" to indicate that theoretical approach which locates the sources of state action in the articulated demands of popular majorities or intense minorities, and in the need for public officials to respond to such demands as the price for their retention of power or office.[10] This need for officials to be responsive to the preferences of its citizens is sometimes evident even in nondemocratic capitalist states where formal democratic mechanisms like free elections and legalized labor unions are unavailable. Despite this disclaimer, when thinking about the citizen-responsive state literature I am thinking primarily of the pluralist and voter-centered literature in the social sciences that pertains to formally democratic societies.[11]

The key relationship at the center of this literature is the one between the citizen and the public official; at some point, it is assumed, the changing preferences of citizens come to be reflected in the changing behavior of public officials. In the long run, the changing behavior of officials comes to be reflected in changes in public policy. A diagram of this process may be found in Figure 1.1.

The home domain of the citizen-responsive state literature is the relationship between individual preferences (of voters, interest group members, or public officials) and public policy. Its scholarly mission has been to explain the origins and transmission of preferences and how the actions of state officials are explained by them. It is assumed in this literature that commitment to the basic property rules of society is given in any stable society, and not subject to the political process. The regime is also taken as given, with

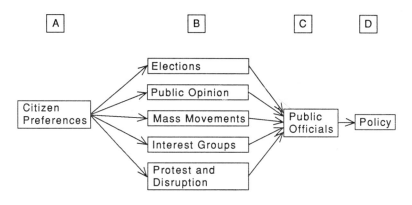

Change in A is transmitted to public officials C through B,
resulting in changes in D. The form of change is incremental.

Figure 1.1. The Citizen-Responsive State Model

consensus on the so-called "rules of the game" of a democratic society what makes settled political life possible at all (Alford & Friedland, 1985; Carnoy, 1984; Dahl, 1961).

Political institutions, including the state bureaucracy, are generally conceptualized in two ways. First, institutions are seen as the precipitate of the political conflict and bargaining process, the place where victories, defeats, and compromises are recorded, and where the machinery for carrying out agreed upon policy is constructed. It is an understanding of state institutions as epiphenomenal, the resultant of other forces. Second, state institutions also are sometimes seen as a multifaceted set of agencies and bureaus that are themselves active participants in the political process. Because of the plurality of the apparatus, it is difficult to administer policy coherently. If each is on its own or is part of some alliance—iron triangles, issue networks, and the like (Heclo, 1978; Lowi, 1969; Ripley, 1976)—then it is hard for a chief executive to get all of the relevant bureaus and agencies on the team. It is for this reason that much of the citizen-preference state literature focuses on the problem of exercising control over the bureaucracy. The bureaucratic apparatus, then, is understood as a pluralistic and open structure and not in holistic or unitary terms as is often the case with scholars working within the state-centric tradition.

Change

The conception of change that is central to this literature is *incremental*. Incremental change is change that comes in small steps that does not involve change in underlying institutions or structures. Change is about small adaptations to problems and opportunities that, even when they accumulate, do not alter the way we would describe the entity being observed. Change, in neoclassical economic terms, is at the margins, representing a conception of continuity in the historical process (North, 1981, p. 62). In this view, the best predictor of institution I or behavior I at time $T^x + 1$ is T^x. Thus it is argued in the classic work on the U.S. budget process by Wildavsky (1974) that the best way to predict the size and commitments in any budget year is the size and commitments of the budget in the previous year.

What Changes?

The model of state change in the citizen-responsive literature involves four basic elements: changes in citizen preferences, mechanisms for the transmission of preferences to state actors, the behavior of state actors, and the translation of official behavior into policy. Property rules and the regime are untheorized and remain outside of the model. Directionality in the model is primarily from citizen preferences, through transmission mechanisms, to state actors, and to public policy (see Figure 1.1). I discuss sources of change in each of the elements of the model below.

A. *Change in citizen preferences.* For the most part, the causes of change in the structure of citizen preferences are exogenous to the theory; change in preference structures, that is to say, is untheorized. While change in social and economic structures is often alluded to by scholars working in this tradition,[12] such change is not an integral part of the overall theory of state responsiveness to citizens. All that it is necessary to know in the model is that citizen preferences do, in fact, change, not why they change. Thus, the main data needed to explain public policy, according to Wildavsky (1974), are such things as "the contemporary climate of opinion," or "the pressing and recognized needs of the times . . . obvious to all." Nor does the citizen-preference state model care much about the content of preferences. All that is essential to the approach is that preferences be transmitted to public officials in some manner, regardless of their origins or content. The only way to judge whether the system works or not is to measure the closeness of fit between preferences and policy.

A few words are in order about the term preferences. First, I use it here in a rather loose sense and mean to include both short-term opinion change and long-term value change. The latter, of course, is less likely to occur than the former.

Second, I have already suggested that most scholars working within this tradition assume that shifting preferences on the political issues of the day take place within a broad societal consensus concerning property rules and the nature of the regime. Nevertheless, since the sources and content of preference change are not theorized, there is nothing in this tradition that would preclude the possibility that citizen preferences might at some point come to call the fundamentals into question. There are the seeds, then, in the citizen-responsive state approach for incorporating nonincremental change, those seeds have not sprouted in this literature.

Third and finally, the model assumes a long-run congruence between citizen preferences and official behavior and policy in a democratic society because the public, in the long run, is the key in this model to the maintenance of office and power. The model is thus generally unprepared to incorporate the tendency among state actors to go their own way, in service of their own interests. The model is also unprepared to incorporate situations in which officials are unable to respond to public preferences because of the constraints of the economy or of the power of privileged social groups and classes. For these, we must look to other models.

B. *Transmission mechanisms.* The particular forms of transmission mechanism that are available for linking citizen preferences to state actors are what largely determine the kind of regime we are talking about. Mechanisms for the transmission of preferences include elections, interest groups, mass social movements, protest, and noncooperation/noncompliance. It is generally agreed that regimes which carry the designation democratic contain all the above mechanisms; autocratic regimes might only have protest and noncoperation/noncompliance available.

None of these mechanisms ever work at 100% efficiency in transmitting citizen preferences, of course. Indeed, much of the work in the political science discipline is devoted to studies of these mechanisms (e.g., voting, elections, lobbying, protest movements) with an eye toward specifying where and to what extent each is defective as a transmission mechanism.

It ought to be noted that each of the transmission mechanisms under consideration here has its own history; each changes, as it were. Political scientists, for instance, have devoted a great deal of attention to the task of identifying changes in the system of elections in the United States and elsewhere (e.g., formal requirements, turnout, partisanship, outcomes); in the patterning of the interest group universe (e.g., the rise and fall of interest groups, the development of corporatism, the changing role of Political Action Committees [PACs] in the United States). Sociologists and others have done the same for mass movements and protest.

It ought to be further noted that, for the most part, the citizen-preference state literature pays little attention to the issue of what might be called patterned, differential power. Power, in the pluralist variant of the tradition, for instance, is seen as fluid, and not the property of any set of groups or classes. Power is, in the pluralist view, nonhierarchical in the long run, differentiated in terms of the particular matters at issue in the political arena, and based on a wide range of distributed resources that cannot be monopolized by any sector of society. Such a reading of power is, of course, a very innocent one that would be well served by an encounter with the structural focus of the capitalist-state model.

C. *Political actors.* In the citizen-preference state model, there is no state *as such* in democratic societies, only public officials and aspiring public officials who, at some point and in the long run, change their behavior in order to conform to citizen preferences as transmitted to them through one or more of the mechanisms described briefly above. There seem to be at least two reasons why actual or potential officials do so. First, being members of the same society and subject to many of the same dislocations, problems, and trends felt by their fellow citizens, political actors change their own preferences in ways that are congruent with the population. Second and more importantly, being rational calculators who wish to stay in office, exercise power, and achieve their own goals, political actors are forced to be responsive whatever their own preferences might be because the population is in a position, in this model, to affect their future. On issues where no clear public opinion exists, or where interest groups are silent, state actors naturally have a great deal of leeway.

In democratic regimes, citizens have some power over the ability of political actors to stay in office either directly through elections or indirectly through interest group activity (by means of campaign contributions, grassroots mobilization, and the like). As rational calculators, however, political actors respond mainly to those individuals and groups that are potentially the most influential in their ability to stay in or achieve office. Thus, it is inescapably the case that, even in formal democracies, significant inequalities in material resources will be translated into differential political power. We have here the classic Schattsneiderian problem of the heavenly chorus "singing with its upper class accent." (Schattsneider, 1960). On this issue of structural inequalities and their effects, the citizen-preference state tradition is essentially mute, though some of its leading lights have begun a major rethinking of this issue (Dahl, 1985; Lindblom, 1977; Manley, 1983).

Even political actors in nondemocratic regimes sometimes may be responsive to popular preferences in the interests of maintaining social peace and legitimacy, and of maintaining the necessary cooperation for economic growth. More often, however, such regimes will only symbolically respond to preferences, deflect popular grievances onto foreign and domestic "scapegoats," or, as a last resort, turn to coercion. While such responses often occur in democratic regimes as well, their incidence is significantly less.

D. *State policy.* If the transmission mechanisms are properly functioning, state policy in this tradition is simply the reflection, in the long run, of the preferences of citizens. "In the long run" is an important phrase and helps differentiate scholars working in this tradition from others. Thus, neither state-centric nor capitalist state scholars would deny that there are occasions when citizen preferences and policy are congruent. Where they part company is on the question of the long-run, fundamental causal factor explaining state policy: in the state-centric model, it is the interests of state actors that is primary; in the capitalist state model, it is the needs of an economically dominant class or of capitalism in general that is determinative. In the citizen-preference state model, the long-run match between preferences (when they exist) and policy is given; there is little appreciation of what Marxists call "constraints," limits on what is possible or for the potential autonomy of officials from popular preferences.

The Capitalist State Model

The capitalist state model is a summary statement of the Marxist and neo-Marxist literature on the state. The central question posed in this diverse literature is the following: Why are states in capitalist societies capitalist states?[13] Scholars and writers working in this tradition believe that the nature of any state must be first and foremost located in the dominant economic and social arrangements of the society in which it is located. Thus a state in a feudal society is inescapably a feudal state. A state in a slave society is inescapably a slave-oriented state. In a society where capitalism is the dominant social form, it is simply taken as axiomatic that capitalist property rules are at the core of the state, and that the behavior of public officials and the policies they promulgate and administer serve either to advance the interests of the dominant capitalist class[14] or to preserve and protect the capitalist system as a whole. The model assumes that any congruence that

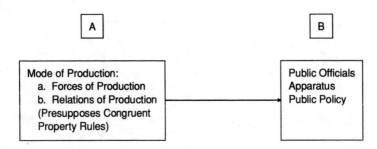

Change in A is reflected in changes in B. B changes either because of the actions of the capitalist class (instrumentalism), or the requirements of system maintenance and reproduction (structuralism), or the balance of political power between classes (class struggle school). The forms of change are either developmental stages or transformative.

Figure 1.2. The Capitalist State Model

might exist between popular preferences and state action is either limited to those occasions and those issues where capitalist class interests or the needs of capitalism as a whole are not engaged, or are the product of the manipulation of popular preferences when they are engaged. As to the tendency for public officials to go their own way in the service of their own interests, a position that is so prominent in the state-centric tradition, this can only be a short-run and exceptional phenomenon. It is assumed that in the long run, the state can only act in ways that favor capitalism and capitalists. It is also recognized, of course, that even within this imperative, there is much room for maneuver on the specifics of policy.

Change

The primary focus of change in this model is in the deep structures of society; state organization and action reflects, in the end, the underlying socioeconomic system. Change in deep structures is the causal factor; state change—whether involving property rights, regime, bureaucratic apparatus, or policy—is an outcome of structural change (see Figure 1.2). State change, that is to say, is the dependent variable in the equation; the independent variables are structural ones.

What, then, is the nature of this deep structure that changes? In the Marxian tradition, deep structure is defined in terms of two elements: the forces of production and the relations of production. Taken together, the forces and relations of production form the essential substructure or foundation of society upon which all else is built; together they determine all of the important aspects of society, including the state. As they change, which it is in their nature to do, all else in society changes accordingly.

The forces of production may be defined as those things that make production possible in any historical period. The forces of production are, as it were, the raw materials of the productive process. These would include what are called the material means of production (e.g., machines, land, resources, factories), as well as labor power. Labor power, in this formula, includes, in addition to sheer effort, the craft and the technological and scientific know-how or knowledge used in putting the means of production into motion.[15]

The relations of production are the fundamental forms of social organization by which the surplus created by the production process is extracted and appropriated. These fundamental social forms, in the Marxian view, always involve relations of domination and subordination based on the differential control over the means of material production. In more prosaic terms, we are speaking here of opposed social classes, one that dominates and lives off of the labor of others, and one that labors and receives back for its own sustenance less than it produces. In capitalism it is the wage system and the production of surplus value that is the basis for the unequal and exploitive relationship that exists between classes.

The state, in this model, is a reflection of and arises out of this basic division between social classes. In capitalism, the state exists, as it were, to maintain the capitalist accumulation process generated by the interaction of the forces and relations of production, to protect the class system upon which the accumulation process is constructed, and to serve the interests of the dominant capitalist class. Class division and capitalist class domination in this model is fundamentally and inescapably inscribed into the very nature of the state, and is reflected in legal property rules, regime form, the nature of the bureaucratic apparatus, and public policy.

Competing Conceptions of the Causes of Change

The fundamental cause of state change, in the capitalist state model, it follows, is change in either the forces or relations of production, or both. It is not entirely clear, however, how changes in the forces of production are translated into state change in the Marxian literature. The same cannot be said for the relations of production. In the literature that the model summarizes, the change in social class composition, consciousness, and relations with other classes and their relationship to the state receives a great deal of attention. Within that literature, however, there remains deep disagreements about the nature of the causal linkages between deep structures and classes and the state. The disagreements tend to congregate around three theoretical nodes. These three are conventionally designated the instrumentalist, the structuralist, and the class struggle approaches.

A. *The instrumentalist approach.* To the question "Why do states in capitalist societies act like capitalist states?" instrumentalists respond that the dominant capitalist class has both the need and the resources to directly influence the state to do its bidding.[16] In the end, this class controls the government and the political process, and writes the rules of the game. Political domination by the economically dominant class is inescapable in any social system. This conceptualization rejects the citizen-responsive state view that the state is somehow a reflection of popular will or of the general interest. Capitalist class political power is exercised in a variety of ways in formally democratic systems: filling high elective and appointive offices; controlling political parties, candidates, and electoral campaigns; molding public opinion; dominating the interest group system; and more (Miliband, 1969).

The state changes in the instrumentalist view as the needs and interests of the capitalist class change. The needs and interests of the capitalist class change as capitalism itself changes, alternately creating problems in the accumulation process, or encouraging subordinate classes and groups to challenge their domination. At its most extreme, in the so-called literature of Corporate Liberalism (Greenberg, 1985; Kolko, 1967; Wiebe, 1967; Weinstein, 1968), even reforms that seem to help subordinate classes (e.g., legalized collective bargaining, social insurance, social welfare), are interpreted as the outcomes of prescient reform advocated by the most farsighted leaders of the capitalist class in order to deflate popular anger and channel it into safe channels.

B. *The structuralist approach.* In this view, the state reflects the systematic and inescapable needs of capitalism because the role of the state is to ensure the reproduction of capitalism and its social relations of production. Most structuralist arguments on the state are functional in form: since capitalism requires x for it to survive and prosper, the state must necessarily do x (Cohen, 1978). Unlike "instrumentalists" whose scholarship is directed at unearthing the linkages between the capitalist class and the state, "structuralists" have been mainly concerned with identifying the tensions and contradictions in capitalism and impediments to the accumulation process (Wright, 1978), and showing how the behavior of state officials and public policy address such tensions, contradictions, and impediments. The implication is that they are not free to choose, or they are free to choose only within very narrow boundaries. Analysis takes the form of examining the capitalist mode of production and its requirements, that is to say, and not the personal biographies of state actors. Because the state must respond to problems in capitalism, it must, in order to preserve the whole, often act independently from the capitalist class and the narrow interests of some of its members, thus the debate over the "relative autonomy" of the state.

State change in the structuralist view, then, may be understood as a reflection of the changing functional requirement of capitalism. Because modern capitalism in non-self-correcting, the state must intervene to correct, manage, and guide it if it is to survive (Habermas, 1975; O'Connor, 1973; Offe, 1975; Poulantzas, 1973). The problems that tend to recur during the history of the capitalist accumulation process include the falling rate of profit, overproduction and stagnation, diseconomies that undermine the accumulation process, working class mobilization, fiscal crisis, and more. The point to be made here is that the state responds to problems and crises thrown up by the capitalist accumulation process. The sources of state change, that is to say, are located in changes generated by underlying economic and social processes.

C. *The class struggle approach.* In this view, while the state primarily reflects the needs and interests of the capitalist class in the long run, officials are constrained in what they are able to do for this class by the waxing and waning political power of the working class. The capitalist class and state actors, in this view, must make accommodations to the working class in those periods when the working class is strong and politically mobilized. Past working class success takes concrete form in state policy and in the creation of agencies and bureaus in the bureaucratic apparatus that administer such policies. Even in periods of working class decline, that is to say, residues of policy and bureaucratic organization remain a part of state policy and the state apparatus.[17]

The location of state change, then, is tied to the ever-shifting contest between social classes. This contrasts with the instrumentalist view that the sources of change may be located in the shifting interests of the capitalist class, and the structuralist view that they are located in the accumulation process.

The Forms of Change

Besides different conceptions of the causes of change, the capitalist state/Marxian literature talks about two essential forms that change may take: developmental stages and crisis and transformation.

A. *Developmental stages.* In this kind of change, a particular mode of production progresses through determinant stages of development (e.g., from small unit competitive to concentrated capitalism, for instance, in the capitalist mode of production); the state responds to the new requirements and power relations of each stage by transforming its own policies and the bureaucratic apparatus that administers policy. The capitalist state, for instance, goes through its own stages of development (e.g., from laissez-faire to managed capitalism) that correspond to the developmental stages within the mode of production. Marxian scholars are not entirely agreed on the nature of these stages, but that stages exist remains unquestioned.[18] Developmental stages for the state within a mode of production, it should be added, refers to changes in regime (rare), the behavior of state actors, policy, and the organization of the apparatus. Because we are within the boundaries of a mode of production, however, the fundamental property rules remain intact.

B. *Crisis and Transformation.* In classical Marxism, when the contradictions between the forces and relations of production become too great, and/or when the conflict between social classes can no longer be contained, the mode of production is itself transformed and transcended. The change from one mode of production to another is such a fundamental and inexorable historical process that existing states cannot, in the end, prevent its occurrence. States no longer have the option, that is to say, of reforming themselves into new developmental stages with the ability to deflect or moderate contradictions. Needless to say, a new mode of production must bring with it an entirely new state, embodying entirely new property rules.[19]

The State-Centered or State-Centric Model

This model embodies a popular new literature that has called for "bringing the state back in" to the analysis of the political (see Figure 1.3). The model rejects both citizen-preference and capitalist state models because of their overreliance on societal factors outside of the state itself for explaining the nature and activities of the state. In the state-centric model, it is argued that the state is not a reflection of social forces whether these forces be voters, groups, classes, or even capitalism, but must be understood in its own right,

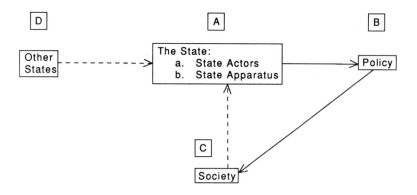

Change in the preferences, interests, and power of state actors as well as changes in state capacities (A) leads to changes in state policy. State policy (B) reshapes society. The state (A) is relatively free from (is autonomous) the influence of society (C). Change in A is either internal to itself or is, on occasion, induced by the actions of other states (D).

Figure 1.3. The State-Centric State Model

as an autonomous entity with its own interests and goals, and with its own capacities to achieve them. At a minimum, in this view, the state "may formulate and pursue goals that are not simply reflective of the demands or interests of social groups" (Skocpol, 1985, p. 9); at the maximum, it may sometimes totally recast the fundamental economic, political, and social structures of society (Krasner, 1984; Trimberger, 1978). The state, that is to say, is not the whim of society or economy but an independent and powerful entity capable not only of holding off powerful social forces, but of imposing its own vision and goals on them.[20]

The home domain of the model encompasses, then, state institutions, state actors, and state actions in the form of policies promulgated and administered. Classes, groups, voters, and economic arrangements are background variables for the calculation of officials and operations of the apparatus. "To bring the state back in" is not, however, a very substantial theoretical guide to those working within this tradition. It is but an admonition to take the state and its institutions and personnel seriously. As a result, state-centric scholars are literally all over the map, and bring a wide diversity of objects under their microscopes for investigation. Out of this diverse literature, one can identify three main tendencies: state actors, the rules of the game, and the system as a whole.

As to state actors, the model conceptualized elected and bureaucratic officials as participants in the political process who seek to advance their own interests or the interests of their agency or institution, and who have a variety of tools to advance their own interests. The model suggests that such actors are relatively free from societal influence because the state, with its monopoly of force and administration, makes important political resources available to its functionaries and officials.[21] Others working within the state-centric model attribute great explanatory power to the "rules of the game" in structuring the nature of politics and processes of governance in society. Katznelson, for instance, suggests that "American exceptionalism" may be explained in large part as the outcome of the way constitutional rules like federalism and a winner-take-all district electoral system structure the struggle between social classes (1985). Finally, there are those who talk of the state in holistic terms, as an entity in its own right. Debates among this branch of the state-centric camp speak of degrees of stateness and state capacities, defined usually in bureaucratic and administrative terms. Talk of weak and strong states is typical (Katzenstein, 1978; Krasner, 1978; Levi, 1981; Nettl, 1968; Nordlinger, 1981; Rueschemeyer & Evans, 1985; Stepan, 1978).

While it does not talk of them in a consistent or theoretically convincing way, the state-centric model is not entirely silent about property rules and regimes. For the most part, they remain either background variables, helping to shape the settings in which the rational calculations of state actors take place, or their transformation may even become, in very rare instances, the objects of attention of officials committed to "reform from above" (Trimberger, 1978).

The state-centric model represents an important corrective to extremist expressions of "society-centered" models in which the state seems to lack any autonomy, officials are devoid of choices, and the apparatus has no independent effect. Any attempt to give the state its proper due is to be commended. To the extent, however, that the state-centric model consigns social, economic, and political factors to background variables, the state to that extent becomes reified and is given an analytic burden it cannot hope to carry.

Change

The influence of societal forces is downplayed in the state-centric model; the state itself is at the center of the explanatory system, though it is often affected by other states and socioeconomic developments. Change, in the end, comes primarily from factors that reside in the state itself. Change in societal factors is not absent; it is simply filtered through the institutions of the state. The state is autonomous; it is capable of responding to societal forces in ways that are consistent with its own interests or even of imposing its own objectives on society.

The analysis of change, then, focuses on the state. Change in state policy may derive, for instance, from a situation in which state officials decide to move to achieve some goal. Why actors may hold certain goals or how they might go about selecting among conflicting goals is left untheorized. All that is important in the model is that state actors have objectives, the power to achieve at least some of them, and a willingness on their part to try to do so. The literature gives no theoretical primacy to any particular part of the process or to any particular objective. Some may act on the basis of their changing conception of the national interest or on their changing estimate of what is necessary to serve the national interest (Krasner, 1978); others may act based on rational calculations of the best manner of extracting revenues from the population (Levi, 1981); still others find that their actions are defined by the need to fend off the threat of other states (Skocpol, 1979); yet others choose to transform the social and economic orders themselves, as in Nazi Germany, post-Allende Chile, and Peru (Trimberger, 1978). Why state actors may choose one over the other is not explained. In terms of the model, it does not matter. The objectives of public officials are not theoretically derived. They simply exist.[22]

Changes in state capacities, so central a factor in the model, also are essentially untheorized. The rise of strong states, for instance, is sometimes attributed not only to the choices of public officials who have an interest in enhancing the tools of their power, but to trends and tendencies in society that seem to contribute inexorably to the growth, reach, and power of states: industrialization, computerization, technical complexity, rationalization, centralization, and planning (Alford & Friedland, 1985; Bell, 1973; Dahrendorf, 1959). All of these historical trends, it is argued, contribute to the ability of states to control given territories, to extract resources from its population, to wage war with other nations, and to manage tools of legitimation on a national scale. How to weigh the relative contribution of each of these factors remains unspecified in the model.

Research Dialogues

The power of theoretical models lies in their capacity to focus our attention on a narrow range of phenomena, allowing us to subject them to searching

Table 1.2 Domains of Models of the State

Change	Aspects of the State			
	Property Rules	Regime	Apparatus	Policy
Incremental			SC	CR
			cs	sc
Developmental Stages		cs	cs	CS
				cr
Crisis Transformation	CS	cs	cs	CS
	sc	sc	sc	sc

CAPS =   home domain
lower case = theoretical forays
CR =   citizen-responsive state model
CS =   capitalist state model
SC =   state-centric model

scrutiny. The weakness of theoretical models is the flip side of their strength: their tendency to ignore phenomena that might be of some import in a practical or theoretical sense. The models reviewed in these pages partake of the normal strengths and weaknesses of the species. They are powerful and illuminating in some respects and limited and deficient in others. Each has a home domain where it is particularly persuasive; each has what might be called a foreign domain where it hardly ventures because it knows little of the landscape or the language. In Table 1.2, I present, by way of summarizing the material presented in these pages and specifying where future research might take us, where each of the theoretical models is at home, where each makes tentative forays, and where each stays away. The table charts each of the models in terms of the two principal concerns of this essay: aspects of the state and change.

There is no space in this essay to make a major foray into the thorny epistemological question of why each of these traditions can be said to have a home domain where it is most comfortable and convincing. The question, moreover, is dealt with at great length by others (Alford & Friedland, 1985). The usual argument is that one theoretical tradition cannot venture onto the terrain of other theoretical traditions without doing damage to its own fundamental assumptions. I would suggest, however, that such an argument is seriously overstated. At any rate, to stake out such a position on a priori grounds without testing its veracity in practice is inappropriate.

A number of things become immediately evident from an examination of Table 1.2. First, we can see that the debate about the state is joined mainly with respect to the policy aspects of the state. Each of the models is most comfortable in this domain, and offers there its most impressive and penetrating scholarship. While no consensus has yet emerged regarding the nature of policy in capitalist states, it is interesting that it is in this area of research one finds the most important intermodel dialogue and cross-fertilization—class fractions as a type of pluralism in the work of Poulantzas, rational choice concepts migrating to Marxism, elements of class entering into the work of leading pluralists like Dahl and Linkblom, state-centric insights on the independent behavior of state officials influencing the work of so-called "post-Marxists" like Fred Block, and so on. The lesson here is that where the issues are joined, one is most likely to find theoretical cross-fertilization. The results support my contention that the strictures against collaboration between theoretical traditions is unwarranted.

Second, it is evident that the prevailing models of the state in the social sciences have very little to say about the property rule basis of the capitalist state (with the notable exception of the capitalist state model, which simply assumes its importance) or about the nature of regimes. While the state-centric model is most at home with respect to the state apparatus, neither of the other two models is comfortable there nor has much to say. It follows, in my view, that scholars working within each of these theoretical traditions must shift focus in such a way that aspects of the state normally outside of the home domain are drawn under the conceptual microscope, as it were. Capitalist state scholars must come to grips with regime forms and the bureaucratic apparatus; state-centric scholars must do better with respect to the property rule basis of the state (and the constraints it imposes) and the nature of the regime. Citizen-responsive state scholars must loosen their grip on policy issues, and confront aspects of the state having to do with the bureaucracy, regime, and property rules. It is only by doing so, I believe, that each of the models will be able to transcend their perceptual lacunae and enter into a dialogue that will have payoffs equivalent to the dialogue on what the state does and why it does it (policy).

Third and finally, each of the models must attempt to venture onto a different terrain on the subject of change. The capitalist state model, for instance, is essentially silent about incremental change, while the state-centric and citizen-responsive state models are mute when it comes to stage/development and crisis/transformation forms of change. Each of these forms of change are ubiquitous in the history of the human species and our institutions, and it does no credit to the models here under review that they have tended to ignore important aspects of the operations of states.

While venturing onto foreign terrain away from the comfort of home domains will not guarantee the emergence of a consensus, it will generate dialogue and debate that can only sharpen and improve each of the models. Advances similar to those already evident in the area of policy mentioned above can be expected to be achieved in other areas related to state change. In saying this, I do not mean to underestimate the difficulties involved. Nor do I believe that such forays will be done in precisely the same way or come up with the same results as traditional approaches. I simply suggest that theoretical understanding demands that we go some distance in this direction.

Essays in This Volume

The essays in this volume have been written with the aim of contributing to this ongoing dialogue on the state. Each of them tackles an important theoretical issue; each ventures outside of the comfortable confines of its theoretical home domain; and each tries to say something about state change. The essays in Part II focus on the fundamental relationships between state and society (understood above as property rules). The essays in Part III focus on state institutions (or regime and apparatus). The essays in Part IV are about state policy, or what the state does.

Part II

In his essay "The Two-Tiered Theory of the State: Resolving the Question of Determination for the Case of the Local State," Mark Gottdiener argues that a theoretical distinction must be made between two aspects of the state. The first is the state as protector and embodiment of a distinct set of property rules and relations. The second is the state as policymaker and actor responsive to labor, capital, and state managers. The first defines the nature of the state; the second highlights what the state does. The first is the realm of determination; the second is the realm of contingency. The first changes rarely; the second is in constant motion. By making this theoretical distinction, Gottdiener shows how change can be quite dramatic in the second-tier without having any discernible effects on first-tier relations. This distinction between what the state is and what it does is then used to illuminate some pressing issues in the recent actions of local governments in the United States.

Thomas Mayer and Tracy Mott, in their essay "Effective Demand and Structural Dependence of the State," address first-tier (to use Gottdiener's term) issues concerning the fundamental nature of the capitalist state by confronting and refuting the well-known Przeworski and Wallerstein argument that the capitalist state is not structurally dependent on capitalism. Using the same formal methods as Przeworski and Wallerstein, Mayer and Mott lend credence to the argument that the capitalist state is structurally linked to capitalism and its dominant class.

Thomas Mayer and Robert Pois present an account of the rise of the Nazi state and the nature of its rule in their essay "Structure and Consciousness in the Rise of the Nazi State." Their story of the Nazi state is a nuanced one that avoids the simplifications of the familiar deterministic and voluntaristic ones that prevail in the literature. They trace the rise of the Nazi state to the fundamental tension between capitalist accumulation and political democracy in a sharply class-divided society. The direction taken by the Nazi state once in power, they suggest, was largely defined by ideologically structured forms of consciousness that ultimately led to disaster. Their essay focuses our attention on the changing nature of the relationship between the Nazi state and capitalism, showing us that it was not an entirely unambiguous one.

Part III

Russell Hanson's attention is on the process of state building in the United States during the New Deal in his essay "Federal Statebuilding During the New Deal: The Transition from Mothers' Aid to Aid to Dependent Children." Hanson shows how changes in welfare policy during the New Deal required the construction of an elaborate bureaucratic apparatus. The form taken by this apparatus, he argues, was fundamentally shaped by the existence of a federal system in which state jurisdictions mattered. Hanson shows in his essay that the form and behavior of this apparatus were highly dependent upon policy legacies, governmental machinery already in place, and the social structural conditions in the states. His suggestion is that state apparatuses in federal and unitary systems are quite different.

Otto Marinen argues not only that the state is relatively autonomous from society but that state agencies are relatively autonomous from the state in his essay "The Police and the Coercive Nature of the State." His point is given force by his examination of the police, a state apparatus so fundamental to the definition of the state as a territorially defined institution that monopolizes the instruments of legitimate coercion.

Taiwan is a much-cited example of state autonomy in the state-centered literature. To many, it is the Taiwanese state that is at the center of that society's economic miracle. In his essay "State-Making and State-Breaking: The Origins and Paradoxes of the Contemporary Taiwanese State," Steve

Chan offers a needed corrective to the prevailing literature by showing how the Taiwanese state is itself a product of three historical legacies—imperial China; Japanese occupation; and liberal, anticommunist America—and constrained by the global system.

In their essay "Change and Continuity in the British Colonial State in Africa: Integrating Theoretical Perspectives," James Scarritt and Shaheen Mozaffar formulate a general analytical model of the state that attempts to synthesize insights from Parsonian, state-centered, and neo-Marxist approaches. They then put this model to use in examining the transformation of the British colonial state in Africa. They show how the constraints of the global system, processes of social and economic change in Africa, and the requirements of rule interacted to give the colonial state a particular form.

Part IV

Most discussions of state behavior in the society-centered literature (which encompasses both the citizen-responsive and capitalist state approaches) are predicated on the notion of relatively fixed interests among the population which are, in one way or another, transmitted to state managers and institutions for their attention. David Levine shows in his essay "The Transformation of Interests and the State" that interests not only are not fixed but are often shaped, defined, and transformed by the state itself. If he is correct, then any consideration of state change must take account of the complexities in the formation and transformation of interests.

How to explain reform? According to Elizabeth Sanders in her essay "Farmers and the State in the Progressive Era," the enormously influential "corporate liberal" explanation, popularized by Weinstein, Wiebe, and Kolko, will not do. Corporate liberalism interprets progressive era reform as the response of the most sophisticated and farsighted corporate leaders to the changing circumstances of capitalism at the turn of the century. Sanders takes scholarship of this type to task for ignoring the influence of other social movements and classes (especially farmers and the white-collar middle class) on progressive reform, for being excessively executive-centered and ignoring Congress and the courts, and for focusing on the national level to the exclusion of the states. Her complex essay represents a case for state-centered and citizen-responsive state approaches, and a rejection of at least one version of the capitalist state approach.

Robert Ross traces the cause of the present move of public policy in the western nations away from the social welfare state to basic transformations in the nature of world capitalism. In his essay "The Relative Decline of

Relative Autonomy: Global Capitalism and the Political Economy of State Change," Ross shows how the recent supercession of "monopoly capitalism" by "global capitalism" has increased the vulnerability of nationally based corporate enterprises to competition. In such a problematic environment, capitalist states have become less responsive to labor, less inclined to regulate corporate activities, and less friendly to the expansion of the social wage. Another way to put this is to say that the decline of the autonomy of the capitalist state (in relationship to the capitalist class) rooted in the transformation of the world capitalist system is the fundamental cause of the retreat from the welfare state.

Notes

1. Unlike classical Marxism in which the state is generally conceptualized as epiphenomenal, derived from the operations of capitalism and not central to its reproduction, most neo-Marxist approaches today conceptualize the state as central to the accumulation process and the reproduction of capitalist social relations of production. From this point of view, the state assumes much greater prominence in contemporary accounts than in classical accounts.

2. For overview of this vast literature see Alford and Friedland, 1985; Carnoy, 1984; Jessop, 1982; and Nordlinger, 1981.

3. Alan Wolfe conceptualizes the state, for instance, as alienated politics (Wolfe, 1977). Many Marxists understand the capitalist state as an institution that carries out some functional necessity for the reproduction of capitalism: to organize the owning class and disorganize the working class (Poulantzas, 1973); to absorb the surplus (Baran & Sweezy, 1966); to organize hegemony (Gramsci, 1971); to overcome crisis tendencies (Wright, 1978); and the like. Many others see the state only in terms of its class and group representations, as if the state were simply a reflection of social forces.

4. Nora Hamilton, in her book *The Limits of State Autonomy: Post-Revolutionary Mexico* (1982), suggests that this Weberian definition of the state was also the definition favored by Engels. See Engels, 1972: 228-233.

5. In borrowing the Weberian definition, it should be obvious that I do not, however, subscribe to the tendency of Weberian oriented scholars to focus their attention exclusively on states as organizations and to ignore issues of societal linkages, class biases, functionally defined objectives, and the like.

6. Both of these are, of course, pure cases. In the real world, the prevailing property rules may be obscure or mixed in form, having elements of different property forms. The determination of precisely what kind of property rules prevail requires investigation and cannot be determined in an a priori fashion.

7. The classic statement of Weber on bureaucracy is, of course *Economy and Society* (Weber, 1978).

8. See Alford and Friedland's *Powers of Theory* (Alford & Friedland, 1985) for a particularly compelling discussion of this literature.

9. Rational choice and rational actor approaches are implicated in all three of the above categories and do not represent, in my view, alternative ways of understanding the state.

10. So-called "economic theories of democracy" (Downs, 1957) present this position in the most parsimonious and testable form: teams of sitting or aspiring officials who compete for electoral support by offering policies preferred by the majority of the electorate.

11. This, of course, encompasses a vast literature. For summaries see Alford and Friedland, 1985; Carnoy, 1984; and Chilcote, 1981. Exemplary works in the pluralist tradition include Bentley, 1935; Dahl and Lindblom, 1953; Dahl, 1961; and Truman, 1951. Exemplary works in the voter-centered literature include Fiorina 1981; Hinich, 1984; and Pomper, 1975.

12. As in the "transformation of elites" notion in Dahl, 1961, or in the many references to urbanization, industrialization, and economic crises.

13. For an introduction to this literature see Alford & Friedland, 1985; Carnoy, 1984; Greenberg, 1986; and Jessop, 1982.

14. This suggests that there are many occasions when such interests are either not engaged or are not apparent because of conflicts and disagreements among capitalists.

15. See G. A. Cohen, 1978, for the most brilliant analysis in the literature of the forces of production and their determinative effects on all of society. Cohen argues that the forces of production produce the relations of production. Other Marxist writers tend to take the forces and relations of production as co-equal and remain silent on the relationship between the two.

16. The most important works in this tradition are Domhoff, 1970; Kolko, 1967; Miliband, 1969; and Weinstein, 1968.

17. For the leading statements in the class struggle school see Esping-Andersen, 1985; Korpi, 1983; O'Connor, 1973; Przeworski, 1985; Stephens, 1979; and Wright, 1978.

18. Alan Wolfe in *The Limits of Legitimacy* (1977), for instance, refers to the "accumulation" state, the "franchise state," and the "diarchy." Wright (1978) formulates a five-stage state system corresponding to functional responses to historical crisis tendencies in capitalism. Ross, in chapter 11 of this volume, describes a three-stage state system corresponding to the change in capitalism from competitive, to monopoly, to global forms. Habermas (1975) formulates a schema of state stages corresponding to crisis stages of various social formations, including liberal and organized capitalism. There is more that could be added, but the point is made without doing so.

19. For an introduction to the literature on transition see Anderson, 1974; Dobb, 1963; Wallerstein, 1974; and Wolf, 1982.

20. The leading works in the state-centric approach are Evans, Rueschemeyer, and Skocpol, 1985; Heclo, 1974; Katzenstein, 1978; Krasner, 1978; Nettl, 1968; Skocpol, 1979; Skowronek, 1982; and Trimberger, 1978.

21. Thus, Weir and Skocpol (1985) analyze major New Deal legislative initiatives as the result of the interactions of public officials and experts, and attributes little influence to social movements and organized labor.

22. That such an important part of the model remains untheorized is not surprising in light of the methodological commitment of most state-centric scholars to what has been called "analytic induction" and their aversion to what they call "grand theory" (Skocpol, 1985).

PART II

Changes in the Relationships Between State and Society

2

The Two-Tiered Theory of the State

Resolving the Question of Determination for the Case of the Local State

M. GOTTDIENER

The explosion of recent work on the capitalist state compels us to recognize the main theoretical perspectives summarizing such efforts. For the purposes of this discussion I follow Greenberg and Page who identify a "democratic-state approach," a "capitalist-state approach," and a "state-centered approach" (Greenberg & Page, 1988). Reviews of the literature invariably uncover a bewildering array of approaches to the state and, as Greenberg and Page note, these often draw upon well-established but irreconcilable theoretical perspectives. On the one hand, there are competing explanations for the same phenomenon, on the other hand, and more perplexing, there are competing theories which claim to address state/society phenomena at different levels of abstraction so that one approach is allegedly more fundamental to explanation than the other.

Is this combat just so many sightless people confronted by an elephant, or, by taking account of the state have we really reached some outer limit of social science itself; a place where its explanatory ability breaks down into some version of relativism or even explanatory chaos? To be sure it is quite right to suggest that we no longer have patience with proselytizers advocating some version of state/society reductionism, most notably by enjoining us to choose between society-centered or state-centered perspectives on the state. If, for example, a successful contemporary school of thought has been launched by exhorting followers to "bring the state back in" (Evans,

41

Rueschemeyer & Skocpol, 1985), it can also be observed that for many societal analysts, especially those involved in the past decade's work on the "new urban sociology," the state has never been left out (Gottdiener & Feagin, 1988).

The real issue in state analysis has never been counterposing one reductionist scheme to another, but examining, instead, the underlying theoretical assertions that make alternate views of the state such a real possibility in the many careful analyses that have been carried out regarding its relation to society. Thus, for example, the "democratic-state approach" is based on a theory of the responsive state (see McDonald & Ward, 1984), "society-centered" approaches involve some theoretical conception of the relative necessity of the state to society, or, its structural dependence on capital (Poulantzas, 1975a; Przeworski & Wallerstein, 1988), while "state-centered approaches" rely on some theoretical conception of state autonomy and the alleged role of state managers as historical subjects whose actions are also viewed by this perspective as "necessary" to society (Block, 1980).

One frequent response to the diversity with which state perspectives emerge in analysis has been to argue for *theoretical pluralism* (see Alford & Friedland, 1985; Saunders, 1983). This is most common in what Harrington (1983) calls "dualist models" that make use of both Marxian and Weberian explanations of state-related phenomena depending on the level of abstraction that is involved (see also, Pickvance, 1984). Theoretical pluralism represents a way out of the impasse presented to researchers of the state. But it effects a synthesis of sorts only at the level of explanation itself (e.g., Alford & Friedland, 1985; Carnoy, 1984) and by overlooking the places where different theories oppose each other at the same level of analysis through counter-claims of explanatory proof. Many of the points of contention among different state theories involve issues that are more than trivial as, for example, in the counterclaims among neo-Marxists and neo-Weberians regarding the concept of relative autonomy. For the former the state's autonomy is hemmed in structurally by its dependence on the well-being of material resource development. For the latter, it is only the state that can represent the general interest of capital, hence, if the state can be viewed as needing the economy, then the opposite is equally true, and we might say that the economy is also dependent on the state.

The following rejects the unsatisfactory position of theoretical pluralism as a means of explaining the presence of separate, plausible state theories. I do not attempt to reconcile separate perspectives at the level of explanation but at the deeper level of ontology. Specifically, before we can address what the state does, it is necessary to examine its nature and particularly the nature of its relation with society. In this manner I shall attempt to pass beyond the impasse that dictates the need for dualist models and theoretical pluralism to some synthetic account of the state/society relation. The state, in what follows, is conceived of as possessing a *two-tiered* structure that houses separately the forces of determinism and contingency which give rise to the varied views of the state. The two-tiered view of the state becomes a way of cutting through the problem presented by these competing perspectives. In what follows I address the more fundamental issue of the nature of the state while leaving aside functional considerations such as the determinants of state action (i.e., the secondary question of why the state does what it does).

A Two-Tiered View of the State

In much of the social science of the past, whenever the nature of the state was addressed it was invariably approached in functional terms and according to the role it played in society (see MacIver, 1969). Among Marxists, for example, it was common to approach social phenomena and their determinants according to a "base-superstructure" distinction. Economic processes and the "mode of production," or the particular arrangement of resource owners and production relations within the institutional framework of production, constituted the fundamental determinant of social organization. The state—its managers, its structure of administration, and its forms of intervention—was viewed by this perspective as belonging to the determined social relations constituting the "superstructure." State change, therefore, always was a consequence of prior changes in the base and the state's role in society always was conditioned by the needs of the base because it determined the functions of state governance.

In contrast, the Weberian tradition views the state as one manifestation of the several formal frameworks of power that exist in any complex society and which reproduce the relation of domination/subordination in social processes. Because it is specialized with a control over the legitimate use of violence, the state is relatively unique and possesses more power than other associations in society. As Weber suggests, "The state is a relation of men dominating men, a relation supported by means of legitimate violence" (Gerth & Mills, 1946, p. 78). Thus the state is both a relation, that of domination/subordination of power, and a structure, a legitimated framework that is reproduced by legal rather than economic relations. In this way the state can be particularized as an institution separate from the global field of power relations analyzed more generically by Foucault (see, e.g., Foucault,

1979). Finally, this particularized relation of state power had its own material base which was, according to Weber, its specific administrative framework and the work force of bureaucrats.

For Weber then, authority relations particularized in the state form are a separate form of power relations existing alongside those emanating from the economic system of expropriation and the relations of production. Marxists, in contrast, point to the origin of legalized authority relations underpinning the state in relations of production and hence "derive" state forms from economic relations (see Holloway & Picciotto, 1979; Jessop, 1982; Pashukanis, 1978). Authority relations are, therefore, part of the superstructure, again, when they are circumscribed in political and not economic frameworks. Rather than constituting an autonomous area of power, political relations remain determined by economic considerations even if only a derivationist argument can be used to demonstrate this link.

Despite the differences between the Marxian and Weberian traditions regarding the autonomy of political relations (see Giddens, 1971), both Marx and Weber enjoyed a common agreement that production relations are constituted neither as economic relations nor political relations per se, but rather as *social* relations. Hence, the terms of disagreement among Marxists and Weberians with regard to the state are themselves conceptually flawed because of a failure to specify accurately the nature of production relations in what Marxists refer to as the base. Put differently, the debate over the autonomy of political as opposed to economic relations is a false way of specifying what both Weber and Marx meant by the relations of production. This in turn sheds some light on the problem for state theorists of base-superstructure determinism. The reduction of relations of production to either economic or political relations which are then viewed as constituting separately some distinct realm of the economic and of the political violates the common agreement of both Marx and Weber that production relations are neither economic nor political but social (see my critique of Poulantzas in this regard, Gottdiener, 1987). By returning to this insight we can acquire a greater understanding of the nature of the state, even if we will not be able to reconcile the differences Marx and Weber had over the specification of power relations in social organization.

The First Tier: Property Relations

Marx, for example, asserted that the fundamental property of the base of society was its structure as the site of ownership relations surrounding the means of production. These ownership relations are *social* in nature and are comprised of politico-juridical as well as economic determinants. As Oskar Lange (1963) has observed, production relations are based on ownership relations which involve not simply mere possession, but more precisely a social understanding of property claims that involve laws, customs, respected social standards, and social mechanisms guarding against the violation of property rules. Following this approach, I suggest that the politico-juridical relations deriving from the state that establish *legitimate* ownership relations of society constitute the deep level structure of the state. This first tier of the state consists of a generic category of property expropriation deployed within a specific mode of production and, in addition, the mechanisms of legitimation and force that protect this system of entitlements.

The fundamental feature of the first tier is that its specification and legitimation of expropriation has two separate components; one pertains to politico-juridical relations establishing the system of expropriation in the economy, such as the wage-labor form under capitalism. The other, however, defines the system of expropriation that pertains to the state itself, or the legitimate claims of the state on property. Under capitalism both the state and the capitalist class, for example, require the legitimate expropriation of surplus value from producers. In fact, the expropriating powers of the state are even more global and include legitimated claims by the state on surplus value held by the capitalist class itself. In effect, then, both capital and the state possess separate but similar legitimated claims on the property of others, and it is these rights that constitute the first tier of the state.

Under capitalism, therefore, there is a *homologous* relation between the state and capital existing at the level of the first tier. It is homologous in the literal sense of being comparable to and of operating in the same way without being the same or deriving from the same exact source. That is, the state and capital function according to separate structures in society, but they also function according to the same process at their deepest level, namely, the expropriation of property. Consequently, at the level of the first tier both the state and capital possess the very same interest, namely, the sustenance and preservation of the power of expropriation over the working class who are the ultimate producers of wealth, and it is the concordance of interest that is most important in understanding the capital/state relation. Because, there are two separate and very different structures existing for the deployment of political power relations and for the relations of production, this concordance of interest between the state and capital is a homologous one. It is not a matter of one interest determining the other, but of relative autonomy between the state and capital at the level of the first tier relations of expropriation. As in previous production modes, the capitalist like the worker must render "unto

Caesar" what is Caesar's according to the state's legitimating principles in a society with a well-developed political framework of power.

Historically, just as capital has reproduced and refined further its expropriation powers while being conditioned by the class struggle, so too has the state moved in its own interest to develop separately but homologously its powers of property expropriation vis-à-vis both capital and labor. The first-tier relations that are involved here pertain to what constitutes a legitimate claim on forms of property, rather than a determination of the rate or quantity of what can be expropriated, as the latter belongs to another aspect of the state. (See below). The latter constitutes for capital its economic crisis base and determines its relation with labor and technology, while the constraints on the rate and quantity of *public* expropriation constitutes the crisis base of the state and determines the fiscal problems that condition the state/capital relation. But this crisis conditioning for the state is not a first-tier phenomenon.

In contrast, just as capital defends its interests against the working class, it also positions itself vis-à-vis the state in a struggle over the latter's claim on its expropriated wealth and on forms of wealth to which the state can legitimately lay claim. It is simply wrong to suggest that, because all wealth is ultimately derived from the process of production, the state and capital do not possess an antagonistic relation with regard to the right to expropriate part of the surplus (see also, Przeworski & Wallerstein, 1988). Furthermore, while the claims made on capital by the state may be more easily worked out in capital's favor relative to the state's demands on the working class, and, while the extent or limits of state claims on wealth may involve struggle and redefinition, the first-tier arrangements that legitimate the right to expropriate property are rarely challenged at all and certainly not by capital.

It is only the exact arrangements and limits of expropriation that are conditioned historically by the three-way relations of the class struggle, on the one hand, and by the separate state/capital and state/citizen property relations. Consequently, it is only the arrangements and limits of expropriation that seem most often to be subject historically to the process of social change. Thus, the struggle over the extent and limits of expropriation belongs to a separate level of state/society relations, while the first tier only consists of the rights of expropriation itself (more about this second level below), which are contested less often as basic rights than are the former relations.

Finally, much of the function of social control ascribed to the state stands in the service of property relations and the defense, often through the use of legitimate forms of violence and surveillance, of those relations. When the state moves against those who have violated capitalist property rights it is also reproducing its own claims on property and is not simply acting in the service of capital through its police powers, as Marxists often suggest. Resisting taxation, for example, even if done by capitalists, can be construed as an act tantamount to revolution.

If the right of expropriation constitutes a first tier of the state, much of its activities lie outside this domain and involve the political relations of administration and public decision making. These activities constitute a second level or tier of the state structure. As I have suggested above, this second tier also involves the struggle over the extent of property claims but never over the basic politico-juridical rights to expropriate property itself.

The Second Tier:
Administrative and Political Relations

The second tier is most commonly the place where analyses of the state commence. Located here we find both state managers, or the historical subjects comprising the state, and its apparatus or structure which also varies considerably within as well as among societies. The second tier houses two separate but related processes: first, the three-way social struggle involving the capitalist class, workers, and state managers over the division of wealth, especially the conditions under which claims against surplus value are made by the three separate social agents (i.e., capital, labor, and the state); and, the struggle over the construction of some "general interest" that can rationalize the fate of capitalism and help direct the process of state intervention through the state's apparatus of decision making.

At the level of the second tier both the particular interests regarding the division of wealth and the more general interests involved in the articulation of policy and in the setting of social priorities are resolved according to the three-way struggle between the state, capital, and labor. The most important feature of this process is that it is both contingent and variable, hence, it can only be grasped by models that are attuned to both society and state-centered determinations and one perspective can never be shown consistently to be more germane than the other as a source of explanation for state actions.

The contingent character of second-tier relations is most important for an understanding of the way the state/society relation has been approached by analysts in the past. Because neither the struggle over the division of wealth nor over the direction of public policy is determined by the logic or even the needs of capital alone, monocausal theories of the state have failed to account for all its manifestations and theoretical pluralism results. I intend by the present argument to show, however, that this pluralism is simply the outcome of trying to take the relations and processes associated with the second tier for the underlying nature of the state itself.

Second-tier relations never call into question the fundamental expropriation rights that lie at the base of particular social formations. When the
three-way struggle at the level of the second tier spills over into such
considerations, such as in conflict over taxation and property rights, or, in the
redefinition of labor claims to surplus value, such as in worker ownership
schemes, then second-tier relations can affect the first tier and fundamental
changes in the mode of production can occur. For this to happen, however,
it is necessary for some struggle to challenge not only the extent or type of
expropriation but also the very *right* of expropriation ascribed by society to
political and economic relations. It is this latter first-tier feature that is rarely
challenged compared with the contingent nature of the struggle at the level
of the second tier.

Thus, it is not possible to lump the entire politico-juridical apparatus of
the state into some level of social relations—call it the "superstructure" or
some "relatively autonomous" system of practices, if you like—which then
can be analytically "particularized" or structurally separated from the base,
as neo-Marxists, for example, assert. At the same time, however, I do not
mean to imply that all political relations are part of the relations of production,
so that at a weaker level of abstraction it is still possible to talk of forms and
processes of domination and administration that are only phenomenal forms
of the more basic production relations, thereby agreeing with neo-Marxian
analysis. What I suggest is that previous approaches to the state fail to
differentiate between two qualitatively separate aspects of the state/society
relation by treating political relations as belonging to the same generic
category of social relations existing at the level of the social formation.

Consequently, the analysis of the state/society relation is almost invariably
a contingent one that can support first a society-centered and then, depending
on different historical circumstances, a state-centered view. There exists,
however, a place beyond which contingent relations cannot pass and that is
in the determination of property relations and expropriation rights. Under
capitalism these first-tier arrangements place the state directly in the same
relation to the producers of surplus value as is the case for capital. This
homological relation gives to capitalist systems their character and circum-
scribes the boundaries or constraints of the class struggle beyond which
politics itself cannot pass.

Finally, the two tiers differ with regard to their roles in social change.
Because the first tier deals with ownership rights it is more fundamental to
change. Changes in first-tier arrangements produce changes in the mode of
production. Private ownership, nationalization, and socialization, for exam-

Table 2.1 The Tiers of the State and their Relation to Social Change and Conflict

	First Tier	*Second Tier*
Features	property rights	division of wealth, relative participation in the rationalization process (i.e., intervention and decision making).
Conflicts	struggles over ownership claims, public/private distinctions, the right to tax and expropriate property (eminent domain).	conflict over tax burden, burden of debt, social wage, subsidization of labor and/or capital. Conflict over policy and power or influence in decision making and administration.
Social Change	change *in* the mode of production: nationalization, private ownership, socialization, etc.	changes *within* the mode of production, balance of power between capital, labor, and state managers; well-being of these three groups. Changes in welfare capitalism and in the extent of states' socialization of capital's or labor's costs of reproduction.

ple, are all different outcomes of first-tier relations as is the case for laws that govern the power (but not the extent) to tax. Struggles over these structural arrangements are fundamental to the nature of society and they effect changes *in* the mode of production.

In contrast, second-tier processes involve the balance of power between capital, labor, and the state over the division of wealth. Conflict at this level for the state concerns the extent of the state's socialization of capital's and labor's costs of reproduction. Changes *within* the mode of production result from these struggles, such as changes in the arrangements of collective provision under welfare capitalism.

The distinctions between the two tiers of the state discussed above are summarized in Table 2.1.

The two-tiered approach to the state can be applied with some success to the study of several thorny issues in the theory of the state, as, for example, in the analysis of the local state (Gottdiener, 1987). In the remainder of this chapter I shall illustrate the utility of the concepts developed above in a discussion of the issues regarding the alleged necessity of the state, a topic that divides Marxian, neo-Marxian and neo-Weberian approaches.

The Necessity of the State

Both neo-Marxian and neo-Weberian perspectives assume the necessity of the state as the system manager and reproducer of social relations. In opposition to these views are those of more traditional Marxists and certain neoclassical theorists who do not conceive of the state as necessary to capital. In Marx's analysis of capitalism found in *Capital,* for example, the wage-labor relation is self-reproducing and does not depend upon collective provision. Specifically, in the circuit of capital accumulation, labor presents itself to the capitalist as a free commodity that can be purchased for a wage. This relation presupposes that the worker is separated completely from all the means of production; a separation that is the direct outcome of capitalist property relations. It is, however, a presupposition that is dependent on a historical process during which time capitalist relations are hypothesized as penetrating those of pre-capitalist relations necessary to the formation of the working class. The process that produces wage labor historically under capitalism is one that involves the definition of property rights.

The traditional Marxian position argues that while the state may be involved in the penetration process of capitalist relations, it is not necessary to that process. Rather the status of the free worker is reproduced by the class struggle itself during which the capitalist smashes the unity of the collective laborer with the means of production taking place through "work" by purposefully fragmenting the link among workers so as to reinstate collective labor as individual labor divorced from the means (see Clarke, 1985). This is accomplished principally through the struggle of the capitalist against organized labor which is not only involves abstract property "rights" but a host of other social control mechanisms. Marxists following this view assert that while the state is a useful instrument in aiding the capitalist class in the class struggle, once the unity of collective labor forms is effectively smashed, the state is no longer necessary to the self-reproduction of the capital/labor relation. Hence the state is not necessary to the reproduction of capitalist relations, only to their constitution.

It is possible to argue against this view by paying careful attention to the historical presuppositions mentioned by Marx as necessary constituents of the capitalist wage-labor form. In particular, these include the dissolution of traditional community networks; the dissolution of proprietory labor (i.e., the artistic-craft ethos that developed culturally around labor as a use-value and an end in itself); the dissolution of collectivized forms of the means of consumption, such as the right to be fed and housed, that are not predicated on one's exchange value; and the reduction of the laborer as a human being to labor-power and as an input to production according to labor-time, labor-productivity, and the like (see Gottdiener, 1987). In the course of capitalist development these preconditions have been represented as tendencies, however, most have yet to be fully realized. Consequently, by virtue of a historical argument it can be asserted that the wage-labor relation is not at present self-reproducing within the dynamics of capitalist production processes alone and that some room remains for the role of the state as the necessary adjunct to capital's efforts in the creation and sustenance of the wage-labor form.

This conclusion is by no means a vindication of neo-Weberian and neo-Marxian arguments on the necessity of the state. A decade of fiscal crisis restructuring, the privatization of former collective consumption activities—most particularly the retreat and dismantling of welfare state provision in many industrialized countries—and new relations between capital and labor that have attenuated the power of organized forms have all worked together to isolate the struggle between capital and labor from previously developed public provision. In a very real sense Marx's historical preconditions regarding the self-reproduction of the labor force are actually coming into being in American cities under the present conditions emerging from two decades of sociospatial restructuring that began with the crises of the 1960s. These changes include, for example, fiscal austerity, the decline of welfare provision, the decline of union strength, the dominance of nonvoters in elections, homelessness, the privatization of childhood education and medical care by consumers themselves as a matter of choice, and the privatization of many city services by local government. Hence, while the state is still required for the self-regulation of capital, its historical role in the production of the wage-labor form is presently attenuating.

Perhaps, then, the state is not as necessary to capital as we have been led to believe, or, as Jessop (1978) has suggested, perhaps, at present the capitalist economy and its democratic shell have begun to part company. For the local state the democratic quality of present arrangements seems to have declined and regulation is presently being carried out more concretely by capital itself. In American cities such a trend is exemplified by the following changes. First, the retreat of the welfare state in general through privatization by government suggests that capital has accepted the responsibility of uneven development and a differentially endowed labor force. In fact, capital even seems willing to accept the presence in cities of a large and self-reproducing underclass and the realm of social pathology that such a population element represents. Second, elements of labor also seem willing to privatize their consumption and to work out arrangements with employers for medical care along with adopting privatized schooling schemes for their children rather than press for a socialization of the costs of labor's reproduction. The split among elements of labor over public versus private means for supporting the quality of life, which always has existed to some extent within cities, has presently taken on the character of a fundamental schism in the urban population. Currently the retreat of collective provision has produced an extreme crisis of inequality within cities as a consequence of the disparity between different groups to sustain their quality of life through increasingly privatized means. This splits the labor force between those able to sustain themselves in a privatized social milieu and those who must continue to rely on state provision.

Third, reproduction of the labor force in general has also shifted from public to private responsibility as capital has internalized many of the costs and activities associated with job training, education, and research and development during the recent period of restructuring. Finally, it must also be pointed out that many of the system maintenance functions that were once ascribed to the state have been internalized as well. Since the 1950s, in particular, this has most commonly taken place through the growth of service-related employment and what is at present the growing number of workers involved in the processing of information by private sector firms.

Results from two decades of capital and state restructuring in the United States, in fact, compel us to talk about regulation rather than reproduction as the function that best characterizes what is a joint capital and state venture in the sustenance of growth (see Gottdiener, 1987; Gottdiener & Komninos, 1989). This mode of regulation involves mutual adjustments of both capital and the state acting through institutional ensembles and cultural processes of normalization according to which the needs of society are met by flexible means emerging from both public and private venues. Disappearing as a consequence of present arrangements are those sharp splits in the functional division of labor between the state and capital that once supported a discourse which made clear distinctions between state-centered and society-centered determinants of state activity.

3

Effective Demand and Structural Dependence of the State

THOMAS F. MAYER
TRACY L. MOTT

> Capitalists get what they spend. Workers spend what they get.
>
> Michal Kalecki

1. Introduction

If the government of a capitalist society is concerned with the material well-being of its people, then government policy must foster the welfare of capital. This is the main claim of structural dependence theory. According to this theory, the need to foster the welfare of capital holds no matter what ideology is favored by government leaders. If they govern within the framework of capitalist institutions, serving the interests of capital is incumbent upon liberals and conservatives, upon the radical left and the radical right, and even upon socialists and fascists. This structural relationship exists because the material means to pursue any personal or any social objective ultimately derive from the success of the capitalist economy, which in turn depends upon the willingness of capitalists to invest. But capitalists are only willing to invest if they can turn a profit by so doing. Thus the government of a capitalist society must strenuously protect the profitability of capital.

In a brilliant article which serves as the focus for much of this chapter, Adam Przeworski and Michael Wallerstein use a formal model to study the internal logic and robustness of structural dependence theory (1988).[1] According to this model the state, with proper taxation and income transfers, can engineer any distribution of income between workers and capitalists without curtailing private investment. Hence they conclude the theory of structural dependence of the state on capital is false when considered in a static sense.[2]

We believe Przeworski's and Wallerstein's general approach constitutes a decisive advance in reasoning about the connection between class relations and the state. Nevertheless we have some basic criticisms of the arguments they use. Most fundamentally we think they misunderstand the economic relationship between wage earners and owners of capital. This leads them to propose a model which misconstrues the functional relations between wages, profits, and investment. Naturally a flawed economic model cannot generate sound inferences about structural dependence of the state on capital.

How does the theory of structural dependence analyzed in this chapter connect with the process of state change? If the theory of structural dependence is correct, the working class in a capitalist society can achieve its interests only by reorganizing the state in a fundamental way. The normal capacities of the capitalist state are simply insufficient to limit the power of capital, and class struggle—if pursued in a rational way—will spawn a political struggle about transforming the state. On the other hand, if the theory of structural dependence is wrong, then a sufficiently unified and sufficiently organized working class might accomplish its class objectives within the framework of capitalist society and without overhauling the capitalist state: the political strategy of social democracy would appear to be vindicated. Thus the true relationship between class struggle and state change hinges upon the validity of structural dependence theory.

In the following section we outline and evaluate the model used by Przeworski and Wallerstein to analyze state dependence on capital. In section 3 we present a modification of the Przeworski-Wallerstein model and explain some of the thinking behind it. Section 4 deals directly with the structural dependence of the state comparing results from our modified model with ones obtained by Przeworski and Wallerstein. A few of our conclusions are discussed in the final section.

2. The Przeworski-Wallerstein Model: Appreciation and Critique

The formal model proposed by Przeworski and Wallerstein depicts capitalist production as it unfolds over time (designated by the symbol τ in the equations below). The personae of capitalist production are workers, capitalists, and the state. Net national income $Y(\tau)$ is divided into three parts: aggregate wages $W(\tau)$, investment $I(\tau)$, and capitalist profits not used for investment $P(\tau)$.[3] This division yields the basic income accounting equation:

$$Y(\tau) = W(\tau) + I(\tau) + P(\tau) \qquad [3.1]$$

Workers control m, the share of national income going into wages.[4]

$$W(\tau) = mY(\tau) \qquad [3.2]$$

Capitalists control s, the share of their own income going into investment, and they are assumed to be the only people able to invest. This monopoly on investment could be considered the defining characteristic of the simplified capitalist economies studied by Przeworski and Wallerstein.

$$I(\tau) = s(1 - m)Y(\tau) \qquad [3.3]$$

$$P(\tau) = (1 - s)(1 - m)Y(\tau) \qquad [3.4]$$

The state intrudes upon an already formed capitalist economy. It can levy taxes of various kinds including overall income taxes, taxes on investment, and taxes on the consumption of either workers or capitalists. The state can use tax revenues to redistribute income between workers and capitalists. By so doing it alters the trajectory of the capitalist economy.

Once workers select a wage share m (which is equivalent to selecting a wage rate) and once capitalists select an investment share s (which is equivalent to selecting an investment rate) these shares are assumed to remain constant over time.[5] The behavior of the state is a little more complicated. In the static version of the Przeworski-Wallerstein model the taxation rates chosen by the state also remain constant over time; but in the dynamic version the state starts off with one taxation schedule and then shifts to a different schedule.

Everyone's economic welfare depends upon the growth of national income, and the rate of growth is assumed proportional to the amount of investment I.

$$\frac{dY(\tau)}{d\tau} = \nu I(\tau) \qquad [3.5]$$

The parameter ν represents the amount of additional output generated by one additional unit of capital stock. The fact that only capitalists can invest gives them tremendous leverage over the society as a whole. This is the basic source of structural dependence in the Przeworski-Wallerstein model.

We disagree with the reasoning underlying equation 3.5. This equation determines growth entirely on the basis of investment, while the model as a whole makes no provision for relating investment to effective demand. Demand is not a constraint on growth in the Przeworski-Wallerstein model. The model implicitly assumes Say's law of markets according to which productive activity automatically generates sufficient demand to absorb the goods produced. This is not merely a technical error in model construction. As we indicated above, it manifests a fundamental misconception about capitalist class relations.

The Przeworski-Wallerstein model suggests a one-way dependency of labor on capital. Capitalists would like to cut wages to zero, but are prevented from doing so by considerations completely outside the purview of the model itself. In reality, the demand furnished by the working class is a vital ingredient of capitalist dynamics. Labor may be dependent upon capital, but the reverse is also true; and the dependence of capital on labor operates in both the realms of production and realization. A state which hopes to intervene effectively within this complex structure of class interdependence has taken on a difficult task indeed.

Investigating the state's dependence on capital, we remind the reader, is the purpose of the Przeworski-Wallerstein model. But if its misinterprets the structure of dependence between the classes of capitalist society can this model possibly illuminate the relationship between the state and the owners of capital?

Having postulated a pattern of capitalist growth, Przeworski and Wallerstein next define a procedure by which capitalists select an optimal investment rate and workers choose an optimal wage rate. Capitalists and workers each try to maximize a utility function based upon expected lifetime income. Capitalists choose s to maximize

$$P^* = \int_0^\infty e^{-\rho\tau}\ln[P(\tau)]d\tau \qquad [3.6]$$

and workers choose m to maximize

$$W^* = \int_0^\infty e^{-\rho\tau}\ln[W(\tau)]d\tau \qquad [3.7]$$

A logarithmic utility transformation is used because of its simplicity and because it embodies the principle of declining marginal utility. Workers and capitalists discount the future at the same rate ρ while, contrary to many Marxist interpretations, capitalists only care about consumption with investment merely providing a means to increased future consumption.

With no government in the picture capitalists maximize their utility by investing at the rate

$$s^*(m) = 1 - \frac{\rho}{v(1 - m)} \qquad [3.8]$$

The important point about this result is that the optimal investment rate s^* declines as wage share increases (i.e., $ds^*/dm < 0$) suggesting that workers cannot increase their wage share without diminishing investment and thereby reducing future economic growth. Przeworski and Wallerstein interpret this to mean that, in the absence of state intervention, workers are structurally dependent upon capital.

Without state intervention owners of capital and workers (assuming they both act rationally) will each consume ρ/v share of national income, and the remainder will be invested. This is usually possible in a capitalist economic system since the rate of discounting the future ρ is ordinarily less than the rate of economic growth v. If for some reason this inequality should be reversed, equation 3.8 implies the capitalists will disinvest irrespective of the share of wages in national income.[6]

Suppose the state enters the scene by imposing a tax on all capitalist income and transferring the proceeds to the workers. According to the Przeworski-Wallerstein model this does not change things at all. Capitalists simply reduce their investment by the amount of the income tax and consume at exactly the same level they would without the tax. If the state cares about maximizing workers' welfare, they the working class will end up with the same share of national income it had before, namely ρ/v. The state which levies a fixed tax on capitalist income thus remains structurally dependent on capital.

Things turn out quite differently, however, if the state only taxes that part of capitalist income which is not invested. Under the income tax discussed above, capitalists could not reduce their taxes by shifting revenue from consumption to investment. With taxation limited to non-invested income, however, capitalists can lower their tax payments by investing more. Once again it is assumed that tax revenues are transferred to the working class. If only the noninvested portion of capitalist income is taxed, Przeworski and Wallerstein obtain the remarkable result that the rate of capitalist investment remains totally unaffected by the tax rate. When the state extracts taxes entirely from capitalist consumption, the investment rate remains that given by expression 3.8.[7]

This is perhaps the most important finding made by Przeworski and Wallerstein. By taxing capitalist consumption the state can increase the workers' share of national income without diminishing economic growth. This happens even if capitalist consumption is taxed down to almost nothing. By pursuing such a policy the state escapes structural dependence on capital. The independence of the investment rate from the taxation of capitalist consumption appears to vindicate traditional social democratic strategy. Advocates of this strategy claimed that a government favorable to the working class could control a capitalist economy so as to provide workers with as many material benefits as they could expect under socialism.

Suppose the state taxes capitalist consumption and transfers the revenue to the workers. By what we have just seen, capitalist investment would remain constant. Under these circumstances workers should reduce their wages and receive income from transfer payments instead. According to the Przeworski-Wallerstein model a wage reduction causes capitalists to increase the investment rate thereby spurring economic growth. In the limiting situation consumption is near zero, workers get all their income in the form of transfer payments from the state, and investment absorbs virtually all production not consumed by the working class.

By such procedures the state, in collaboration with the working class, can implement any desired division of national income between consumption and investment. Socialism becomes superfluous because capitalists can be induced to become mere instruments for investing capital. All vestiges of structural dependence have been eliminated.

In reaching these conclusions, Przeworski and Wallerstein assume capitalists will behave in an amazingly passive and myopic fashion. The capitalists simply accept the choices made by the working class and the state, assume these choices will remain in effect indefinitely, and try to make the best of the situation. Real capitalists have a much broader strategic perspective. They will not accept abhorrent wage and taxation rates as fixed in stone. The vulnerability of labor organizations and progressive governments to capital strikes is well known. Real capitalists fully understand that their control over investment (and many other elements of the economic system) gives them the power to compel changes in wages and taxation. They also understand that long-term capitalist welfare is sometimes maximized by enduring short-term losses. A broad strategic perspective on the part of capitalists is all the more likely in an economic structure characterized by imperfect competition and oligopoly.

Przeworski and Wallerstein develop their model in a neoclassical way largely because they think

> the problem of structural dependence cannot arise within a Keynesian framework where increasing wage-earners' consumption accelerates investment and may even increase current profits. Indeed, one of the political appeals of Keynesian theory was the denial of any conflict of interests between wage earners and capitalists. (Przeworski & Wallerstein, 1988, p. 27, n. 6)

We do not agree with this assessment. The problem of structural dependence does arise within the Keynesian framework, but it assumes a more complicated form. The working class and the state remain dependent upon the willingness of capitalists to invest and must refrain from activities which choke-off this willingness. But, as we have already indicated, capitalists also are dependent upon working-class consumption.

This mutual interdependence does not imply harmony of interests between workers and capitalists. In addition to conflicts about wage rates, class struggles concern the organization and intensity of work, appropriate production technology, and overall control of the production process. Within the confines of a capitalist system neither workers nor capitalists can dispossess the other. They struggle to improve their economic positions fully recognizing that advantages gained by one will sometimes be liabilities for the other. They are structural allies but also structural antagonists. Our proposed modification of the Przeworski-Wallerstein model attempts to capture this structural ambivalence.

3. A Neo-Keynesian Model of Structural Dependence

Our model of structural dependence builds in considerations of effective demand thus enabling us to investigate the implications of the complex class relations discussed in the previous section. The formulation we present below is a straightforward modification of the Przeworski-Wallerstein model. The only difference is in the growth equation 3.5, and their model turns out to be a special case of ours. The Przeworski-Wallerstein growth equation depends entirely upon investment. Our growth equation depends upon both investment and demand factors. It is just about the simplest conceivable growth equation based upon the interaction of supply and demand considerations.

$$\frac{dY(\tau)}{d\tau} = \nu_1 I(\tau) \left\{ \nu_2 \frac{W(\tau)}{Y(\tau)} + \nu_3 \left[\frac{I(\tau)+P(\tau)}{Y(\tau)} \right] \right\} \qquad [3.9]$$

In this equation $I(\tau)$ represents the contribution of supply or production forces to economic growth, while the term in parentheses measures the fraction of productive capacity which will actually be used given the existing level of effective demand. More specifically W/Y, the share of wages in national income, represents the working class component of demand while $(I + P)/Y$, the share of total profits in national income, represents the capitalist component of demand.

Because "workers spend what they get" while capitalists may not, we shall usually assume that the following inequality holds between parameters v_2 and v_3:

$$v_2 > v_3 \qquad [3.10]$$

Workers, this inequality says, have a higher propensity to spend than capitalists.

If $v_2 = v_3$ then equation 3.9 reduces to equation 3.5 and our model becomes identical with the Przeworski-Wallerstein model. From this it follows that the latter is a special case of the former. Consider what it means if $v_2 = v_3$. This implies that wage dollars and profit dollars are equally important as sources of demand (i.e., that workers and capitalists have equal propensities to spend). Income can be arbitrarily shifted between workers and capitalists without affecting the volume of demand. Such uniform propensity to spend (or intensity of demand as we shall sometimes refer to it) is the condition under which the Przeworski-Wallerstein model becomes valid.

Using the assumption of constant wage, investment, and uninvested profit shares in national income (i.e., equations 3.2, 3.3, and 3.4), differential equation 3.9 becomes

$$\frac{dY(\tau)}{d\tau} = Y(\tau)s(1 - m)[v_6\, m + v_5] \qquad [3.11]$$

where

$$v_5 = v_1 v_3 \quad and \quad v_6 = v_1(v_2 - v_3) \qquad [3.12]$$

and inequality 3.10 implies that[8]

$$v_6 > 0 \qquad [3.13]$$

Equation 3.11 is a linear first-order differential equation which is easily solved to give

$$Y(\tau) = Y(0)\exp[s(1 - m)(v_6 m + v_5)\tau] \qquad [3.14]$$

In the absence of state intervention, the capitalists' consumption function equals

$$P(\tau) = (1 - m)(1 - s)Y(\tau) \qquad [3.15]$$

and using equation 3.6 we obtain the capitalist utility function[9]

$$P^* = \frac{1}{\rho}\left[\ln P(0) + \frac{s(1 - m)(v_6 m + v_5)}{\rho} \right] \qquad [3.16]$$

Note that an increase in the wage share of national income can, under certain circumstances, have a positive effect on capitalist utility. In particular, if wages constitute less than half of the national income, and if a unit of wage income generates at least twice the amount of demand as a unit of capitalist income, then capitalist utility will be enhanced by a small increase in the wage rate.[10]

According to our assumptions, capitalists choose an investment rate s by maximizing equation 3.16. This turns out to be

$$s^* = 1 - \frac{\rho}{(1 - m)(v_6 m + v_5)} \qquad [3.17]$$

Contrary to what would be expected under the Przeworski-Wallerstein model, a rise in the wage share does not always cause a fall in the investment rate. If workers' income is sufficiently low, and if the demand generating capacity of wages is over twice that of profits, then a rise in the wage share will induce a corresponding rise in the investment rate. The derivative of the optimal investment rate $s^*(m)$ with respect to the wage share is

$$\frac{ds^*}{dm} = \frac{\rho(v_6 - v_5 - 2v_6 m)}{(1 - m)^2(v_6 + v_5)^2} \qquad [3.18]$$

from which we see that

$$\text{if} \quad v_5 < v_6 \quad \text{then} \quad \frac{ds^*}{dm} < 0 \qquad\qquad [3.19]$$

and

$$\text{if} \quad v_5 < v_6 \quad \text{then} \quad
\begin{aligned}
\frac{ds^*}{dm} &< 0 \quad \text{if} \quad m > \frac{1}{2}\left(1 - \frac{v_5}{v_6}\right) \\[2mm]
\frac{ds^*}{dm} &> 0 \quad \text{if} \quad m < \frac{1}{2}\left(1 - \frac{v_5}{v_6}\right) \\[2mm]
\frac{ds^*}{dm} &= 0 \quad \text{if} \quad m = \frac{1}{2}\left(1 - \frac{v_5}{v_6}\right)
\end{aligned}
\qquad [3.20]$$

Equations 3.19 and 3.20 also refute the claim made by Przeworski and Wallerstein that ds^*/dm will necessarily be positive in a Keynesian model "since wage increases put more money in the hands of people with a high propensity to consume" (Przeworski & Wallerstein, 1988, p. 27, n. 6). Even in our very simple model things are much more complicated than this statement suggests, indicating once again that a neo-Keynesian *cum* Marxist approach has considerably greater flexibility than Przeworski and Wallerstein seem to think.

With no government presence, owners of capitalist property consume

$$\frac{P}{Y} = (1 - s^*)(1 - m) = \frac{\rho}{v_6\, m + v_5} \qquad\qquad [3.21]$$

share of the national income, and the share they invest is

$$\frac{I}{Y} = s^*(1 - m) = 1 - m - \frac{\rho}{v_6\, m + v_5} \qquad\qquad [3.22]$$

Under the Przeworski-Wallerstein model capitalist consumption as a share of national income is independent of the wage rate, while the investment share decreases as wages rise. In our model a rise in wages causes a decline in share of capitalist consumption. Moreover an increase in the percentage of national income going to workers would almost certainly depress the investment share, but could conceivably have the opposite effect.

What about the workers? In the absence of government what share of national income will they allocate for wages? Our model makes things more complicated for the working class. Its members already had to balance their own desire to consume against the necessity of encouraging capitalist investment. According to our formulation, workers or their political representatives must also compare working-class consumption propensities with those of the capitalists. This leads to a less elementary formula for the workers' optimal wage share:[11]

$$m^*(s) = \frac{s(v_6 - v_5) + \sqrt{s^2(v_5 - v_6)^2 + 8s\rho v_6}}{4sv_6} \qquad [3.23]$$

Let us assume, as Przeworski and Wallerstein do, that workers take the initiative and choose an optimal wage share to which capitalists respond as best they can. Given such a procedure, rational workers should assume that capitalists will make the best possible response to the workers' wage share choice; that is they should assume capitalists will act according to equation 3.17. Under these assumptions the wage share becomes

$$m^{**} = \frac{v_6 - v_5 + \sqrt{(v_5 - v_6)^2 + 8v_6\rho}}{4v_6} \qquad [3.24]$$

and the total profit share may be obtained by substituting equation 3.24 into equation 3.17.

All the results presented so far suppose the absence of state intervention. Before turning to the question of structural dependence, let us reconsider the relationship between our model and the Przeworski-Wallerstein formulation. As we have already demonstrated, the two are equivalent if the demand generated per unit of capitalist income equals the demand generated per unit of workers' income (i.e., if $v_6 = 0$). Our assumption is that workers generally consume most of their income thus producing a high and largely invariant demand intensity. But this is not true of capitalists. The goad of necessity does not compel them to spend what they get, and they may choose not to invest it. Capitalist demand intensity, we submit, approaches workers' demand intensity only at the very peak of the business cycle when there exists little unemployment and almost no excess productive capacity.

The Przeworski-Wallerstein model is approximately valid for a full-employment, full-capacity utilization economy, but not at other phases of the business cycle. It describes tolerably well the relations between capital and state under conditions of full employment. This hypothesis is supported by observing that our own model yields results in glaring contradiction to Przeworski-Wallerstein predictions precisely when wages are very low and the ratio of worker-created to capitalist-created demand intensity very high; conditions which accompany high unemployment and excess capacity.

4. The Structural Dependence of the State

Let us assume, as Przeworski and Wallerstein do, that the state intervenes in the economy exclusively through taxation. To better address the question of state dependence on capital, let us further suppose we are dealing with a pro-worker government subscribing to the working-class utility function and which typically taxes capitalist income and transfers it to wage earners. We shall conceptualize taxation a little differently than do Przeworski and Wallerstein. We consider two kinds of taxes: a tax on capitalist investment and a tax on capitalist consumption (or more correctly, on the noninvested part of capitalist income). Both are assumed to be fixed percentages of the income category they tax.

Let t_i and t_c be the respective fixed proportions of capitalist investment and capitalist consumption extracted as taxes. If $t_i = t_c$ we have the uniform capitalist income tax of which Przeworski and Wallerstein speak. Let

$$T_i(\tau) = t_i I(\tau) \quad \text{and} \quad T_c(\tau) = t_c P(\tau) \qquad [3.25]$$

define the respective volumes of the income and consumption taxes at time t. Then the economic growth equation becomes

$$\frac{dY(\tau)}{d\tau} = v_1(I - T_i)\left[v_2\frac{(W + T_i + T_c)}{Y} + v_3\frac{(I + P - T_i - T_c)}{Y} \right] \qquad [3.26]$$

$$= Y(\tau)s(1 - m)(1 - t_i)\{v_6 m + v_5 + v_6(1 - m)[st_i + (1 - s)t_c]\}$$

The solution to this linear first-order differential equation is

$$Y(\tau) = Y(0)\exp(\kappa\tau) \qquad [3.27]$$

$$k = s(1 - m)(1 - t_i)\{v_6 m + v_5 + v_6(1 - m)[st_i + (1 - s)t_c]\}$$

We first consider the possibility of a uniform tax on all capitalist income, that is $t_i = t_c = t$. If such a tax is in effect, then the optimal capitalist investment rate would be

$$s^*(m, t) = 1 - \frac{\rho}{(1 - m)(1 - t)[v_6 m + v_5 + v_6 t (1 - m)]} \qquad [3.28]$$

What does expression 3.28 tell us about the structural dependence of the state on capital? Let us adopt as an indicator of such structural dependency the propensity of investment to decline as the income tax rate t rises. Computing the partial derivative of $s^*(m, t)$ with respect to t, we find that $\partial s^*/\partial t$ is negative, positive, or zero as t is greater than, less than, or equal to the quantity

$$\frac{1}{2}\left[1 - \frac{m + (v_5/v_6)}{1 - m} \right]$$

provided that $m < 1$.

This tells us that a uniform income tax cannot circumvent structural dependence if $v_5 > v_6$ (or equivalently, $v_2 < 2v_3$), or if $m > \frac{1}{2}$. However, if the wage share is low and if worker demand intensity is very high relative to the demand intensity of capitalists, then a uniform tax on capitalist income can shift the distribution of national income in favor of workers without reducing capitalist investment. Under these circumstances the state would not be structurally dependent on capital; however, the income tax rate would have to remain quite low in order to avoid disinvestment. The Przeworski-Wallerstein model, on the other hand, implies no escape from structural dependence is possible with a uniform income tax.

Next we consider a tax on capitalist consumption only (i.e., $t_i = 0$). This is the crucial case for Przeworski and Wallerstein. With this form of taxation, they establish the feasibility of redistributing income without reducing investment. Actually the results of our neo-Keynesian model under the assumption of an exclusive tax on capitalist consumption are a bit disappointing; or perhaps we should say the solutions are too complicated to provide much substantive insight. Certainly our results are very different than those obtained by Przeworski and Wallerstein. The optimal investment rate is by no means independent of the rate at which capitalist consumption is taxed. Depending on the circumstances, an increase in the consumption tax could either spur or retard the rate at which capitalists invest. If workers' demand intensity is significantly higher than capitalist demand intensity, the state would not be free to maneuver in the way suggested by Przeworski and Wallerstein.

However, we have already articulated a more fundamental critique of the Przeworski and Wallerstein approach to analyzing structural dependence: when confronted by a pro-worker government, capitalists will not assume taxation policies are immutable and adjust accordingly, they will try to change the objectionable taxation schemes. Such action is all the more likely within the context of political democracy since pro-worker governments can be voted out of office, and since electorates everywhere are highly responsive to economic trends. How will capitalists behave when faced with a hostile government? Surely they will not try to maximize their static utility function in the manner prescribed by Przeworski and Wallerstein. Why bow to a hostile fate when the means to avert it lay at hand?

Capitalists might try to gain political leverage by attacking the working class with which the hostile government is closely identified. In economic terms this would mean choosing an investment rate s so as to minimize the worker utility function W^*. Such a strategy, however, could severely damage capitalist interests and thus is not likely to be adopted. A more attractive strategy would be to maximize the difference between the capitalist and the worker utility function, that is to maximize $P^* - W^*$. This approach balances the objectives of attacking the working class and safeguarding capitalist interests. To be sure, it may diminish the overall utility of property owners, but only insofar as its diminishes wage-earners' utility (and by implication the utility of state managers) even more.

What happens if capitalists select an investment rate s with the objective of maximizing $P^* - W^*$? To make things more interesting, let us suppose the state imposes a tax exclusively on capitalist consumption. It is easily seen that

$$P^* - W^* = \ln P(0) - \ln W(0)$$
$$= \frac{1}{\rho} \ln \frac{(1 - m)(1 - s)(1 - t_c)}{m + (1 - m)(1 - s)\, t_c} \qquad [3.29]$$

and

$$\frac{\partial (P^* - W^*)}{\partial s} = \frac{-m}{\rho(1 - s)[m + (1 - m)(1 - s)\, t_c]} \qquad [3.30]$$

In order to insure that $\partial(P^* - W^*) / \partial s$ exists let us assume that

$$0 < m, t_c < 1 \quad \text{and} \quad s < 1 \qquad [3.31]$$

It follows that, in all situations consistent with equation 3.31, capitalists will disinvest at the fastest rate possible. If negative investment rates are excluded from consideration, then s^* will equal zero. If negative rates are permitted, then s^* will equal the lowest permissible investment rate. The state, once perceived as unfriendly to the interests of property, cannot prevent such capitalist disinvestment through its choice of a taxation rate t_c. This result is entirely independent of the v_i parameters meaning that it holds for both the Przeworski-Wallerstein model and our own.

If the political process is such that capitalists, when confronted by what they deem a hostile government, shift from maximizing P^* to maximizing $P^* - W^*$, then the state remains dependent upon capital even in what Przeworski and Wallerstein call the static situation and even when the state uses their preferred taxation instrument, an exclusive tax on consumption. Maximizing $P^* - W^*$ is not a long-term capitalist strategy. Its purpose is to compel a change in government or at least a change in government policy. When this has been achieved capitalists presumably would return to the strategy of maximizing P^*.

Suppose capitalists despair about the possibility of changing state policy. Matters would not proceed just as they had before. Increasing ρ, the rate at which the future is discounted, would be a plausible capitalist reaction. Both in the Przeworski-Wallerstein model and our own, under all wage rates and all the proposed taxation schemes, an increase in the future discount rate causes a decline in the optimal rate of investment. Whether this decline would negate the benefits accruing to the working class from tax-based income transfers is hard to say, but it easily could. The capitalist consumption annihilating taxation rates envisioned by Przeworski and Wallerstein would probably induce steep rises in ρ, and in all models optimal investment is highly sensitive to the level of the discount rate.[12]

Considerations like these cast further doubt on the notion that the state could escape dependence on capital while leaving investment decisions in private hands. By way of contrast, Przeworski and Wallerstein conclude their static analysis on a rather optimistic note:

> There may be limits to the ability of the state to redistribute consumption without discouraging private investment. . . . But all of these reasons are less general then the claims of the theory of structural dependence. Our analysis reveals a large range

of economically feasible policies. . . . The state is not structurally dependent. (1988, p. 21)

Keynesianism is sometimes said to be the economic theory of social democracy (Przeworski, 1985, p. 36-38), and the analysis presented above certainly owes a great deal to Keynesian ideas. But our results do not confirm the upbeat tenor of the passage above, nor would it be confirmed by appeals to historical evidence (though Przeworski and Wallerstein seem at least dubious about the relevance of historical evidence).[13] Mature capitalism generally improves the welfare of the working class, and the state has a significant role in this process. This we do not contest. There seems every reason to believe, however, that the state in capitalist society—meaning a state which accepts capitalist social relations—will find itself structurally dependent upon capitalist economic institutions. If so, the necessity of protecting the economic interests of the capitalist class will place rather tight limits on how much the capitalist state can help other constituencies.

5. Conclusion

State intervention, argued Michal Kalecki, could tame that part of the business cycle created by purely economic forces, but it would lead to what he called a "political business cycle" (1971, chap. 12). According to this theory, the capitalist class feared the *political* effects of full employment. Therefore the state in a capitalist society would not always maintain full employment even though it had the means of doing so, and even though full employment raised capitalist profits. The capitalist class, argued Kalecki, wanted the state to be dependent upon capital and opposed state spending to create employment because it might reduce such dependency. Business interests feared public investment would compete with private investment, and subsidizing mass consumption would undermine the work incentive. A condition of full employment could hamper workplace discipline and render the working class more aggressive.

The post-World War II experience of social democratic governments has basically supported the views of Kalecki.[14] The problems confronting social democratic governments have been aggravated by the openness of their economies to international competition.[15] Whenever rising wages threatened profits, social democratic governments (or conservative governments elected in their place on an austerity platform) enacted restrictive policies which, by lowering effective demand, ultimately hurt profits as well as wages.

Nevertheless our analysis suggests that social democracy can make capitalism work better for both workers and capitalists at least some of the time; but a social democratic state soon encounters barriers to the continuation of these achievements. These barriers result partly from the defensive reactions of capitalists themselves and partly from the international context within which the capitalist state functions.

The fact that capitalism is a world system does not qualitatively change the problems encountered by social democratic strategy; it simply means these problems surface a little sooner (and perhaps a little more severely) because the nation-state cannot control most features of the international capitalist environment. Social democratic governments are confronted with a difficult choice between (a) isolating their country from the world capitalist system to establish more effective controls over domestic economic processes and safeguard structural reforms (at the expense of diminishing short-term economic welfare and possibly impairing economic growth), or (b) participating in the international capitalist system to gain the advantages of foreign markets and the world division of labor (at the risk of submitting to the system's economic logic thereby subverting major internal reforms). To date no social democratic government has had either the political strength to attempt the first course of action, or the political imagination needed to escape the horns of the dilemma altogether.

Our analysis also points to the relevance of the business cycle for understanding the phenomenon of structural dependence. When investment spending is low, a social democratic government can redistribute income toward workers without jeopardizing capitalist investment. In fact such redistribution will probably increase investment by increasing workers' consumption and thereby augment effective demand. Yet this very process pushes the economy toward a condition from which redistributive policies are no longer Pareto-optimal and the issue of structural dependence appears in a quite different light. When investment spending is high and production approaches full capacity, redistributive policies will either decrease investment and hence the rate of economic growth or, if capitalists try to maintain their income by raising profit margins, will cause inflation, currency depreciation, and financial capital flight (in highly open economies). Under these circumstances the social democratic state (or any other government for that matter) keenly experiences its dependence upon capital.

Due to the salience of economic fluctuations for issues of structural dependence, an adequate model of the latter must include the business cycle within its purview. This would mean abandoning the exponential growth model used by Przeworski and Wallerstein and, with certain modifications, continued in this chapter. It would also mean relaxing the assumption that investment constitutes a fixed share of national income, and treating the investment share as an endogenous variable instead.

The results presented in this chapter generally support claims that the state is structurally dependent upon capital. However, our model also points to another form of state dependency: dependency of the state on wages. Neither the capitalist class nor governments strongly identified with it can push the wage share of national income below a certain point without creating serious realization problems endangering both economic growth and capitalist welfare and possibly precipitating a fiscal crisis of the state. Just as pro-labor governments within democratic capitalist societies do not move vigorously against capitalist interests, so pro-capitalist governments within these societies will observe unexpected restraint in assaulting the economic interests of the working class. The much and deservedly abused administration of Ronald Reagan is a case in point.

Capitalism, like all class-divided societies, is a system of exploitation; but it is also a system imposing limits on the extent of viable (that is, sustainable) exploitation. The logic of capital coercively imposes itself upon pro-capitalist as well as upon pro-worker governments.

Notes

1. The formal model developed in this chapter builds upon ideas from Przeworski's earlier book *Capitalism and Social Democracy* (1985) several chapters of which were coauthored by Wallerstein.

2. A somewhat different result emerges when changes in the taxation and income transfer policies of the state come into the picture. During the period when such changes are anticipated but not yet implemented, investment rates are altered in the way predicted by structural dependence theory. Przeworski and Wallerstein therefore think the state may be dependent on capital in a dynamic sense.

3. Przeworski and Wallerstein generally treat $P(\tau)$ as if it were equivalent to capitalist consumption. Our approach, however, recognizes the existence of income neither consumed nor invested in the expansion of productive facilities. As we shall see, this can be a significant component of capitalist income and can have great import for the evolution of capitalist production.

4. The idea that workers, even in the absence of state intervention, can control the share of national income going to wages and choose a wage share optimizing time-discounted working-class utility is highly unrealistic to say the least. Przeworski and Wallerstein have no illusions on this score. They make the assumption of working-class control in order to model strategic conflict between workers and capitalists within the economic sphere. The essence of strategic conflict is that each party controls some aspect of the conflict situation, but must consider other participants' reactions to the choices they make. Unless workers control something there can be no strategic conflict between workers and capitalists, although a conflict of interest can still

exist. Once the structure of strategic conflict has been established, it is possible to investigate how the state can intervene.

5. The stipulation of constant wage and profit shares is one of the strongest assumptions made by the Przeworski-Wallerstein model and one of the first which should be relaxed in obtaining a more realistic representation of class relations in a capitalist economy. In order to achieve the maximum comparability between our own results and those obtained by Przeworski and Wallerstein we have maintained this assumption in the model presented in this chapter. However, this constant share assumption has been eliminated in several of our other alternatives to the Przeworski and Wallerstein model. In these alternative models wage and profit shares are endogenously determined.

6. This relationship plays a part in our own analysis of how structural dependence works.

7. A little reflection will help the reader understand why this happens. This investment rate in the Przeworski-Wallerstein model reflects the trade-off between present consumption and prospective future consumption. Naturally this trade-off will depend upon both the rate of discounting the future ρ and the effectiveness of investment spending in creating economic growth v. The consumption tax reduces present and future consumption in the same proportion, but does not alter the growth-inducing efficiency of funds allocated for investment. Hence it does not change the trade-off between present and future consumption, and thus does not effect the investment rate. The income tax, on the other hand, does reduce the efficiency of funds allocated for investment because it takes some of these funds for taxes. Therefore it alters the trade-off between present and prospective future consumption to the latter's disadvantage resulting in a compensating shift from capitalist investment to capitalist consumption.

8. Unless otherwise indicated, all the v_i parameters are assumed to be nonnegative.

9. If $v_2 = v_3$, then $v_6 = 0$, and equation 3.16 reduces to the corresponding expression of the Przeworski-Wallerstein model (1988, p. 24, expression [A − 1]).

10. That is, if $v_2 > 2v_3$, and $m < \frac{1}{2}$, then $\partial P^* / \partial m > 0$.

11. This expression is obtained by observing that

$$W(\tau) = mY(\tau)$$

and using this to calculate the workers' utility function which is

$$W^* = \frac{1}{\rho} \left\{ \ln[mY(0)] + \frac{s(1-m)(v_6 m + v_5)}{\rho} \right\}$$

The optimal wage share is chosen so as to maximize W^*.

12. Przeworski and Wallerstein "treat investment in a neoclassical fashion as the result of intertemporal allocation of consumption by owners of capital" (1988, p. 27, n. 6).

13. After discussing the experiences of Salvador Allende in Chile and Michael Manley in Jamaica, Przeworski and Wallerstein write: "These experiences cannot speak to the issue of limits and possibilities: one can always cite some counterfactual actions which would have perhaps avoided the disasters. The issue concerns possibility and possibilities cannot be determined on the basis of limited historical experience" (1988, p. 14).

14. We should also call attention to other neo-Keynesian thinkers who have advanced similar arguments such as Nicholas Kaldor, Stephen Marglin, Luigi Pasinetti, Joan Robinson, and Josef Steindl.

15. "Social democracy in one country" does not seem feasible.

4

Structure and Consciousness in the Rise of the Nazi State

THOMAS F. MAYER
ROBERT A. POIS

We shall argue that fascism arises from tensions between capitalist development and political democracy. National Socialism prevailed in Germany because it could transform the German state in ways which temporarily resolved these tensions between capitalism and democracy. Of all the political contenders, only the Nazi party could gain wide adherence in post-World War I German society characterized as it was by deep class antagonisms and structural problems demanding radical change. Yet these same class antagonisms and structural problems generated forms of consciousness deeply antagonistic to social change. The basis of Nazi power lay in the contradictions between structure and consciousness, between the necessity for and the resistance to fundamental social change.

Structural Considerations in the Rise of the Nazi State: Democracy and Accumulation

The concept of structural causality emerges from the scarcely controversial notion that human society can be viewed as a *system* of social relations. The word "system" here has a double significance. It means that the various elements of human society fit together and jointly constitute a coherent (but not uncontradictory) whole. It also means that human society possesses a structure whose existence does not depend upon the awareness of its participants. The connection between human action and human society conceived as a system of social relations is twofold. The system influences the kinds of human actions that occur, while human actions reproduce and/or transform the social system itself. The concept of structural causality refers to the *reciprocal* determinations between human action and the system of social relations.

The word "reciprocal" bears special notice. By some accounts structural causality would only pertain to the determination of action by system, not the other way around. However, we think emphasis on the reciprocal aspect of determination is critical for avoiding the rigid determinism and neglect of human agency which mar some forms of structuralism.[1] As we shall see below, action often constitutes structure. An important example of this is the way in which classes are constituted by class struggles.[2]

Certain features of German social development have been associated with the rise of National Socialism by writers with widely different theoretical orientations (e.g., Gerschenkron, 1943; Dahrendorf, 1979; B. Moore, 1966). One of the features most commonly associated with the rise of German fascism is the purported absence of a successful Western-style bourgeois revolution. This supposedly allowed a pre-capitalist agrarian elite to retain a powerful position within a modern capitalist economy, preserved traditional social status as a crucial dimension of the stratification system, and created a bourgeoisie deeply influenced by feudal values and modes of operation.[3]

The importance of the state in accomplishing industrialization is another aspect of German social development sometimes thought to favor the rise of fascism. The resulting interpenetration of political and economic institutions fostered a German state with overweening power, and simultaneously discouraged the emergence of autonomous capitalist industry as an institutional counterweight. A third factor, closely related to the ones already mentioned, is the weakness of parliamentary institutions and democratic ideology throughout Germany; a weakness enervating opposition to authoritarian movements of all sorts.

While some or perhaps even all of these factors help explain the emergence of German fascism, we think structural analysis should focus upon the system of capitalist democracy that existed in Weimar Germany. The term "capitalist democracy" may not be an oxymoron, but such a system combines political and economic structures of, at best, marginal compatibility. The most obvious contradiction in any system of capitalist democracy lies between private property and popular sovereignty. If citizens really have political power, why should they tolerate enormous property inequalities like those characteristic of capitalist economic organization? Conversely, why should the tiny elite which own and control vast amounts of capitalist property support a political system that could at any moment place their ownership in jeopardy?

The contradictions implicit in any system of capitalist democracy make its social reproduction problematic. A common response to the problems of reproducing capitalist democracy involves increasing separation between the executive functions of the state and its representative or democratic aspects. The structure of German society made social reproduction of the Weimar Republic form of capitalist democracy particularly difficult. Faced with severe economic depression the Weimar form of capitalist democracy simply could not reproduce itself.[4] National Socialism as a system of state power entails an extreme separation between the administrative and the representative components of the polity.

The key strength of National Socialism was its capacity to make reaction popular. It solved the structural problem of authoritarian rule in a democratic age by elaborating the distinction between participating in the political process and controlling the state. The forms of democracy were transmuted into the substance of dictatorship. The German people were connected with the Nazi state by (a) rejecting popular sovereignty in favor of mass politicization, (b) making activity rather than decision the heart of citizenship, (c) interpreting majority rule as emotional identification with the state and its leader, (d) heightening the affinity between submission to and identification with the state, (e) functional substitution of civic rituals for elections, (f) intensifying communal consciousness through militarism and racial nationalism, and (g) establishing a collective social project through imperialist expansion (Bracher, 1970, pp. 8-9; Talmon, 1961).

The form of unity cultivated by National Socialism was not an association of individuals based upon mutual benefit. The communalist solidarity favored by the Nazis was more akin to the forms of unity prevailing within family life. Elections are intrinsically hostile to such communalist structures because they cast participants in the role of self-interested individuals thereby atomizing the collectivity, and also because elections reveal (and encourage) internal conflicts rather than the unity of the whole. Just as violence can have a certain acceptance within family life, terror has a place within certain communalist forms of political solidarity. Terror emphasizes the patriarchal authority of the leader, establishes obedience not only as an externally imposed necessity but as a self-imposed moral obligation, stresses the distinction between insiders and others (and the value of being the former), and demonstrates the determination of the violent leader and hence the transcendent importance of the cause which commands loyalty to it.

The capacity of National Socialism to make reaction popular and its methods of binding the masses to the state were evident long before Hitler's elevation to the Chancellorship. It was this which converted the abstract preference of the dominant class for authoritarian rule into a real possibility. It is not quite accurate to say that National Socialism gave capitalism a mass base. National Socialism provided a mass base for a specific type of authoritarian capitalist state which then secured capitalist property (at least temporarily) and facilitated capital accumulation.

A fundamental source of anticapitalism is the social divisiveness of a capitalist economy. The accumulation process tends to divide the community into a small elite which controls the major concentrations of capitalist property and a large mass of people essentially excluded from ownership of the means of production. The communalist solidarity of the Nazi movement eroded this partition, not of course by ending exploitation, but by diminishing its salience relative to the *Volk* unity of the German people. When juxtaposed to their common membership in the German racial nation, the social relevance of the antagonism between worker and capitalist diminished significantly.

Under National Socialism anticapitalism evolved into anti-Semitism. It was not so much that Jews appeared in popular consciousness as the rulers of industry; but they were commonly perceived as well adapted to and relatively successful within the capitalist system. Thus they could function as plausible targets for resentments about unemployment, business failure, inflation, competitive stress, and the other ineradicable insecurities of life under capitalism. For many Germans victimized by the Depression, anger about relative success or lack thereof was a stronger emotion than sentiments about huge but socially distant concentrations of power.

Jews frequently occupied intermediate positions within the capitalist economic framework. They were small bankers, wholesalers, department store managers, grain dealers, real estate agents, pawn shop owners, and so forth. In these positions they encountered middle-class Germans as palpable agents of finance capital, absorbing much of the anger which might more properly have been directed against it. Notwithstanding their comparatively weak position within the larger economic structure, Jews could thus become rather effective tokens of capitalist exploitation. The subsequent expropriation of Jewish property satisfied some of the anticapitalist desires of the German masses, not because it enriched the middle or working classes (the main beneficiaries were giant corporations), but rather because it suggested the possibility of further and more extensive expropriations (which never happened) (Neumann, 1944, pp. 121-123).

National Socialism also transformed anticapitalism into aggressive expansionism. When Hitler came to power, the socialist aspects of the Nazi movement were thoroughly repressed. Expansion provided an outlet for the frustrated energies of Nazi anticapitalism. It was, after all, an endeavor requiring the joint participation of all classes in German society from which everyone might anticipate certain benefits. If anticapitalism meant mitigation of capitalist class conflict, then imperialist expansion was, at least in this limited sense, formally anticapitalist. It was formally anticapitalist in other ways as well. Expansion within the European continent implied a militarized economy featuring state planning rather than market organized production, administered rather than competitively determined prices, and controlled employment rather than a free labor market. We have here the substance of capitalist development cast in the forms of "post-" if not "anti-" capitalism.

The contribution of National Socialism to the reproduction of capitalism becomes even more evident when we consider the interaction between the rapid pace of German industrialization and the tardiness of German unification. The coincidence of these two realities meant that capitalist class conflict emerged in the context of unresolved nationality problems and sometimes in the midst of severe regional antagonisms. The latter was particularly true of southern Germany and the former multinational Austro-Hungarian Empire, the nurseries of National Socialism. The two forms of conflict sometimes became thoroughly entangled with part of the animus of class struggle being channeled into national chauvinism. Both the organization of National Socialism and its seemingly confused ideology express this entanglement.

When historical circumstances somehow limit the possibilities of successful working-class struggle, the class-conflict nationality-conflict ambivalence will be resolved in favor of the latter which then absorbs the total energies generated by antagonistic social relations. Because the structure of the Nazi movement embodied this ambivalence, it could use the opportunities created by the frustrated working-class struggles of the Weimar period, redirecting these antagonisms in ways that preserved capitalist property and accelerated capital accumulation.

The tension between capitalism and democracy which provides the focal point of our structural analysis connects with the issue of a German bourgeois revolution. The denial of any fundamental tension between capitalism and democracy—and even more the thesis of an inherent nexus between the two (Lindblom, 1977)—is often accompanied by the claim that the bourgeoisie (or fractions thereof) functions as the class carrier of political democracy; from which it follows that the bourgeois revolution is also a democratic revolution. We reject this argument.

A bourgeois revolution secures the conditions needed for the reproduction of capitalism and establishes overall bourgeois cultural dominance. A bourgeois revolution need not be a democratic revolution and, given the structural tension between capitalism and democracy, there are strong pressures against any such association. Political democracy is the result of class struggle, not a consequence of bourgeois social supremacy.

The supposition that the bourgeoisie, by its inherent nature, supports democracy is substantively mistaken; but even more importantly it reveals a misguided concept of social class. Classes are best understood not as abstract entities to be inferred from the structure of social relations, but as contingent historical entities whose existence is at least partially engendered by class struggle. The paradoxical conclusion of this reasoning is that class struggles create classes.[5]

The German bourgeoisie was formed through a class struggle which inclined it toward social hierarchy and political authoritarianism rather than toward liberalism and democracy. The authoritarian cast of the German bourgeoisie stemmed quite logically from its own internal divisions, from its confrontations with a socialist labor movement on the one hand and an agrarian aristocracy on the other, and from its reliance upon an authoritarian state to secure the conditions of capitalist development (Blackbourn & Eley, 1984, p. 147). The absence of democracy in pre-World War I Germany did not necessarily signify the absence of a bourgeois revolution; it merely indicated the politically reactionary character of the German bourgeoisie. Conversely, the cause of National Socialism cannot be located in the political weakness or political inadvertence of the German bourgeoisie.

The conservative complexion of the German bourgeois revolution had several consequences relevant to the emergence of National Socialism. Most immediately it produced a capitalist class that could easily adjust to a dictatorship provided the latter respected the imperatives of capitalist property. It also preserved traditional status (in the Weberian sense of social honor) as an important dimension of the German stratification system effecting, among other things, the viability and robustness of interclass political coalitions. The continuing relevance of traditional status allowed remnants of the landed nobility to survive as something more than an agrarian bourgeoisie, a circumstance which surely abetted the vitality of a politically reactionary military establishment. The conservatism of the bourgeois revolution fostered alliances between capitalists and the military both under the *Kaiserreich* and in the Weimar Republic: the former alliances being founded upon preparations for war and a joint desire for imperialist expansion, the latter ones being cemented by common fears of proletarian revolution and common suspicions of the democratic state.

By the same token, the emergence of political democracy from the ashes of World War I posed serious problems for the highly fractionalized German bourgeoisie. Prior to 1918, bourgeois unity—to the extent mandatory for overall capitalist stability—had been achieved largely through the mediation of the state, and on the basis of a program emphasizing imperialist expansion through war and suppression of socialism. Weimar democracy, despite the eagerness of its leaders to cooperate with the capitalist class, thoroughly disrupted this arrangement. It governed a nation recently defeated in an imperialist war, and had itself been established largely through the initiative of socialists. Weimar democracy politicized the economic conflicts between fractions of the bourgeoisie thus allowing the class formation processes sketched above to cleave asunder the capitalist class itself. Moreover, Weimar democracy, in conjunction with economic crisis, made the financial security of the working class dependent on its access to political power, a connection which lured the bourgeoisie even further into the political arena and further aggravated its internal divisions.

Structural Considerations in the Rise of the Nazi State: Class Relations

Why could National Socialism overcome the internal divisions of the German bourgeoisie? Mainly because it could escape the domestic and international shackles which prevented imperialist expansion and could successfully repress all manifestations of working class radicalism. This enabled it to resurrect, in a more extreme form to be sure, the essential policies underpinning the limited but functionally adequate capitalist class unity of the *Kaiserreich*. Hence, the Nazi state was better positioned to combat unemployment and other ravages of depression than the Weimar Republic had been.

In a democratic context, big business is apprehensive about the social consequences of many measures the state might use to combat depression even though these measures would increase profits. For example, big business might oppose public investment because it sets a bad precedent and competes with private investment; and it might oppose subsidizing mass consumption because this undermines the work incentive. In a capitalist democracy, big business typically fears full employment because it tends to weaken workplace discipline and make the working class more aggressive.

Fascist dictatorship removes many capitalist objections to full employment. Because the fascist state has suppressed trade unions and all other manifestations of working class autonomy, the capitalist class need no longer rely upon economic pressures for purposes of workplace discipline. Because government spending concentrates upon armaments it will not compete with private investment. Under fascism the capitalist class can tolerate the full range of state-initiated antidepression policies (Kalecki, 1971, pp. 138-145). Under the Weimar Republic, significant fractions of the bourgeoisie opposed public works programs fearing they might favor the German labor movement. Under National Socialism, with trade unions gone, no capitalist objection was raised to government spending done on a far greater scale.

Marx defined Bonapartism as a form of the capitalist state in which the bourgeoisie abandoned political power in order to preserve its social domination. A number of authors including Antonio Gramsci and August Thalheimer have identified this relationship between the bourgeoisie and the state as the fundamental characteristic of modern fascism.[6] More recent evidence suggests that, under conditions of economic or political crisis, the state in advanced capitalist societies increasingly separates itself from direct control by the capitalist class. By separating itself in this fashion, the state does not turn against the capitalist system as a whole. Quite the contrary, to support the system effectively under crisis conditions the state must be highly independent from any particular elements of the capitalist class.[7]

The autonomy of the National Socialist state from control by the capitalist class or any of its fractions enhanced its ability to unify the bourgeoisie. Ultimately this generated a condition in which the political priorities of the state completely overshadowed the economic interests of the capitalist class in the determination of public policy. By the concluding years of the Third Reich the capitalist class had learned that its complete abandonment of political power, even if undertaken voluntarily, could pose deadly dangers of its own.

Besides contributing to the unity of the dominant classes, National Socialism also strengthened the popular legitimacy of their dominance. We have already discussed some of the ways this happened, but our analysis remains incomplete. The Nazi movement, as has often been noted, received disproportional support from the middle classes who felt squeezed between organized labor and monopoly capital, and whose divergent material interests made it hard to achieve autonomous political organization. The structural incoherence of middle-class interests often attracted the petty bourgeoisie toward political movements which deemphasized the importance of class struggle, and the Nazi glorification of race and nation were appealing for roughly the same reasons. The undiminished significance of noneconomic status considerations within the German stratification system greatly hindered formation of any stable political alliance between the middle and working classes.

While the support given by the middle classes to National Socialism cannot be gainsaid, we think it more important to emphasize the wide class basis of the Nazi movement which:

united a broadly based coalition of the subordinate classes, centered on the
peasantry and petite bourgeoisie but stretching deep into the wage-earning population. (Eley, 1983, p. 75)[8]

The Nazi coalition was based upon racist ideology, imperialist expansion,
and a distinctive form of organizational dualism.

Prior to the acquisition of state power, organizational dualism took the
form of a split between National Socialism as a dynamic formless movement
and National Socialism as a hierarchical structure penetrated by a drastic
leadership principle. Afterwards the same organizational duality was
expressed in the bifurcation between party and state. This duality, we submit,
is related to National Socialism's remarkable ability to hold together a broad
class coalition: It permitted the integration of forces for change and forces
for order within a functioning political unit; it provided for practical expression of wildly antagonistic ideological impulses without disrupting the
coherence of the organization; it allowed for the promulgation and disciplined execution of unexpected political initiatives which kept opponents off
balance and strengthened organizational elan; it explains why sober German
capitalists, fully aware of the NSDAP's anticapitalist rhetoric and penchant
for crackpot economic nostrums, could entrust their political future to
National Socialism; it created a complex and contradictory political reality
providing disparate social classes with subjectively meaningful objects of
identification and support.

Conversely, the imperative of solidifying and energizing an exceptionally
broad class coalition motivated continuation of a dualistic organizational
structure after National Socialism had acquired state power. This imperative
also encouraged renewed imperialist expansion.

World War I inevitably had a brutalizing effect on all the main combatants.
In the German situation, it increased the acceptability of civic violence, a
phenomenon evident not only in the tolerance extended to the private armies
of National Socialism but also in the consistent political bias of the Weimar
court system. The war discredited the classes which had led the imperialist
endeavor, but it did not discredit imperialist expansion as such. Nor did the
revolution of 1918 alter those class relations which for half a century had
propelled German expansionism.[9] The tenuous class equilibrium of German
capitalism depended upon the prospect and reality of imperialist expansion.
This welded together the dominant groups in German society and helped
them forge essential links with the subordinate classes. Expansion and
production of the military wherewithal this might require had been used to
cope with one economic crisis after another. German society was structurally

addicted to imperialism and military defeat had done nothing to alter this addiction.

National Socialism, for all its bizarre attributes, was actually in tune with the structural needs of German capitalism, while the class-immobilized Weimar democracy was not. Racism is in many ways the logical ideology of imperialism. Open domestic class struggle would impair and possibly destroy the imperialistic enterprise. The seemingly irrational racial anti-Semitism of the Nazi movement incubated the seed of renewed imperial expansion. The violent activities of National Socialism conditioned society for the violence needed to throw off the Versailles straitjacket within which German imperialism languished. Over the course of inflation, depression, class disunity, and frequent changes of government an increasing number of Germans perceived a congruence between the Hitler movement and the structural requirements of a class-fragmented monopoly capitalist society which had turned its back on social revolution.

Citing Hungary, Germany, Spain, Greece, and Chile as examples, the Yugoslavian Marxist Branko Horvat argues that failed socialist revolution "almost invariably" leads to fascism (1982, p. 387, p. 643, n. 13). It does so by weakening democratic social forces while simultaneously creating both the incentive and the social basis for a reactionary coalition bent on eliminating, by means of brutal repression, any future threats to capitalist property and petty bourgeoisie social status. Other social theorists have also linked fascism with counterrevolution. August Thalheimer associated fascism with a defeat of the working-class revolutionary movement plus a continued possibility of social revolution due to the bourgeoisie's incapacity to rule effectively (Rabinbach, 1974, p. 133). Geoff Eley interprets fascism as a "counterrevolutionary ideological project" mainly directed against working-class socialism (1983, p. 81).

The acquisition of state power by a fascist movement is indeed a crushing defeat for working-class socialism, but it certainly does not represent an unmitigated triumph for the propertied classes. National Socialism came to power due to a crisis in reproducing political democracy within a capitalist context. Through repression of the labor movement, military production, and aggressive imperialist expansion, the Nazi state promoted capital accumulation and managed to pull the German economy out of the doldrums of depression. But the stronger it became, the less deference National Socialism exhibited to the interests of the bourgeoisie. The fascist state in Germany never ceased promoting capital accumulation, but it emancipated itself almost entirely from the political influence of the capitalist class. In fact, the history of National Socialism after 1936 seems to show that economic conditions fostering capital accumulation need not coincide with political conditions which secure capitalist property.

Consciousness and Rise of the Nazi State:
Forms of Class Awareness

Historians understand consciousness as the perceptions historical actors have of their material and spiritual situations within society, perceptions which are sometimes articulated in comprehensive belief systems. Through reason-informed empathic understanding, the historian tries to grasp the consciousness of the historical actor, and thus to comprehend—within certain limits—what people thought or felt about themselves and the world around them.

Consciousness must be contrasted with, but also related to, the structural realities of social organization. It can influence these realities or even create its own mental realities at variance with those which historians regard as objective or structural.[10] The role played by nationalism in obscuring concrete structural problems has often been cited by historians.

For the majority of workers who saw their interests represented by the Social Democratic Party and the nominally Social Democratic labor unions, class consciousness was an operative reality, and this determined their position towards the Weimar state. After all, the Social Democrats, along with the Catholic Center Party and the increasingly superfluous German Democratic Party, had formed the original "Weimar Coalition." The Republic was, in a certain sense, their state. Notwithstanding precious little Social Democratic participation in the cabinets—and between 1920 and 1928 not a single Social Democratic chancellor—the Weimar Republic remained a state dedicated to social equity. Workers represented by the Social Democrats identified with the Republic out of recognition that state institutions could and often did serve their interests.

Of course, the Communist Party and the workers who supported it claimed to have a more realistic view of Weimar Germany. Recognizing that certain crucial social realities remained unchanged from Imperial days, the Communists saw the Republic as a pious sham which, ultimately, favored the interests of the bosses. In the end, one could expect little from a "Republic" headed by the party that had presided over the murder of Rosa Luxemburg and Karl Liebknecht.[11]

However divided the various factions of the German capitalist class may have been, they all thought they embodied the true interests of German society. If one identified German interests with the conditions necessary for sustaining industrial power, this belief rang true. Threats to industry—among others, unfavorable balances of trade, declining profits, arbitration arrangements biased toward labor, and an extremely costly social welfare system—appeared as general threats to the well-being of the nation. German industrialists of all kinds could plausibly think their class interests were identical to the national interests of Germany.

German farmers and land owners faced hard times even before the Great Depression. Increasingly aware of their marginal economic position, rural folk, including those once positively disposed toward the Weimar Republic, became progressively embittered against a government seemingly more responsive to the demands of rioting workers and export trade profiteers than to the urgent necessities of people who fed the country (Conway, 1966, p. 150-151). According to electoral data, the NSDAP received relatively more support in rural than in urban areas (R. Hamilton, 1982, p. 36-45).

All classes in German society were sensitive to economic conditions. The middle classes differed from the others in being acutely aware of their *special* interests, and in rejecting most forms of class thinking about broader political and social issues. This sort of consciousness led to extremely narrow "interest politics" making government coalitions impossible to form at the very time Germany began to feel the full impact of the Depression. Such "interest politics" increasingly caused middle-class people to oppose the Republic, and were mainly responsible for what a distinguished historian has called "the dying middle" (Jones, 1972).

Nevertheless, the longing of middle-class and agriculturalist folk for the *Volksgemeinschaft* and their sometimes strident rejection of class thinking had a basis in reality. Feeling trapped between large-scale capitalist interests and an aggressive politically organized working class, the middle sectors of German society were terrified of any serious class confrontation. In any such an encounter they would surely emerge as the big losers.

Consciousness and the Rise of the Nazi State: The National Socialist Mystique

The National Socialist ideology had at its core strongly articulated religious elements. In fact, it can be plausibly described as a religion (see Pois, 1986; Rhodes, 1980; Sironneau, 1982). The central task of the National Socialist religion was fostering the emergence of the new "Aryan Man." This implied destroying or at least weakening the enemies of "Aryan Man," and here we can accurately speak of an "anti-Jewish Revolution."[12] Many Germans who voted National Socialist, and even many who joined the Party, were not fanatical anti-Semites.[13] But anti-Semitism lay at the very heart of Hitler's belief system, and the structural forces discussed above gave enormous power and autonomy to the ideology of the supreme leader.

The National Socialist ideology was also a form of "biological mysticism" (Rauschning, 1939, p. 240). National Socialist ideologies saw their movement as grounded in what they liked to call "laws of life." Man's estrangement from the natural world would be ended through participation in the movement. Grounded in "laws of life," actions taken by the National Socialist leadership were justified by their very commission. This way of thinking allowed the Nazi leadership extraordinary tactical flexibility; flexibility probably unequaled by any modern political movement.

In many areas of popular concern the National Socialist "religion" was genuinely petit bourgeois.[14] Women must be liberated from women's liberation. Patriarchal usages at all levels of social life must be preserved. Annoying experiments in modern art must give way to a healthy national art. Above all, divisive class thinking must be dissolved within a comforting if history-defying *Volksgemeinschaft*.[15] These were the "laws of life" with which the German public soon became familiar.

The violence of National Socialism was one of its most attractive features. Violence seemed to embody dynamic youthful courage and idealism utterly lacking in middle-class parties and even in the Social Democrats. World War I had brutalized German social, political, and cultural life to an extent unimaginable in the Imperial age. For embittered soldiers who returned to a society in flux which could hardly accommodate them, for young men despondent at having missed the glorious adventure and feeling betrayed by the outcome, and for others like them the brutal Free Corps exercised considerable appeal.

While not all Free Corps members later joined the SA, the anomic nature of immediate postwar German life, and the violence-prone organizations it bred provided a spiritual bridge to National Socialism. Disaffected young people of all classes were drawn to a movement which connected violence with idealism in an ideology of national renewal.

A political messianism which eschewed all varieties of class consciousness plus the appeal to generally held petit bourgeois values, allowed National Socialism to achieve synergy with much of the German people. Once in power, an utterly unprincipled pragmatism allowed the Nazi elite to implement economic policies which, at least until the late 1930s, satisfied both working-class and capitalist interests. Rearmament, various public works projects, plus favorable trade balances with countries of Eastern Europe, virtually ended unemployment; and the owners of German industry, despite controls on profits, did rather well indeed.[16]

Hitler's rise to power created a major organizational difficulty: How would the National Socialist movement relate to the German state?[17] Audaciously thumbing his nose at long established precedent, Hitler deemphasized the state in favor of the movement. The state had never been sacred in the eyes of leading National Socialists. It provided mechanisms that could be useful to the movement, particularly in such mundane spheres as economics, transportation, agriculture, and the like. But crucial decisions—those directly concerning the National Socialist mission—were generally made outside of the formal state apparatus. In certain key areas such as racial policies and military decision making, one might even say that the Nazi movement *was* the state.[18]

If Germany had remained at peace, a system which tried to be all things to all people could not have lasted. Such a system would have required truly totalitarian social controls, something probably not feasible with the relatively primitive technology of the time. However, Hitler's "biological mysticism" implied policies requiring war, and war came perhaps a bit earlier than the Nazis had anticipated.

The Dynamics of State Change

How did structure and consciousness interact in the rise of the Nazi state? A structural crisis emerging largely from tensions between capitalist accumulation and political democracy weakened the Weimar Republic and eventually rendered it unviable. The crisis was overcome by placing in power a movement without strong ties to any social class, but able to satisfy some of the claims of each. The chaotic nature of National Socialist ideology proved to be a great advantage in its efforts to rise above all social classes while appealing to each. The turbulent and almost incoherent character of Nazi bureaucracy greatly enhanced the importance of the supreme leader. Organizational incoherence and personal ascendancy also made the movement less competitive with, and thus less threatening to, established elites—especially big-business elites.

The dominance of Hitler in the Nazi state had definite structural causes. But this very dominance made Hitler's ideology extraordinarily important in determining the path taken by the Nazi state. As the Nazi movement increasingly evaded any form of class control, so Hitler's ideologically driven policies increasingly renounced any allegiance to rational objectives. The murder of the Jews is only the most horrendous example of this mind-boggling irrationality. Ideology (that is, formalized consciousness) was in command; but the dynamics of class structure gave it that position.

The revolutionary credentials of National Socialism were largely spurious. But even while old social relationships remained intact and became even more adversarial, people somehow came to feel that a revolution was in progress. Workers remained workers, but now they were praised for it. The lot of farmers improved little but their role as the embodiment of spirit of Germany was continuously emphasized.

The middle classes, an important source of Nazi support, gained new career opportunities in the military and in the Nazi Party itself. They did benefit to some degree from the rise of the Nazi state. Yet relative to their *bête noire,* big business, the position of the German middle classes changed very little; if anything it declined. Hostility towards big business—a primary reason for middle-class support of National Socialism—did not and could not find resonance in a capitalist economy preparing for war (Geyer, 1987, p. 63-64; Schoenbaum, 1968, 275-276).[19]

In one limited sense the Nazis did carry out a bourgeois revolution. During the Nazi period the social prestige and political power of the nobility declined rather precipitously. Simultaneously, however, some members of the aristocratic caste found places in that "new" nobility of race, the SS, an organization then developing various enterprises of its own (Schoenbaum, 1968, p. 258).

Like everyone else, the capitalist class had its problems under the Nazi regime. Industrialists saw limits placed on profits and investments regulated. They were often caught between policies emanating from the Ministry of Economics, and directives issuing from such newly created institutions as the Hermann Goering Four Year plan (concerned mainly with rearmament). In the absence of a full-scale assault on corporate wealth, however, the capitalist class could usually protect its interests. Naturally capitalists were the prime beneficiaries of rearmament, of policies assuring Southeastern Europe access to German finished goods, and above all else of a now quiescent labor force. Later on, astounding military victories placed abundant new resources, human and otherwise, at the disposal of the capitalist class.

Whatever contradictions these class relationships presented to the Nazi leadership did not matter much because they saw the "National Socialist State" as an aspect of a far-reaching ideological enterprise within which economic concerns were of quite secondary importance.

The German public was not entirely oblivious to the sacred tasks of National Socialism. The most effective propaganda campaign in history saw to that. All forms of aesthetic communication were mobilized, as never before, in support of the national mission.[20] Nonetheless, the eventual goals of National Socialism—supplanting established Judeo-Christian culture and creation of a new being beholden to nature's "laws of life"—and the means to be used in attaining these goals had to remain largely secret (Pois, 1986). What most Germans could see was that National Socialism:

(1) ended unemployment and established an apparently viable economy

(2) restored national pride

(3) preserved bourgeois values threatened by "big city degeneracy" often identified with the Weimar Republic

(4) ended the gnawing uncertainties posed by a pluralistic political system

(5) purged people whose influence on public life was proclaimed pernicious

(6) claimed to break down class barriers

(7) achieved diplomatic and military successes not seen since the days of Napoleon.

These things could be seen as part of an idealistic revolution of consciousness in which the rawest national enthusiasm and the crudest prejudice were ennobled by their service to the *Volksgemeinschaft*.

Without foreign expansion and military success the Nazi state could not have endured long. Class consciousness and class conflict could not have been superseded indefinitely. In the absence of expansion and victory the economic policies of the regime would have encountered increasing opposition from various class fragments and might have broken down entirely. The bureaucratic incoherence of the Nazi state would have posed an increasingly formidable barrier to its own reproduction. National Socialist ideology required the validation of military success. Without this the irrational enormities of Nazi policy would have encountered far broader and more determined opposition, if they were attempted at all. And without successful expansion, the viability of National Socialism as a means of handling the structural contradictions between capitalist accumulation and German political democracy could only have been relatively short-lived.

During the halcyon days of uninterrupted victories, Hitler was unwilling to place inordinate demands on the German population. Peacetime rearmament had been extensive in breadth but not in depth; total economic and social mobilization for war took place only after Stalingrad.[21] While Germans endured measures like fuel and food rationing before then, and while durable commodities such as automobiles became increasingly scarce, prior to 1943 the production of consumer goods remained surprisingly high. Tank and aircraft production increased rather slowly and, in keeping with petit bourgeois social values, truly effective use of women in the war effort remained astonishingly limited.[22] Hitler apparently feared that rigorous demands on the public would induce a collapse of the home front such as he thought had occurred in 1918 (Spielvogel, 1988, p. 241).

Concluding Remarks

Earlier we hypothesized that fascism was most likely to occur after a failed working-class revolution. This suggests that the failure of the Weimar Republic may not have been the principal cause of National Socialism's ascendancy. Perhaps the truly decisive event was the failure of the 1918-1919 revolution. The defeat sustained by the German working class at that time made the demise of the bourgeois republic probable if not inevitable were it confronted with a serious challenge of any sort. This bourgeois republic could count on the support of few bourgeoisie. The mainstay of the Weimar state proved to be the Social Democratic Party whose leadership had played an ignoble (though perhaps unavoidable) role in suppressing the 1918-1919 revolt. But despite its indubitable service to the preservation of capitalist property, the Social Democratic Party could not escape the hostility of the capitalist class.

The republic which emerged from the abortive 1918-1919 revolution was itself an abortion plagued by massive structural problems irresolvable within the existing socioeconomic framework. The mere recognition of these problems, to say nothing of their solution, was rendered virtually impossible by the manifold forms of false consciousness they themselves generated.

The state which emerged from the context of failed revolution was itself transformed by a movement whose existence and popularity testified to both the human capacity for self-delusion and the prodigies of false consciousness feasible during episodes of capitalist crisis. While Nazism (in contrast to more generic fascism) was a rather singular phenomenon conceivable only in the German historical context, the defeat of progressive forces has often made possible the emergence of institutions fundamentally antithetical to human needs. Failed revolutions can stimulate vicious strains of political pathology more properly the subject of psychoanalytic interpretation than of conventional historical explanation.

We may debate whether Theodore Adorno was correct in declaring that, after Auschwitz, the writing of poetry is barbaric; but the absolute imperative of preventing further such atrocities is beyond dispute. Unfortunately knowledge has never provided a very strong defense against evil. To imagine that understanding the transition to a Nazi state can diminish the likelihood of a reoccurrence may be nothing more than academic conceit.

Notes

1. Erik Olin Wright has made a useful attempt to clarify and elaborate the concept of structural causality (1978, pp. 9-29).

2. Adam Przeworski provides an insightful analysis of how the struggles of workers constitute the proletariat as a class in his paper "Proletariat into a Class: The Process of Class Formation" (1985, pp. 47-97).

3. Geoff Eley has presented strong arguments against the above thesis. He maintains that Germany did experience a successful bourgeois revolution, but not in the form of liberal democracy (Blackbourn & Eley, 1984, pp. 144-155).

4. A similar argument is made by Timothy W. Mason (1977).

5. In a seminal discussion of the formation of the working class Adam Przeworski writes: "Classes must . . . be viewed as effects of struggles structured by objective conditions that are simultaneously economic, political, and ideological. . . . Precisely because class formation is an effect of struggles, outcomes of this process are at each moment of history to some extent indeterminate" (1985, p. 47).

6. For discussion of these theories of fascism see *Fascism and Dictatorship* (Poulantzas, 1974, pp. 59-61), and Anson Rabinbach, "Towards a Marxist Theory of Fascism and National Socialism" (1974, pp. 132-133).

7. This, the reader will recall, is precisely the analysis made by Nicos Poulantzas in *Political Power and Social Classes* and *Fascism and Dictatorship*.

8. Richard F. Hamilton (1982) shows that the upper-middle class gave strong support to National Socialism, at least in the large cities.

9. Bracher finds a direct connection between the unfinished democratic revolution of 1918 and the fascist counterrevolution of 1933 (1970, pp. 71-72).

10. For an excellent study of how varieties of "false consciousness" can be of decisive importance in influencing behavior, see Barrington Moore, *Injustice: The Social Bases of Obedience and Revolt* (1978).

11. The Free Corps and regular army units which put down the Spartacist Revolt in January, 1919, were under the *de jure* control of Gustav Noske, Security Commissar, who was in turn responsible to Friedrich Ebert. Both were Social Democrats and, after the resignations of three Independent Socialists, so were the other four members of the radical-sounding Council of Peoples' Commissars. Friedrich Ebert would be, of course, the first president of the Weimar Republic.

12. George L. Mosse has introduced this term (1964, Chap. 17).

13. This is one of the theses of Sarah Gordon's *Hitler, Germans, and the "Jewish Question"* (1984).

14. On the bourgeois nature of National Socialism with regard to social issues, see Mosse (1978, p. 23) and Pois (1985, pp. 89-90).

15. For a good treatment of the antihistorical nature of National Socialism see Weinstein (1980, pp. 124-126, 137-138).

16. For an interesting study of how Nazi trade policies toward at least part of *Mitteleuropa* were rooted in previous concerns see Hopfner (1983).

17. One of the best treatments of the relationship between the National Socialist movement and the German state, remains Franz Neumann, *Behemoth* (1944, pp. 41-68). Also see David Schoenbaum (1968, pp. 193-233).

18. In this context, the notion of the "Movement" State was particularly important (Neumann, 1944, pp. 61-82).

19. Labor Front leader Robert Ley took the anti-big-business aspect of Nazi ideology very seriously, but attempts to translate this into meaningful policies foundered when the Nazis came to power because they needed the support of major industrialists (Smelser, 1988).

20. For a fine Marxist approach toward Nazi efforts to blend together *völkische,* yet progressive (or at least forward-looking) aesthetics with increased production, see Rabinbach (1976).

21. On the "in breadth" nature of German rearmament see Deist (1981). For a pioneering work emphasizing the relatively inadequate nature of German rearmament see Milward (1965).

22. An excellent comparative study of how women were mobilized for war has been provided by Rupp (1978).

PART III

Changes in the Institutions of the State

5

Federal Statebuilding During the New Deal

The Transition from Mothers' Aid to Aid to Dependent Children

RUSSELL L. HANSON

With the passage of the Social Security Act in 1935, a bifurcated welfare state was established in the United States. A wholly national program of social insurance was created for retired workers and their dependents. Acceptance of this program was swift, and subsequent amendments to the Act made coverage nearly universal. More recently, cash benefits have been liberalized, and medical insurance has been added. As a result, "social security" has become an immensely popular and effective income-support program, one that is widely credited with alleviating poverty among the elderly.

The Social Security Act also established several programs of public assistance, among them Aid to Dependent Children (ADC), now known as Aid to Families with Dependent Children. These programs were *federally* organized: state governments could, at their discretion, participate in programs that had broad national guidelines and requirements, and receive

AUTHOR'S NOTE: I gratefully acknowledge the financial support of the Ford Foundation's Project on Social Welfare Policy and the American Future, which enabled me to do the research on which this chapter is based. Edward Greenberg and Thomas Mayer provided very helpful comments on an earlier draft of this chapter, which was presented at a conference on State Change sponsored by the Institute of Behavioral Science, Program for Research on Political and Economic Change, University of Colorado at Boulder.

partial reimbursement from the Congress for their efforts on behalf of certain classes of poor people. These categorical assistance programs have never been popular or well-supported, nor have they been very effective in combating poverty among groups they are intended to help.

Because of these shortcomings, reformers often lament the arrested development of public assistance, and urge the establishment of truly national programs. National regimes are more centralized than federal ones, and because they are more centralized they have greater capacity for action—or so it is presumed. Indeed, the apparent success of national insurance programs provides a standing recommendation for structural reform of welfare, so long as we ignore the differences between assistance and insurance, or deny the relevance of such differences to questions about the best way of organizing a system for delivering goods and services to the poor.

This simple view is rather appealing, and it is common not only among political activists, but also professional scholars. It appears in historical studies of statebuilding, the process by which institutional capacities for successful policy-making evolve (or do not evolve, as the case may be.) Typically, the process of statebuilding is seen as consisting of different moments that may be ordered in terms of varying degrees of centralization, and the burden of scholarship is to map regimes' progress or lack thereof along some continuum of centralization and decentralization (or better, noncentralization, as decentralization implies a devolution of authority from above). Scholars then seek to explain why certain regimes have become more centralized, and hence have greater capacity, than others, or why some exceptional cases show little or no movement in the direction of greater centralization and the achievement of a policy-making capacity.

Unfortunately, this way of proceeding excludes from the outset the possibility that statebuilding is a process that is both multidimensional and multidirectional, and consequently that different regimes may follow quite distinctive statebuilding paths. Yet it is surely possible that *federal* statebuilding is an alternative to national statebuilding. It is not necessarily a process that represents an intermediate stage in the (possible) movement toward a centralized, national state. Nor is federal statebuilding a process that yields institutional arrangements that have an obviously inferior capacity for action, by comparison to national arrangements. Rather, federal statebuilding proceeds in a different direction altogether, and involves a very different kind of capacity for action than is implied in models of centralized policy-making. It is therefore a serious mistake to assimilate federal statebuilding to a national statebuilding model under the guise of "incomplete nationalization."

What is needed instead is an appreciation of federal statebuilding as a process that is distinct from national statebuilding. This understanding must begin with the realization that federal statebuilding is a very complex process of institutional development. Whereas national statebuilding typically involves efforts to endow a single institution or agency with policy-making capabilities, federal statebuilding focuses upon intergovernmental relations and efforts to establish the capacity for *joint* action by agencies at several levels of government. Because these agencies may be financially, politically, or even constitutionally independent of one another, the problems of coordinating action are substantially more difficult than those encountered in national statebuilding enterprises.

In saying this I certainly do not mean to overstate the ease with which national statebuilding occurs; even the creation of a central agency with narrow policy responsibilities may be difficult or impossible in some political situations. I only mean that once it is established, a central agency has important powers over subordinate actors charged with policy implementation. These actors are in fact part of a nominal chain of command, and while they are far from powerless to resist directives with which they disagree, the central agency does control budgets and other resources. It also enjoys a position of legal authority and, in principle, if not always practice, the central agency is therefore well-equipped to enforce compliance with its directives.

That is not true under federal arrangements, where even a nominal chain of command often does not exist. In the case of public assistance, for example, states are not required to provide aid to certain categories of poor people; their involvement must be induced by financial incentives, as the central agencies "in charge" of these programs have no constitutional authority to require state participation. Furthermore, states retain important statutory authority in defining assistance programs, once they agree to provide aid, and of course they are always free to seek Congressional redress for any conflicts that arise between them and central agencies. Similarly, where states require local governments to implement programs, the local governments may enjoy a great deal of political independence, if not constitutional autonomy, in the conduct of their actions. As a result, federal policy-making is less hierarchical than is national policy-making, and tends to be more political than bureaucratic in style.

Necessarily, then, the capacity for action of a federal organization involves questions about the joint capacity of several more or less independent actors. This further distinguishes federal statebuilding from national statebuilding in two important ways. First, it is clear that the joint capacity of a federal organization is determined by the capabilities of the "weakest" partner, typically local government. Since a federal policy-making venture depends on *each* actor carrying out appointed tasks at appointed times, the existence of a strong, capable central agency is no guarantee of success. The actual delivery of assistance to those in need will instead depend on how well the weakest actor performs its job; if that actor fails, the joint undertaking is compromised.[1]

This is closely related to a second difference between national and federal statebuilding: "joint capacity" is likely to be quite uneven across states. The capacity of national, state, and local partners may be extremely high in some states, perhaps even higher than it might be under a purely national system, and extremely low in other states, where states and localities have a very limited capacity for action. To an important extent, this unevenness is ineradicable; it is even reinforced by federalism, when that has an open or permissive character. The fact that such unevenness is part of the very structure of federal organizations makes them quite different from national regimes, which push toward uniformity, and where standardized practices are a measure of high capacity.

These rather programmatic observations suggest that it is during program implementation that the distinctive problems of federal statebuilding arise. Consequently, if I am right about the differences between national and federal statebuilding processes, they should be most apparent during the implementation of the Social Security Act of 1935, which simultaneously involved both kinds of process. Since the national insurance programs have already been examined thoroughly by those who see it as a critical moment of statebuilding, I shall turn to a case study of the implementation of the public assistance provisions of the Social Security Act, which established a federal structure for aiding dependent children, the blind and disabled, and the aged. By examining the process of institutionalizing these programs we may see how certain peculiarities of federal statebuilding unfolded in the United States and at the same time gain a better appreciation of how different this process was from those which involved national statebuilding.

Aid to Dependent Children

Prior to 1930 few states and localities had well-developed programs for assisting poor and unemployed people. Assistance for orphans and other poor people was niggardly and often punitive; the county poor farm was hardly a model of rehabilitative services. In-home assistance, in the form of cash or food or other services, was far from universally available. For example,

Mothers' Aid, which provided cash assistance to widows and women whose husbands had deserted them and their children, was available in only about one-half of the counties in the United States in 1931 (Committee on Economic Security, 1937, p. 236). And by 1934 only 28 states and two territories, mainly in the West, had established old-age pensions (Committee on Economic Security, 1937, pp. 160-161). Moreover, the programs that did exist were generally quite restrictive and woefully underfunded; even in the best of times they provided little protection from poverty for their intended beneficiaries.

The weakness of these safety-net programs was exposed very early in the Great Depression, as was the inability of state and local governments to adapt them to meet the needs of a vast army of unemployed and unemployable people. Congress moved quickly to provide "temporary relief," establishing the Federal Emergency Relief Administration (FERA) in 1933 under the leadership of Harry Hopkins. In its three years of existence, FERA distributed more than $3 billion from the national treasury, with states contributing an additional $450 million in matching funds, and localities another $600 million (Whiting, 1942). At the same time, FERA represented a fairly centralized approach to the problem of relief, and though subnational policymakers welcomed the influx of national monies, they strongly resisted Hopkins's efforts to direct the uses to which the money was put.

The resentment of state and local officials toward FERA figured prominently in Congressional efforts to fashion a more permanent solution to the problems of "unemployable" people (i.e., those whose plight was unlikely to improve when the Depression receded). The categorical assistance provisions of the Social Security Act were a partial reversion to the relief policies and philosophy that preceded FERA, as the Committee on Economic Security made clear in its report to Franklin Delano Roosevelt on the need for new legislation:

> As for the genuine unemployables—or near unemployables—we believe the sound policy is to return responsibility for their care and guidance to the States . . . [and] we strongly recommend that the States substitute for their ancient, outmoded poor laws, modernized public assistance laws, and replace their traditional poor-law administrations by unified and efficient State and local public welfare departments, such as exist in some States and for which there is a nucleus in all states in the Federal emergency relief organizations. (Quoted in Brown, 1940, p. 303)

Dependent children were spared this fate; they were to be assisted under a permanent grant-in-aid program, Aid to Dependent Children. Under this program, the national government would pay one-third of the cost (up to $18 per month) of assisting a single dependent child, and one-third of the cost (up to $12 per month) for each additional child. The dollar amounts were the same as limits on payments to the children of servicemen killed in World War I, and the matching fund provisions were similar to those under FERA, while other program details were based on Mothers' Aid programs recommended by the U.S. Children's Bureau (Brown, 1940; Witte, 1962).

The impact of ADC was both immediate and profound. Previous gains under Mothers' Aid and FERA were consolidated and extended, and the number of children who were assisted increased dramatically. Most state caseloads increased by huge proportions upon the adoption of ADC. Even states which had liberal Mothers' Aid programs saw their caseloads double or more inside of three years after adopting ADC. Pennsylvania went from a Mothers' Aid program with 8,286 recipients in December, 1935, to an ADC program with 30,245 families in December, 1939, and 48,778 families in December, 1940. By the end of the decade Pennsylvania's ADC program was three times as large as California's, and one and one-half times the size of New York's. Even so, the greatest impact was undoubtedly felt in states that had no Mothers' Aid programs, or which had underdeveloped and underfinanced plans for assisting widows: Alabama had no Mothers' Aid in 1935, but in December, 1936 there were 5,316 families on ADC. Arkansas, Georgia, South Carolina, and Tennessee had similar experiences, as aid became widely available for the first time.

The tremendous impact of ADC on indigent children and state and local budgets brought with it great changes in intergovernmental relations. With so many new cases eligible for national matching funds, it was necessary to oversee the operation of state ADC programs, as well as their local implementation, if for no other reason than to insure against "raids" on the national treasury. Opportunistic state policymakers might shift cases from general assistance, which was paid wholly out of state and local funds, onto categorical assistance under the Social Security Act, thereby avoiding part of the cost of aiding needy people. They might even ignore or misinterpret eligibility requirements in order to do so, or at least some national policymakers feared they would.

The Social Security Board was charged with the responsibility of ensuring that state ADC programs met the conditions for participation in the matching funds available for ADC. In order to qualify for matching funds, states had to designate a "single state agency" responsible for administering ADC, or for supervising the administration of ADC by local political subdivisions. For many states this represented a significant departure from past relief policies, which had given localities almost exclusive control over the provision of welfare. Many localities were unwilling to cede control over the administration of welfare to state governments, in part because they preferred to let matters of eligibility and assistance be determined according to local custom, and in part because those who were responsible for relief were reluctant to accept any reductions in their power and influence. As a result, it was sometimes difficult to establish a supervisory relationship that was acceptable to the Bureau of Public Assistance, and its overseer, the Social Security Board.[2]

Of course, problems of supervision were much less serious in some states than others. This was particularly true for states which had well-institutionalized Mothers' Aid programs that required only minor changes in order to meet the conditions for participating in ADC. For example, states in the northeast and the southwest were especially likely to have centralized Mothers' Aid programs. Connecticut, Maine, New Hampshire, Rhode Island, and Vermont all administered Mothers' Aid at the state level, which also provided the bulk of the financing. New Jersey and Delaware did the same, while state agencies in Massachusetts and Pennsylvania supervised the administration of Mothers' Aid by local poor relief boards, and partially reimbursed them for expenses. New York, too, supervised the actions of local subdivisions, though it did not help pay for Mothers' Aid. Thus, all states east of the Ohio River and north of the Mason-Dixon line had more or less centralized programs, with the greatest degree of centralization being achieved in New England.

A second, much smaller, cluster of centralized Mothers' Aid programs emerged in the Southwest. The diversity of states within each of these two regional groupings, and the differences between the groups themselves, make it difficult to generalize about the reasons for their inclination toward centralization. However, there is no question that these states, with one or two notable exceptions, made the transition from Mothers' Aid to Aid to Dependent Children easily and without incident. A review of their experiences in the transition from Mothers' Aid to ADC will show the stark contrast with other states' difficulties in establishing adequate supervision, highlighting the difficulties of organizing joint capacity for action in a federal system.

State Administration of ADC

Connecticut, Maine, New Hampshire, Rhode Island, and Vermont adopted Mothers' Aid later than most other states, but when they did enact legislation it was quite systematic. Their programs were all administered by agencies of the state, not local subdivisions, and the state provided substantial financial resources, as well. As a consequence, Mothers' Aid was available everywhere in these states, and payments were actually made in all counties during the Depression years 1931-1936, except in Rhode Island. Because these programs were already under a single state agency, supported by state funds, and available in all political subdivisions, they met the basic conditions for participation in ADC as outlined in the Social Security Act. For the same reason, the capacity for joint action on ADC really involved only two levels of government, not three, as in other states.

In addition, all but Connecticut construed dependency broadly. Mothers with children whose fathers were dead were eligible in all five states. Maine, New Hampshire, Rhode Island, and Vermont also aided families in which the father had deserted, or was incapacitated or institutionalized. Maine, New Hampshire, and Rhode Island even provided assistance to divorced mothers. Thus, these states' programs contained relatively liberal eligibility provisions that closely resembled those recommended in the Social Security Act. Furthermore, assistance was relatively generous in these states. Connecticut, Maine, and Rhode Island all ranked well above the national median in terms of annual expenditures per capita for mothers' assistance, and New Hampshire and Vermont ranked above fifteen other states. As of 1934, the average monthly payments per family ranged from $17.86 in Vermont to $47.00 in Rhode Island (Committee on Economic Security, 1937, p. 247).

Liberal eligibility requirements and relatively generous benefits, combined with reliance upon state government for a significant portion of the funds necessary to sustain them, gave New England legislatures a powerful financial incentive to adopt and implement ADC quickly. By doing so New England legislatures were able to take special advantage of the matching fund provisions of the ADC program, which allowed states to shift a portion of the costs to the national government. State and local governments were no longer responsible for the entire share of assistance costs, and their *average* cost per case was therefore reduced. So long as these reductions were not offset by *marginal* increases in expenditures associated with heavier caseloads attending the adoption of ADC, states and their localities could actually save money by abandoning Mothers' Aid in favor of Aid to Dependent Children. In fact, two of the New England states—Maine and Vermont—did save money by shifting to ADC. New Hampshire broke even on the change, and Rhode Island's state and local governments spent slightly more during the first year of ADC than they had in the last year of Mothers' Aid, while assisting more families (Committee on Economic Security, 1937).

Connecticut was the only small New England state that failed to adopt ADC immediately. It was not until 1941, when the Democrats regained control of the lower chamber and the governor's office, that ADC legislation was passed. Patterson (1969, p. 159) explains the tardiness of Connecticut this way:

Confronted by well-organized Republican opposition in the legislature and by sharp intraparty dissension [Governor Cross, a Democrat] was not adept enough as a party leader or inspiring enough as a speaker to put across a comprehensive program. Cross led Connecticut away from the indolence of the Republican machine of the 1920's but not far enough to enact a little New Deal.

Cross's inability to enact a "little New Deal" may also have been due to the fact that the political opportunities for adopting programs like ADC were relatively short-lived in states like Connecticut where the Democratic realignment was not really completed until after World War II (Sundquist, 1973, p. 219). Democrats swept into office on Roosevelt's coattails were, by the end of the 1930s, suffering defeat at the hands of resurgent Republican party candidates, particularly after the failure of the Supreme Court packing scheme in 1937. It then became much more difficult to pass New Deal measures opposed by legislators who rejected the New Deal on ideological grounds, or were unwilling to raise taxes in order to fund them.

And the adoption of ADC probably would have cost Connecticut money. Unlike the other New England states, Connecticut imposed strict conditions of eligibility on recipients of Mothers' Aid; only widows could receive assistance on behalf of their children. As a result caseloads were stabilized at a relatively low level, with only modest increases associated with the early years of the Depression, and very slight increases thereafter. Because ADC defined eligibility more broadly, and extended aid to relatives other than mothers of dependent children, state policymakers might reasonably have expected a rather sizable jump in caseloads upon the adoption of ADC. This could easily have increased the costs of assistance to the state and its localities, even after taking federal matching funds into account.

However, the matching rate was increased in 1940 to 50%, so that fully one-half of the costs of assistance were borne by the national government. This meant that caseload increases associated with the transition to ADC could be substantially larger without requiring greater outlays on the part of subnational governments. Furthermore, the improving economy promised to moderate the expected surge in caseloads. Thus, the terms of adoption had

shifted decisively by the time the Democrats gained control of state government in 1941, and upon the adoption of ADC, Connecticut, too, saw its
outlays for assistance reduced from those made under Mothers' Aid.

State Supervision of ADC

As we have seen, the transition to federal assistance was generally smooth
and uneventful in states where the provision of welfare had been fairly
centralized. The difficult problems associated with the division of authority
between state and local officials vis-à-vis administrative and financial
responsibilities had already been resolved in favor of arrangements that
approximated those required under the Social Security Act. This was not
entirely fortuitous; the adoption of centralized Mothers' Aid programs was
consistent with the general recommendations of the U.S. Children's Bureau,
the leaders of which played an important role in drafting Title IV of the Social
Security Act. To the extent that state policymakers were inclined to follow
the advice of the Children's Bureau, they correctly "anticipated" program
requirements later associated with Aid to Dependent Children.

On the other hand, states with well-developed, but decentralized, programs
for Mothers' Aid often found themselves at odds with agencies of the national
government, which demanded alterations in long-standing patterns of state-
local relations (i.e., greater centralization) before releasing matching funds
for ADC. Where state governments allowed local political subdivisions to
establish and maintain programs that were relatively autonomous, the institutionalization of Mothers' Aid created political and administrative arrangements that were inconsistent with those required for ADC. For example, the
Social Security Board refused to accept judicial authorities—the traditional
administrators of Mothers' Aid—as officials charged with responsibility for
implementing ADC. The members of the board believed such recognition
would compromise states' ability to supervise local activities as required
under the Social Security Act, since judicial officials are independent.
Federal statebuilding therefore entailed difficult problems of institutional
adaptation in states where earlier statebuilding processes followed a logic of
development incompatible with the centralizing dynamic of federalization.[3]

The adoption of enabling legislation that permitted, but did not require,
local political subdivisions to provide Mothers' Aid was typical of midwestern and western states, and it no doubt reflected rural-urban political cleavages. In these states, support for Mothers' Aid was strongest in urban

counties, which had the largest number of potential recipients, as well as the greatest concentration of municipal reformers. Rural dwellers were less receptive to social welfare measures, and their representatives were therefore reluctant to "mandate" the responsibility for mothers with dependent children to their own counties. This conservatism was buttressed by financial considerations: a mandated program would necessitate increased taxation by local governments, and perhaps by state government as well, if state funds were used to pay some or all of the costs of Mothers' Aid. State funding, in turn, raised concerns about rural taxpayers footing the bill for poor relief in cities, the residents of which were regarded with suspicion and downright hostility by rural residents.

Rural representatives, who in most states enjoyed a disproportionate influence in politics by reason of malapportioned legislatures and county-unit nominating procedures for state office, were able to resist efforts to establish statewide programs in aid of mothers with dependent children. They enacted legislation that protected their interests, while permitting urban subdivisions to implement—and finance—programs supported by reform constituencies. This had important consequences for the development of Mothers' Aid, and ultimately for the adoption of ADC, which had to be available in all political jurisdictions of a state before federal matching funds were released.

In particular, the institutionalization of Mothers' Aid as a county option made it extremely unlikely that these states would move toward ADC programs directly administered by the state. For obvious political reasons, this meant that when ADC was implemented, it was done by local governments under the supervision of a state agency. The state agency was therefore caught between the Social Security Board, which expected it to force local governments to comply with program requirements, and local officials who enjoyed substantial political leverage over state administrators through their influence on the legislature. And local officials did use their power to resist state efforts to force them into compliance on ADC.

In Michigan, for example, there was great resistance to ADC from probate judges who presided over juvenile courts, for they were the principal administrators of Mothers' Aid, the program to be replaced by ADC. Dancey (1939) reports that in Michigan this type of opposition was sufficiently great that when the state created the necessary administrative apparatus for ADC in 1936, it left the Mothers' Aid program intact, so that about one-third of the counties in Michigan operated both programs simultaneously. These counties continued their Mothers' Aid programs even after ADC was adopted by the state, mainly because probate judges refused to relinquish this function. The power of the judges and their allies was clearly demonstrated in 1938, when they rebuffed the legislature's attempt to eliminate Mothers' Aid by reorganizing state welfare programs.[4]

Similarly, ADC was not adopted in Illinois until 1941, although that state had adopted the first law allowing all counties to provide Mothers' Aid. Among the opponents of implementing legislation for ADC was the judge of the Cook County Juvenile Court, who was joined by many officers of the court, as well as township supervisors. Apparently, their resistance stemmed from fears that their prerogatives would be reduced by moving from Mothers' Aid to ADC. The judge was rumored to have campaigned actively among downstate judges and local welfare boards to cement their opposition, which was already strong, given downstate fears of statewide programs dominated by Chicago interests (Glick, 1940). The active support of ADC legislation by the American Legion was insufficient to overcome this opposition. Whereas Old Age Assistance had passed early and easily because the clientele it served was numerous and active, ADC had fewer friends able to bring pressure to bear on the Assembly.

Then, too, Illinois's experiences under FERA and Old Age Assistance (OAA) probably made it more difficult to pass ADC legislation. Under FERA, national and state officials often had come into conflict over what the former perceived as an inadequate fiscal effort on the latter's part. State officials, on the other hand, pointed to the ambiguity surrounding the notion of a state's "fair share" of relief expenses, and tended to appropriate relief funds on a temporary and opportunistic basis (Miles, 1941, p. 248). Eventually, this led to a withholding of national funds for a short while in 1935, as pressure was brought to bear on the Assembly by FERA administrators.

As Miles (1941) observes, the chief effect of this action was to antagonize the Assembly, and solidify its determination to support states' rights in these matters. Illinois retreated to a system of poor relief, only adopting OAA under great political pressure, after ensuring that the necessary legislation guaranteed a high degree of state autonomy from national administrators. Naturally, the exercise of that autonomy, in the form of allowing localities to operate OAA programs in the virtual absence of state supervision, brought Illinois into conflict once again with national administrators. This time it was the Social Security Board that withheld OAA funds in order to force the state to take a more active role in the administration of OAA. Eventually the state did so, but the conflict reinforced the general suspicion of many legislators toward federal assistance programs, including ADC.

When ADC was eventually adopted in 1941, the problems of transition were enormous. In Cook County, there were funds for only 11,000 families, and many more were placed on "waiting lists" until further funds were available. And because Cook County payments for Mothers' Aid were higher than state standards for ADC, some families actually received less money under the new program. Thus, in December, 1941, the average monthly payment per child under Mothers' Aid was $19.46, and maximum payment levels were at $25 for the first child, and $15 for each additional one. But in December, 1942, the average monthly payment per child under ADC had fallen to $14.57, and the maximums were lowered to $18 and $12, respectively (W. Clark, 1943). On the other hand, six times as many cases were being assisted in Cook county, mainly because ADC defined eligibility to include the children of divorced or separated mothers, and paid benefits on behalf of children to relatives other than the mother, which together accounted for as many as one-third of the cases in the county. Furthermore, in other Illinois counties, ADC made larger payments to far more families than had Mothers' Aid. The southernmost counties in "Little Egypt" were spending six times as much as they had before, and payments were, on average, three times as large. In effect, ADC established a minimum level of assistance in Illinois, raising standards in areas where Mothers' Aid was poorly institutionalized, but lowering them in Cook county, where Mothers' Aid had been well-established (W. Clark, 1943). As the editors of the *Social Service Review* (1941) noted, "the life of a law is in its administration," as those who had hoped the battle for ADC had been won with the passage of an enabling law were just discovering.

Integrating Assistance Programs: OAA and ADC

The supervisory, or in some states administrative, role of state government in ADC had profound implications for the organization of state government itself. The "single state agency" designated to perform this role had to be established where none existed, or else existing agencies had to be given new responsibilities and powers.[5] In either case, the administrative constellation of power was altered, creating serious problems of political integration and coordination at the state level. Various reorganization experiments were conducted in the states to meet these problems, with mixed results (Stevenson, 1937; 1939).

Jane Hoey (1937), Director of the Bureau of Public Assistance of the Social Security Board, discussed some of the difficulties encountered by states as they attempted to integrate departments of public assistance and other state agencies, including those responsible for administering general assistance. Whereas emergency relief programs, because of their "temporary character and mushroom growth," did not ordinarily utilize the services of other state departments, the new bureaus of public assistance were part of the regular machinery of state government and had to "fit themselves into the general pattern which operates throughout state government." Hoey noted that "In some instances, the 'old line' agencies have not been adequately equipped to carry out their responsibilities, or were more concerned with their traditional prerogatives than with the importance of such matters as expediting the payment of aid to persons in urgent need." For their part, "assistance administrators, especially those who had been accustomed to the relative flexibility of emergency programs, have sometimes rebelled at the rigidity and the overlegalistic limitations which frequently characterize the operations of the older state agencies" (e.g., state treasuries; Hoey, 1937, p. 5).

Thus, at the same time as they were struggling to establish adequate supervision of the activities of local subdivisions charged with implementing ADC, state administrators also were faced with the need to accommodate other state officials with related policy-making authority. The latter problem was no less politicized than the former, especially in a context of limited resources. The inevitable bureaucratic rivalries for favored treatment by the legislature and the governor placed great pressure on state ADC administrators, whose programs did not serve politically important constituencies, and whose employees were often viewed with suspicion, both because of their "social work" background, and because their activities often brought them into conflict with local officials.

Two aspects of this problem are worth emphasizing. The first concerns the dilemma facing ADC administrators with respect to the Old Age Assistance (OAA) program, also a part of the Social Security Act. The tremendous popularity of OAA made it somewhat easier to implement ADC, insofar as the former accustomed state policymakers to the idea of accepting matching funds for categorical assistance in exchange for meeting certain administrative and financial requirements. Hence OAA, which was adopted very quickly by all states, established an important precedent for ADC, as well as a structure of administration upon which ADC was often grafted.

The very popularity of OAA also posed a threat to ADC, however, for it inevitably attracted a disproportionate share of the resources state legislatures were willing to commit to "relief" activities. As a result, ADC was often underfunded because too few resources remained after OAA was supported at politically popular levels. Typically, this meant that ADC payments were much smaller than those authorized by law, and that long waiting lists formed once appropriations were depleted altogether. For recipients (and would-be recipients) this was disastrous, but for administrators, too, the ensuing difficulties were great as they attempted to regulate their activities in accordance with revenue flows.[6]

Furthermore, the subsidy for ADC was not as attractive as that for OAA, for which the national government paid half of the assistance costs, up to a maximum of $30 per person per month. This, along with the political appeal of OAA in light of the Townsend movement, may explain the quick diffusion of OAA, compared to ADC, as well as the relatively more generous payments made available to recipients of OAA. Nowhere was this danger so evident as in the West, where the popularity of old-age pensions made it difficult to institutionalize ADC on a sound fiscal basis.

Colorado provides a good example of the way in which OAA restricted the development of ADC. By the middle of 1935 the Colorado legislature had already passed the necessary enabling legislation for public assistance programs under the Social Security Act, and in early 1936 it created a State Department of Public Welfare to administer the funds on a statewide basis. The legislature also enacted a 2% sales tax, with the revenues specifically earmarked for financing public assistance (Wickens, 1975).

OAA received the lion's share of this money. The state of Colorado provided the most generous benefits in the nation to the aged, and as a result fully three-quarters of all relief expenditures went to the elderly, who constituted a large and well-organized political force in the state. Francis Townsend had once lived in Colorado, and both Townsend clubs and the National Annuity League (a splinter from the Townsend movement) were actively courted by Governor Johnson and others who sought their electoral support. In 1936 a constitutional amendment was enacted which lowered the age of eligibility from 65 under the state pension to 60 under OAA, and established benefits at $45 per month (Patterson, 1969, p. 94).

Even with earmarked revenues it proved difficult to sustain Colorado's exceedingly liberal OAA program, though Republican Governor Ralph Carr (1939-1943) cannibalized the state's education fund to meet assistance needs in the midst of a fiscal crisis brought on by revenue shortages. In fact, the state was seldom able to pay the full old-age benefit, although it managed to protect the elderly much better than children (Wickens, 1975).

An even more extreme case was Texas, which had no ADC program, and which previously spent no state and local funds on Mothers' Aid. However, it did enact an OAA program in 1936 which quickly enrolled 42,000 more recipients than New York had on its rolls, despite the fact that the population of Texas was about half that of New York. Governor Pappy O'Daniel was apparently quite serious when he announced

> I am not saying that all of Mr. Roosevelt's plans are sound and right, but as long as he has the national grab-bag open and as long as all other states are grabbing, I'm gonna grab all I can for the State of Texas and will do all I can to bring within the borders of our grand and glorious state every dollar we can get. (Patenaude, 1983, p. 100)

O'Daniel's admission nicely illustrates policymakers' sensitivity to funding arrangements under the Social Security Act. The availability of matching funds made welfare programs much more attractive than they had ever been before, and in the case of old-age assistance led many states to commit far more resources than were needed, economically speaking. At the same time, state policymakers demonstrated a clear understanding of the subtleties involved in matching fund differentials, thereby undermining the position of those programs (e.g., ADC) characterized by inferior matching rates and unimportant political constituencies.

Integrating ADC and National Relief Programs

The effect of national policies on matching funds was particularly pronounced in the South, which was undoubtedly the region least able to finance assistance in the first place. The combination of matching fund limitations, the availability of alternative, nationally-financed work programs, and an intense preoccupation with the effects of welfare on wage levels made it extremely difficult to establish ADC in that region. Moreover, the absence of any previous experience with Mothers' Aid meant there were no political and administrative foundations upon which to build a welfare state.

This last obstacle is worth emphasizing. Federal statebuilding took quite another path in states with little or no previous experience in social welfare policy than it did in states with prior histories of assisting the needy. Where Mothers' Aid was not institutionalized or only weakly enforced, ADC was seldom implemented with vigor, in part because the same political considerations (e.g., conservative attitudes toward relief-giving and chronic revenue shortages associated with economic underdevelopment) that worked against Mothers' Aid also inhibited ADC. Moreover, the absence of viable Mothers' Aid programs meant there were no administrative foundations upon which to build Aid to Dependent Children, except perhaps for those established under the emergency relief and works programs of the New Deal.

The experience of state governments under these programs could not make up for the lack of prior involvement in providing assistance to the needy. In fact the existence of national programs—for example, the Works Progress Administration (WPA), and before that the Federal Emergency Relief Administration (FERA)—may have deterred some states from establishing stronger ADC programs. The national programs often became "dumping grounds" for women with dependent children, relieving political pressure upon state and local policymakers for assisting the needy, while enabling them to shift all or most of the costs of assistance to the national government.

State governments were so successful in this endeavor that the burden of Southern relief during the Depression was borne almost entirely by the national government. Whereas many other states were able to borrow the majority of funds used for relief, some Southern states were unable to do so because of constitutional restrictions. In Alabama, Florida, Georgia, and Louisiana it was necessary to enact a constitutional amendment authorizing the legislature to borrow, and this required approval by an extraordinary majority (three-fifths or two-thirds) in the legislature, as well as approval in a popular referendum (Lászlóecker-r, 1936a; Shawe, 1937). In Virginia, passage of the necessary amendment required approval in two successive meetings of the legislature *and* a referendum—a truly demanding political test. (In Arkansas, Oklahoma, and South Carolina amendments required approval in a referendum only, and in Mississippi, North Carolina, and Tennessee legislative approval was all that was necessary.)

Since other revenue sources had been devastated by the Depression, and because it was difficult to win authority for borrowing, most Southern states simply did not finance relief. Instead, they relied upon localities, the traditional providers of relief, to make small, but important, contributions toward the nonfederal "fair share" of relief funds (Lászlóecker-r, 1936b). As a result, FERA became almost the sole source of assistance for mothers with dependent children in the South.[7]

While the primary goal of FERA was to help states and localities provide assistance to employable persons and their families, the terms of the act under which it was created did not exclude unemployables from relief programs. However, Rule No. 3, as promulgated by the administration of FERA, stated that direct relief could not be provided out of national funds "where provision is already made under existing laws—for widows or their dependents, and/or aged persons" (Williams, 1939, p. 91). A letter from the Federal Administrator to State Emergency Relief Administrations in April, 1934 recalled that the emphasis of the FERA program is being placed upon work relief or subsistence activities for normally employable persons. We feel, particularly now, that it is important that states and localities continue responsibility for various types of chronic cases and also continue and extend such services as pensions for widows, aged, etc. (Brown, 1940, pp. 161-162)

The same letter requested information on the extent to which states and localities might be "dumping" unemployables onto FERA work relief rolls so as to avoid the costs of assisting them. This was followed by a fall order commanding six Southern states to purge their rolls of unemployables.[8]

The demise of FERA at the end of 1935 might have led Southern states to exploit ADC in 1936 as they had FERA, except for the creation of the Works Progress Administration. The WPA, which was a fully subsidized program for "employables," was subject to the same problems of fungibility as FERA, and this may account for the slowness of some Southern states to adopt ADC and other categorical assistance programs that were not fully subsidized, and which in fact required substantial state and local outlays. More importantly, whenever possible these states preferred to use WPA rather than ADC and OAA, hobbling efforts to institutionalize these nascent programs.

So, for example, state administrative practices were designed to encourage mothers with dependent children to enroll in the nationally financed work programs. It was apparently quite common to exclude from ADC women with only one dependent child, on the theory that such women ought to be able to make it on their own (Lenroot & Field, 1937, p. 242).[9] As Abbott (1937, p. 284) noted, this was precisely what made ADC and Mothers' Aid necessary, for

Employment of mothers with dependent children on WPA is to be deplored, as experience shows that unless the Mothers' earnings are sufficient to enable them to employ competent assistance in the home, the children will be neglected and the Mothers' health will break under the double-burden of serving as wage earners and homemakers.

More importantly, when ADC did become available, assistance levels in the South were established at abysmally low levels. This had two effects. First, it made the means test for ADC assistance quite stringent, and second, it made ADC stipends inadequate to sustain qualifying families. Both results led many women to seek employment (i.e., to become "employable") so as to qualify for participation in WPA.[10]

The Southern situation must be understood in terms of a more general preoccupation with maintaining an abundant supply of cheap labor. Without cheap labor, one of the few significant factors of production on which the South enjoyed a competitive advantage, industrialization would not progress and the South might find itself "thrown back into the fearful prospect of bitter end competition between white and black for the means of subsistence, with all that this meant for the racial values of the region" (Cash, 1941, p. 348). Nowhere was this better illustrated than in Georgia during the gubernatorial tenure of Eugene Talmadge, who railed against the disruptive effects of FERA wage and hour guidelines upon prevailing wage levels in his state. For similar reasons, Talmadge opposed the Georgia legislature's efforts to enact laws necessary to establish public assistance programs under the Social Security Act. In his veto message Talmadge explained, "It is not the purpose of the state to support its people," and that he was "opposed to all kinds of pensions except a soldier's pension," for he did "not want to see the incentive of the American people to work and lay up something for their old age destroyed" (Lemmon, 1954, p. 230).

Meade (1981, p. 40) notes that Talmadge had other reasons for opposing assistance programs. During his 1936 Senatorial campaign against Richard Russell, Talmadge repeatedly attacked the Social Security Act on the grounds that it would destroy the supply of black farm labor and tax Georgia's white people, while giving 90% of the benefits to blacks. Talmadge lost to Russell, and his gubernatorial veto was eventually overturned, but only with great difficulty. At that time the constitution of Georgia made no provision for using either state or local tax revenues for social welfare programs. Nothing less than two constitutional amendments were required before the legislature could enact laws implementing public assistance. The necessary amendments were approved by a two-thirds majority in each chamber of the legislature, and then by voters on June 8, 1937, who by a very wide margin agreed to allow tax monies to be used for Aid to Dependent Children.

Yet ADC never flourished, either in Georgia or elsewhere in the South. The capacity of state and local governments for financing welfare was small, given the underdeveloped economic base of the region. The existing structure of economic and racial power further reduced policymakers' latitude on such matters, even as programs such as the WPA provided an avenue of escape. Of course, the low capacity of the Southern states, combined with the relatively high capacity of New England states, made for a highly uneven capacity in the federal system as a whole, as I show in the last section of this chapter.

Conclusion

States' previous experiences under Mothers' Aid, as modified by programs like FERA and WPA, had a marked impact upon their response to Title IV of the Social Security Act, which established the ADC program. States that had centralized Mothers' Aid programs moved quickly and with little institutional or political turmoil to adopt ADC, since the structure of their Mothers' Aid programs was consistent with administrative requirements set out in Title IV. States with "optional" or noncentralized Mothers' Aid programs adopted ADC more slowly, and with considerable political difficulty, as they moved to require ADC in counties which had not provided Mothers' Aid, and as they withdrew responsibility from local authorities in counties that had provided aid, so as to place it in the hands of new administrative bodies consistent with the requirements of the Social Security Board. As a result, the implementation of ADC was halting and quite uneven across the states and territories.

Unevenness was not restricted to administrative and financial arrangements. It extended to policies on eligibility and assistance, thereby making the experiences of citizens quite uneven. This is the other side of the statebuilding process, so to speak, for welfare institutions ultimately exist for the purpose of rendering services to those in need of assistance. Hence, the process of statebuilding is as much a matter of making connections between citizens and governments, as it is a process of institutional creation and adaptation, and whenever the latter proceeds unevenly, the former will also.

With respect to the early years of ADC, the uneven extension of assistance to the mothers of indigent children is quite striking. By the end of 1942 there were still seven states which had not adopted ADC at all, and it was estimated that as many as 194,000 families in those states were excluded from assistance by this inaction (Bureau of Public Assistance, 1941, p. 58). Moreover, several other states had programs that were not well established, or which conceived the giving of assistance in extraordinarily narrow terms. Clear differences between these "laggards" and more liberal states emerged quickly, and expanded over time.

In fact, interstate differences were greater *after* the passage of the Social Security Act than they were before. Contrary to the expectations of some advocates of ADC, support for children became less uniform than it had been, as some states used matching funds to increase their fiscal effort on behalf of children by a much greater amount than others. Where it was adopted, federal assistance did improve the lot of the poor, but in the absence of any language on minimum standards, that improvement was far from uniform, as liberal states extended the gap between their ADC expenditures and those of less liberal states.

In part these differences reflected underlying variations in political and economic circumstances. The "leader" states were typically those with industrialized economies, and fairly lucrative tax bases. They could afford more generous welfare policies than agrarian states with inadequate fiscal resources. At the same time, "leader" states often had competitive party systems with at least one party identified as a liberal contender, often with a social welfare platform, whereas poor states were likely to have little organized political support for such policies. Thus, differences in political will and economic capacity were associated with differences in ADC policy.

This nonuniformity is in some respects a limitation of *federal* statebuilding processes. The federalization of Mothers' Aid under ADC did not eliminate interstate differences in care for dependent children, as reformers hoped it would, and as a national program might have done. Instead it permitted unevenness to continue, and even accelerate. If the mark of a system's capacity for making policy is its ability to produce uniform outcomes, then federal arrangements are clearly less capable than national institutions.

Yet we must proceed cautiously here. If we intend to explain policy outcomes in terms of institutional capacities for action, then we must be able to ascertain those capacities *independently* of the outcomes in question. Otherwise our reasoning is circular: national systems have greater capacity for producing uniform results than do federal systems, because the results of national processes are more uniform than those of federal processes. A more satisfying conclusion, and one that recognizes that federalism is not oriented toward uniformity in the first place, is that it is quite possible for a federal system to have extraordinarily uneven capacities for action, and is therefore unlikely to produce uniform outcomes. That need not mean that the actors in a federal system are incapable of joint action; in some locales the capacity for such action may be very great, and it simply would be wrong to deny that. In other areas the capacity is poorly developed or virtually nonexistent, and it would be equally wrong to deny that. All of which means that judgments about the relative capacity of federal systems are not analogous to evaluations of the capacity of national systems, at least not in any straightforward way. Once we understand this, we will also understand the need for a bifurcated theory of statebuilding, to go along with our bifurcated practice of providing welfare.

Notes

1. Not surprisingly, one of the distinguishing features of federal statebuilding is the extraordinary effort by central agencies to expand and improve the financial, administrative, and human resources of state, and through them, local governments.

2. As V. O. Key, Jr. (1937) noted, the Social Security Act's requirement that assistance programs be available throughout a state meant that states could not use a traditional device for gaining local compliance, namely, the threat to withhold funds. Denying funds to recalcitrant locales would place a state assistance program in noncompliance with national law, and could result in a withholding of all national funds for the program by the Social Security Board.

3. This may account for another apparent exception in New England, Massachusetts, which did not have the highly centralized Mothers' Aid program typical of other states in the region (Derthick, 1970).

4. The political position of the judges was eroded by economics, however. Nine counties abandoned Mothers' Aid by the end of 1936, 10 more did so in 1937, and three more in 1938, leaving 26 counties with dual programs as of February, 1939 (Dancey, 1939, p. 645).

5. In 14 states, ADC was administered by a state agency, either directly (DE, NH, RI, VT), or through county or district branch offices of the agency (AZ, AR, ID, ME, MO, NJ, NM, OK, TN, WV). Twenty-four state agencies supervised the administration of ADC by local political subdivisions, chiefly county departments of welfare and the local boards of public welfare that either advised or oversaw their operation. AZ, DE, ME, NH, NJ, RI, and VT previously had Mothers' Aid programs administered by state agencies. However, Mothers' Aid programs were locally administered in AR, ID, MO, NM, OK, TN, and WV, so that the move to ADC was accompanied by a significant centralization of power.

6. Most state legislatures made fixed biennial appropriations for ADC, and even though the federal government was willing to supply matching funds beyond such appropriations, these appropriations effectively limited the resources available for assistance. If those resources were inadequate, payments had to be made smaller in order to stretch the funds, or else eligible recipients were put on waiting lists, which often were not eliminated until after ADC had been in operation for several years.

7. Lenroot and Field (1937, p. 241) estimated that about 109,000 families with 280,500 children were receiving Mothers' Aid in 1934, while some 358,000 similar families with 719,500 children were on emergency relief. At a latter point in their analysis, they recognize the disincentives this created for states that received large FERA grants to liberalize Mothers' Aid.

8. The states were Alabama, Arkansas, Louisiana, Mississippi, Oklahoma, and Texas (Brown, 1940, p. 440). Relief was ultimately "federalized" (i.e., removed from state control) in Louisiana because of this "shirking" of responsibility by the state and localities (Williams, 1939; J. Moore, 1975).

9. Single-child families constituted the largest group of families with dependent children in most areas of the country (Lenroot & Field, 1937, p. 243).

10. The *Final Report on the WPA Program* (1946, p. 4) mentions the fact that "in areas where aid to dependent children or general relief were unavailable or inadequate, WPA employment was for many needy women the only available program of assistance."

6

The Police and the
Coercive Nature of the State

OTWIN MARENIN

Military coups are a commonplace event. Elected governments and military regimes are replaced by armed rivals, sometimes violently yet often with little bloodshed. Ruling groups have not been able to call on the other coercive agency of the state, the police, to save them.

The police could offer resistance to military force—they are often as numerous as the military; they are armed, trained, and widely dispersed, and they work in a semi-military and authoritarian organization.[1] The police have sworn an oath to uphold the laws and order of the country so clearly violated by the military's intervention. The police protected the regime and the order it represented against political challengers and mass unrest. In addition, the police have a "professional" interest in the maintenance of order. Yet the police do not intervene to save the existing government, nor are they likely to do so in the future. Sometimes they help instigate a coup and, in the end, they always join the winning side.

The answer why they do not attempt to save the existing regime seems obvious. The police do not save the government because they have little to gain and much to loose by stepping in. It is simply not in their interest as organization or individuals to risk their lives, status, and organizational survival to oppose the other men with guns.

Yet this obvious answer points to a puzzle. How can the state be based on coercion and rule by force—ultimately, if not immediately—(not an uncommon image in analyses of the state) if its hold on the instruments of coercion is so ineffective and unpredictable? How can the police be so nonavailable on the day of the coup when the day prior they were a mainstay of the existing regime? In short, how do we incorporate the inactions of the police (that is, their autonomous interests) into a theory of the state and its changing forms and nature?

This chapter will focus on the impact of police autonomy and behavior on the reproduction of the state in its various forms. Theories of the state and descriptions and analyses of the police at work, though about the same topic, exist in parallel intellectual universes and are, with few exceptions, unconnected in theory (e.g., Brogden, 1982; Reiner, 1986, 1988). Yet theories of what the state is about and what it does ought to be influenced by our knowledge of what agencies of the state do. The state cannot be a coercive agency if it cannot control its agencies of coercion. I will argue that policing, which is relatively autonomous in its determinations, affects the reproduction of the state directly by the exercise of force and indirectly by the impacts of policing on processes of legitimation. To make the argument, I will sketch a model of the state, justify the autonomy of the police, and link police behavior to changes in the state.

Recent arguments about the nature and structure of the state are sketched in the first section. Analyses of the police at work will be summarized in a model of police decision making which stresses the self-interested aspects of police work, and a rough measure of police performance is outlined in the second section. In the concluding sections, I will argue the theoretical implications of the relative autonomy of the police for theories of the nature of the state; the argument will focus on the (hypothesized) impact of policing on processes of state legitimation.

The State

Theories of the state are in turmoil (Carnoy, 1984). Yet common themes exist as well. Recent writings argue for a conception of the state which stresses these characteristics.

(1) States are historical subjects with interests of their own (Evans, Rueschemeyer & Skocpol, 1985; Skocpol, 1979; Miliband, 1983, pp. 63-78). The state's interests are not reducible to or congruent with the interests of social groupings (e.g., classes) or a hypothesized common good.[2] (2) States are aggregates of agencies which sometimes act in unison and often do not.[3] (3) Analyses should focus on the way in which the state is reproduced within the changing configurations of its social formation rather than derive the

nature of the state from prior theoretical assumptions about social life. (4) States require specific legitimations, namely that they present themselves as representing in their intentions and policies the common good rather than the particular interests of social groups or of the state itself.[4] (5) States are organizations which embody social contradictions, including those between themselves and their societies.[5] The effectiveness of the state as a manager of interests will depend on "the pattern in which these contradictory tendencies are combined, both in its internal structure and in its relations to the social structure as a whole" (Rueschemeyer & Evans, 1985, p. 148). (6) States exist at different levels of stateness. Their capacity to act as states is a contingent phenomenon and ranges from states of near nonexistence to overpowering dominance of its social formation.[6]

States, then, must be understood in their concreteness and totality (Jessop, 1982). They are not embodiments of a historical or functional logic nor do they arise in an uncontested way as reflections of social consensus. They are simultaneously players in, the arena for, and the prize of social contests. They are managers for three interests—their own, those of social groupings, and of the dominant conception of the social good. They are complex organizations which must be continually recreated in their autonomy, form, and stateness by the actions of social and 'stately' actors (Marenin, 1987, 1988).

The themes sketched above suggest three aspects of the state (autonomy, organization, stateness) which together delineate the basic, structural characteristics of the state which, when they change, are changes in the state. One basic dimension is the degree to which the state is controlled by social forces, that is, its level of autonomy. States can range from relatively nonautonomous states—those captured and used by social groups—to states which are, to paraphrase Clapham (1985, p. 154), states of themselves, by themselves, and for themselves. States can be agents (direct control by social groups over the state and its agencies), managers (delegated control), or hegemons (control by the state of society).

A second dimension concerns the organizational norms and technologies used to reproduce and sustain the managerial abilities of the state. States must be understood as organizations having internal and external dynamics. "States, like all formal organizations, are decision-making bodies; classes are not" (Therborn, 1986, p. 208). The organizational technologies employed to reproduce the state are, in effect, "forces of production" equally as important to an understanding of the nature and actions of the state (and the promotion of interests) as are material or ideological forces (Therborn, 1978, p. 41; also Wright, 1978, pp. 181-225). Therborn suggests three basic types of organizational technology: bureaucratic, patrimonial, and mass/cadre. Organizational norms and technologies can distort the state away from its socially desired goals. For example, the descriptions of neo-patrimonial states in Africa (Callaghy, 1984; Charney, 1987; Chazan, 1988) depict the distortion of ruling-class goals and nominally bureaucratic (Weberian) norms by the particularistic preferences and organizational norms of state agents.

The third dimension is the level of stateness, the ability of states to act as one and make and implement decisions and policies. The widely used labels strong and weak states refer to this dimension. States are not always cohesive organizations. Rather, they tend to be balkanized (Evans et al., 1985, p. 357). State agencies often have a tenacious life of their own and often are at odds with their "stately" superiors. The disunity of the state reflects the autonomy of state agencies from the executive centers of the state (Pal, 1986; Palmer, 1985). The values and preferences of agents and agencies may or may not coincide with what the "state" wants. Social groups frequently seek to capture one agency of the state rather than the state as a whole; it is easier and the benefits gained are more immediate and direct.

States (in their three dimensions)[7] do not grow like plants but are reproduced by interested actors (groups and individuals within society and the state) who seek to control and use this potentially powerful means of promoting interests for their own benefits. Theorists, of course, differ in designating which interested actors can control the reproduction of the state and what means are effective. Some theorists focus on class and political conflicts as the source of state reproduction (e.g., Therborn, 1986, pp. 219-228). Others focus on ideological means, on hegemonic forms of consciousness, or the powers of ideologically influenced conceptions of rationality. In a capitalist social formation, argue Bennett and Sharpe (1985, p. 45), the "very position of the state makes it rational for state managers to promote the general interests of capital." Others conceptualize the state as the outcome of interest-group competition. Still others stress the organizational and process mechanisms by which interests become embedded in existing stated structures (e.g., Therborn, 1978).

What I want to argue is that "stately" actors also reproduce the state. Agencies and agents seek to reproduce themselves and their preferred policies, and often, only incidentally, the state as such. The state is, in the end, the result of agencies acting in particular ways. Those ways have many determinants. In the next sections I will focus on the organization and determinants of policing and on the impact of police autonomy on the reproduction of the state.

The Police

What do we know of state coercion in real life? Studies of the police at work stress three themes: the police exercise discretion in the performance of their work; police performance has multiple determinations; and the police can be autonomous from the state and from societal forces. Changes in the nature of policing are changes in levels of discretion and autonomy and in the relative importance of determinations of police work. Existing radical and conventional theories of the state and the police tend to misread the importance of these characteristics for their own theorizing; therefore they provide little guidance on how to incorporate studies of the police into explorations of the coercive nature of the state.

Discretion lies at the heart of police work (Bittner, 1980; Goldstein, 1977). Agencies and individual officers have significant discretion in how they wish to use the authority and coercion at their disposal. Their discretion defines and delimits concretely the coercive capacity of the state (and the law, force, and justice experienced by citizens) and, theoretically, suggests that coercion is an ambiguous core characteristic of the state.

The multiple determinations of police discretion at the street level can be described, analyzed, and evaluated (e.g., Reiner, 1980; Sherman, 1980). Five general external sources of pressures on the individual officer are organizational environment, public demands, legal norms, professional codes, and work-group allegiance. Internal pressures on individual officers include personality, personal norms, values, and ideologies. Situational factors also shape the exercise of discretion. All factors can be combined in an integrated model of individual officer decision making (Marenin, 1982, 1985).

The police organization allocates duties and rights, lays down a plethora of important and petty rules which seek to control and guide officers' actions within the department and on the street, and employs typical reward, sanction, leadership, supervisory, and management techniques to ensure officer accountability, increase efficiency, and limit the abuse of power. Formally, the organization is the dominant shaper of police conduct. The organization mediates public, legal, political, and professional demands and protects its own interests as well.

Public demands reach the police as demands for services (e.g., crime, control, maintenance of order, emergency services) and proper and individualized treatment in encounter situations; and in mediated ways through the political process, commonalities of political cultures, and dominant conceptions of the appropriate local order (Bayley, 1985a).

Legal norms justify policing powers and processes, create rules which enable and constrain officers in the exercise of discretion, and channel police attention and work into specific forms and targets of law enforcement and order maintenance. Professional codes of conduct are internalized in formal and in-service training and acquired through the informal interaction of working colleagues and interest associations.

The work group mediates and interprets external pressures by the contingencies of police work. The desire to do one's work in a safe, convenient, and effective manner expresses the autonomous interests of the lower echelons of the police organization, the cops and detectives on the beat and in the streets.

Decisions reflect, as well, the impact of personality (world views, moral assumptions about the utility of force, idealism and cynicism, judgments of conformity and deviance) and calculations of self-interests and satisfactions—the desire to lead a meaningful life, and the need to control work and clients, satisfy superiors, avoid complaints, make a living, keep a job, maintain self-respect, and deal with the potential for corruptive personal gain and abuse of powers (M. K. Brown, 1981; Lipsky, 1980; Muir, 1977).

Finally, what officers do in specific situations depends on the unique configuration of each encounter—time and place; the nature of the event; perceived danger; and the acts and character of offenders, victims and bystanders (Black, 1971).

The pressures generated by these three sets of factors—external demands, personal traits, and unique circumstances—are resolved by the police in operational styles of work. Departments (J. Q. Wilson, 1975) and officers (Hochstedler, 1981; Muir, 1977; Reiner, 1978) develop styles of policing which stress some and deemphasize other goals, means, occasions, and targets of policing. Styles incorporate conceptions and norms of what policing is all about, how it should be done effectively and fairly, and which external demands are legitimate and which are not. Operational styles or patterns of decisions are the policies on law and order, the mix of service and repression, and the concrete existence of coercion one can observe in any social formation (that is, such decisions as which meeting to raid, which demonstration to break up, which houses to protect, who to single out for attention in a crowd, which encounters to initiate and which to forego, or modes and styles of dealing with people). These actions of the police are the coercive nature of the state. Immediately, and sometimes ultimately, control over coercion rests not with a social group (or class) or the state, but with the agency which coerces. The police are not unthinking tools given to blind obedience to state commands.

Police agencies typically do not function as neutral transmitters of external pressures and demands (Cordner & Girvan, 1988; Harring, 1981; Reuss-Ianni, 1983). The police, like other agencies of the state, have interests of their own which they seek to protect as they carry out their duties. They seek to influence the thrust of state policy-making and implementation in ways that suit their needs, experience, and professional expectations (Ericson, 1982). Such organizational and individual mediations of social and "stately" demands constitute the autonomy of the police. In turn, the resultant exercise of force affects the fortunes of other "state" actors and of societal groups.

The concept of "relative autonomy" rediscovered the state as a historical subject. The next step is liberating the agencies of the state from the state. If the state is "relatively autonomous" agencies can counteract state control, and work groups and individual officers can mediate the guiding hand of administrators.[8]

Arguing that organizations have autonomy is not a difficult empirical or theoretical task. The vast literature on organizations, both private and public, supports the existence of organizational interests and points to the variety of means by which organizations can protect themselves even against their controllers. Formally accountable agencies have and can use many means to evade control and impose their self-generated preferences.

Similarly, individuals working in organizations do not spend time strictly according to the dictates of managers or the formal delimitations of their roles. Instead, as Lipsky (1980) spells out in great detail, agents redefine their work by their own interests and devise coping routines which enlarge their powers, discretion, and comfort. Police officers are practically *urtype* street-level bureaucrats. As craftsmen and professionals they believe themselves entitled to do a dirty, dangerous, and difficult job as they see best within specific circumstances. The struggle over control and definition of the job is a major worker-management conflict in any organization. (The first struggle is over the price of labor.)

Agencies and individuals are autonomous when their actions are self-determined and based on assessments of interests and values and less autonomous when actions follow vectors of external pressures (Nordlinger, 1981). The relativeness of autonomy is the ratio of effective external to self-generated determinants of actions. There are empirical difficulties in sorting out the relative importance of factors which go into the making of short- and long-range policies, and what are external and self-generated pressures in specific cases, but these are not insurmountable.

The autonomy of the police can range from slight to substantial. Their relative autonomy from the state and from society is sustained by a rhetoric of professionalism, by political actions on the part of the police (e.g., Baldwin & Kinsey, 1982; Brogden, 1982; Taylor, 1986), by the incapacity of the state to overcome the resistance of the police against external control (Fogelson, 1977), and the incapacity of societal groups to force a different reproduction of the state including its coercive agencies.

In sum, police work is determined by historically given constraints and organizational and personal preferences; it is always the existing endpoint of multiple pressures which seek to construct a particular form of coercion and service. The relative autonomy of the police can be observed in the working life of order, service, and repression demanded by interested groups in society and enacted by interested police forces.

The Police in the Reproduction of the State

The linkages of state and coercion can be seen in different ways. Rather than discuss all aspects of policing in the state, I will focus on the impact of police autonomy and the use of force (conceptualized below as a repression/protection ratio) on changes in the state. Existing theories of the police have little to say on this topic.

Radical analyses of the police stress the repressive functions of the police in a class society. Control by the state over its police is seen as relatively unproblematic and little mediated by individual or organizational interests (e.g., Danns, 1982; Gleizal, 1981; Harring, 1977, 1983; Quinney, 1980; Robinson, 1978; Spitzer, 1981; Takagi, 1983). The police do what the state and the ruling class behind the state want done. The police cannot be autonomous. In short, radicals tend to neglect the theoretical implications of the multiple determinations of police work.

Radical writers may be quite accurate in what they describe but, starting from an instrumentalist or (modified) structuralist conception of the state and force, they are unable to consider the theoretical implications of their descriptions, namely that the state itself may be reproduced by a variety of interests, including those specific to the police and other agents of the state. Their descriptions are elaborate but cannot test or change the originally accepted conception of the nature of the state.

Conventional explanations of the police tend to focus on organizational variables and practices, and the effects of personal and situational factors on the exercise of discretion. The police are not tools of partisan interests but seek to promote and protect order and routine against crime, disruption, and change (e.g., Bayley, 1985a; M. K. Brown, 1981; Skolnick & Bayley, 1986;

Walker, 1983; J. Q. Wilson, 1975). In this view, the problem of police autonomy is how to control the occasional misuse of discretion by individual officers and organizations and how to isolate the police from partisan political demands. Conventional writers tend to neglect the importance of discretion for theories of the state. More precisely, they take the state as a given constraint for police actions.

In radical and conventional thinking, control of policing is not a problem which challenges the dominant understanding of the state as either instrumental or structural agent, or as the arena of competition for social forces. The alternate formulation of the reciprocal relations between the state and the police presented below argues that the relatively autonomous actions of the police and their discretion in the exercise of force affect the reproduction of the state in three basic ways. The police constrain social actions, help shape the structure of social interests, and affect processes of state legitimation.

Coercion comes in many forms and serves many functions which need to be specified before their impacts on the state can be hypothesized. A rough measure of police performance and the interests served by policing is the protection/repression ratio. Police functions range from "normal" protective services which promote order (assistance to victims, crime control) to repressive, even terrorist actions (death squads, torture, midnight raids, undercover provocation, and harassment) which protect the interests of particular groups, including the police and the state (Brodeur, 1983). The uses of coercion by the police can span the poles from repressive force to protective force.

Repressive force is force exercised in arbitrary ways, against any group or individual in society, for the protection of particularistic interests, frequently by barbarous means. Protective force is controlled by established and accepted guidelines, provides services useful and necessary to the lives of all members of society, and is used against specifiable groups or individuals in a limited, non-barbarous way. All police work contains elements of terrorism and protection, repression and service.

Police forces differ widely in the ratio of repressive to protective force they use. Some police organizations are highly repressive and provide, as far as one can tell, little protection while other forces have a high protection to repression ratio in their work. Both repression and protection theoretically are independent of the form of the state or the autonomy of the police, though empirically there may be affinities between types of states, levels of police autonomy, and the uses and misuses of coercion (Bayley, 1979).

It is not always easy to judge what constitutes repression and what constitutes service in specific situations because such judgments inevitably draw upon existing interpretations of the social formation in which the police work. From a radical perspective, a capitalist system is always repressive though it may mask its repression by appearing to offer, and sometimes actually offering, protection and service. Repression only appears naked when authentic challenges to the system arise, when other means of control have failed, or when particular factions in control of coercion are directly challenged. From a more conventional point of view, repression in a capitalist system is an aberration and if used is used to a good purpose, for the suppression of those who would attempt to subvert a system which functions well for all and which all support in its essential structures, values, and rules. Repression is the aberration of corrupt and inefficient agents of coercion. Abuses are the limited failures of limited individuals with limited skills and ethics.

Both protective and repressive police work are "political" in the sense that priorities for police work, the structure of policing organizations, and controls on abuse reflect the distribution of politically organized power. The distinction between repression and protection lies not in the politicized exercise of coercion nor in coercion itself, but in the distribution of interests which are served by the actions of the police—that is, the degree to which the police protect and promote their own or the general or particular interests.

In terms of means—the "serving" of interests—brutal, barbaric, tortuous, and unlimited means always are a sign of repression. Limited and non-barbaric means may be a sign of protection.

Defining the ends, the "interests" served, is more difficult. In the abstract, the police can pay attention to all or to a few groups, and to a wide or narrow range of actions. In practice, due to limitations of time, resources, and willingness, the police only pay attention to selected aspects of social life. What matters, then, is the attention which the police pay, routinely and systematically, to groups, individuals, and acts. What are the rules which guide them in determining which individuals and acts merit attention?

When the rules for selecting and limiting targets are drawn loosely and when the range of acts worth paying attention to is wide and inclusive, then repression is at work. Everything is suspect and everyone can be threatened. Conversely, a narrow range of acts and detailed and open rules for selecting targets indicates protection. In sum, police coercion openly aimed at defined subgroups in the population and exercised in non-barbaric ways indicates protection. Unchecked or covert coercion against a wide range of groups and acts indicates repression.

Levels of repression and protection of social groups are partially determined by the police themselves, as the police distort "rules for attention" by their own interests. Both repression and protection affect the state but through different mechanisms. Repression functions largely in a directly instrumentalist way for the state, but ultimately also can have legitimating or delegitimating consequences. Protection mainly affects the ideological processes through which states become legitimized. One can postulate that protection, since it affects legitimations more directly, is the more important long-term service rendered by the police to themselves and the state.

The impact of police repression/protection levels can be traced in changes in the three dimensions of the state outlined earlier: autonomy, organizational style, and stateness. Specific impacts of the police on the state would include the following. Repression, if successful, will enhance the autonomy of the state (almost by definition) and the ruling capacity of the state. The effects of repression on state unity are less clear. Repression may destroy unity if used against other state actors or it may enhance unity by removing some groups which are in conflict. There seems to be little relation between repression per se and the organizational structure of the police; bureaucratic, patrimonial, and mass/cadre police forces can be massively repressive. The organizational technology embodied within the police, though, will affect the dominance of particular technologies in other state agencies. For example, a police organized along patrimonial lines which is also repressive will hinder the emergence or reproduction of bureaucratic or mass/cadre forms of organization in other state agencies.

Protection will likely enhance ruling capacity and autonomy. Unity may be both reduced or enhanced by effective protection. The effects of organizational technology embodied in policing are indeterminate, though one can speculate that a patrimonially organized force is little capable of offering protection.

As a whole, repression protects the interests of the police, may protect the interests of other agencies of the state and of some social groups, and harms the interests of other social groups. Protection, on the other hand, tends to serve the interests of most social groups and may serve the interests of other agencies of the state and of the police.

Both repressive and protective policing affect the legitimations a state is capable of sustaining. Existing theories of legitimation can be classified into "bank account," "internalization," and "historical evolution" theories. Bank account theories argue that legitimating orientations toward the state follow changes in state performance, if sustained above a minimum threshold level (Lipset, 1963, pp. 64-79). Every policy which finds favor with social groups enhances the legitimacy of the state as people "deposit" an increment of allegiance in the support account of the state. Every policy which fails withdraws good will and diffuses support. Support for the right of authorities to make decisions and enforce implementations fluctuates as people see their interests served or misused. A clear-eyed calculation of costs and benefits, in the short- and long-run, leads to the acceptance or rejection of the state's right to rule.

Internalization theories argue that legitimating orientations are learned in a process of socialization or mystification. The dominant norms of the system are internalized by new members through their participation in social life (Beirne, 1979; Easton & Dennis, 1969). Socialization may result in legitimating orientations without conscious evaluations or judgments by groups or individuals of the policies and interests served by the state or of its moral worth.

Historical evolution theories focus less on how individuals or groups arrive at their orientations and attempt to explain, instead, why certain norms are dominant in the social formation. Changes in consciousness reflect shifts in economic and social structures and the efforts by intellectuals who seek to shape consciousness toward preferred modes of thinking (Ferrero, 1944; Gramsci, 1957; Habermas, 1975).

The police affect all three modes of legitimation. The police are judged by their performance and deposit or withdraw goodwill from the state's account by the manner and effectiveness of their work. Effective performance enhances the legitimacy of the police and the government which the police work for and represent (Carter & Marenin, 1981). State agencies and states which serve the utilitarian interests of social groups gain legitimacy, and those which do not delegitimate the agency and the state. In general, effective protection legitimates and effective repression may do so, while both ineffective protection and repression delegitimate, though probably at different rates.

The police are important symbols in the child's socialization and incorporation into an ongoing social system (Easton & Dennis, 1969, p. 240). The police themselves manipulate symbols of their authority and travails in an attempt to instill in society a sense of proper moral order (as defined by the police, themselves) and dominant legal and political norms (Manning, 1979, pp. 1-13; Taylor, 1986).

The police, by their impact on the fortunes of groups within or without the state, can affect the nature and substance of hegemonic norms. Repression contains actions by stately and social actors. If successful, repression subdues challenges to the state, distorts political life and fates, and limits change (Bayley, 1985a; Bunyan, 1976). The police can threaten other groups within the state or stage "internal" coups (Jakubs, 1977, pp. 96-97; Turk, 1982, p. 159). Repression alters the capacities of stately and social actors as they seek to impose their conceptions of moral worth and general interests on the state and society.

Repression affects legitimating processes in specific ways. Repression helps reproduce the challenged or emergent state by "buying" time for the state to shift to other means of inducing legitimation and by helping to shift power away from local to central levels of the state. Historical analyses of state-local relations and conflicts over the control of coercion bring out the often complex and ambiguous processes by which groups in conflict used coercion to establish and delineate the legitimacy of respective spheres of authority and sanctioning (e.g., Bayley, 1985b; Monkonnen, 1981; Rock, 1983; Spitzer, 1981; Steedman, 1984; A. Williams, 1979). Historically, "the extension of moral consensus and the police as instruments of legitimate coercion [went] hand in hand" (Silver, 1967, p. 14).

Yet repression tends to undermine the legitimacy of the state if unsuccessful, overused, or used ineffectively. Ineffective repression will strip the state of its normative justifications and undermine its capacity to perform hegemonic or utilitarian functions (which, in turn, reproduce legitimating orientations). A state which rules by repression only is not likely to last as pure repression is a notoriously inefficient tool for ruling. Appeals to legitimacy are a more effective way to induce compliance. Legitimations link historically given structures and the interests they serve with individual and social needs and interests in a process of voluntary compliance. Control of legitimations, hence, becomes a key process of governance. The distribution of rights and benefits, of exploitation, discrimination, service, and favors is most powerfully protected if all perceive such an order to be morally right and submit voluntarily to the requirements and commands of that order.

In short, there is a fourth process and model of how states become legitimated. "Coercive legitimation" can induce legitimating orientations just as effectively as can bank account or socialization processes or historical evolution modes. If repression is sustained over time it may legitimate state rule; the "transformation of power into authority is accomplished by conditioning the great majority of people to accept power relationships as real, inevitable, unavoidable and perhaps even right" (Turk, 1982, p. 78). Repression and protection are not alternative forms of police behavior (or the exercise of coercion by the state) but exist in all policing, though in different ratios. In the first three models, legitimacy and coercion are conceptualized as opposites balanced on a scale; when one rises the other declines. Legitimacy is a voluntary choice in thought and behavior; coercion coerces. In coercive legitimations voluntary motives for compliance may arise from coercion, rather than reflect rational judgments, experienced socialization, or the power to shape hegemonic norms. It is the police who control much of the "coercive legitimation" process.

Coercion and the State

Force has a dual character. It guarantees the reproduction of order and domination, represses challenges, allows for habituation, and, with the passage of time, converts revolutionary and illegitimate conditions into honored tradition. Yet force also undermines legitimacy. The use of force by the state and the police against social groups or state actors indicates a failure of legitimation and can lead to further disenchantment and resistance. The state stands in a paradoxical position to its own force potential. It does not always control force yet needs the capacity for coercion; it must use coercion at times but the large-scale use of forces undermines its capacity to rule. Force may insure compliance at the same time that its use delegitimizes the state. The police are not an easy or unproblematic instrument for the state and its capacity for legitimation because they do not represent one pole of a force-consensus continuum, but their intermingling. Policing reveals the dual nature of social order, at once repressive and protective, ultimately and simultaneously based on force and moral judgments.

The nature of both contradictions is captured perfectly in the phrase "legitimate force," that is, the acceptance by interested actors of coercion even against themselves as right and proper. Policing is the testing ground of domination. The powers and interests of the state and of state agencies clash with the needs and values of social groups and are resolved in legitimate forms of organized coercion and compliance (Humphries & Greenberg, 1981; Levi, 1981; Tilly, 1975, p. 59; Turk, 1982).

Coercion is neither an integral aspect of the state nor absent from its changing forms. Coercion is one of the means by which the state is reproduced and it is at the core or periphery of the state by its importance compared to other means of reproduction. The ultimately coercive nature of the state is but a logical syllogism which is not always made concrete in the historical experience of states.[9]

The general effects of the police on the state then depend largely on changes in the repression/protection ratio. As the ratio of repression to protection shifts so will the weight and likelihood of the impacts hypothesized above. In the long run, the legitimating impacts of policing are more important than the repressive aspects, since repression itself is most effective when a new process of legitimation comes into being: coercive legitimation.

The police, then, affect the reproduction of the state in its changing forms by their partially autonomous exercise of coercion and, specifically, through the effects of their coercive acts on the capacity of states to sustain existing legitimations or create new ones.

Notes

1. The normal answer to this question argues that the ruling class has not been replaced, merely one faction has been replaced by another. The form has changed but the essential nature of the state—its functions and relations to social forces—remains the same. This answer sidesteps the issue—for in what way does the state remain the same if its policies, personnel, organizational structure, and governing ethos change? At some point, changes in form(s) mutate into changes in nature.

2. For example, Bennett and Sharpe, 1985; Clark and Dear, 1984; Davis, 1984, pp. 123-124; Evans, Rueschemeyer and Skocpol, 1985, p. 360; Jessop, 1982, pp. 222-223; Pal, 1986; Palmer, 1985; Pierson, 1984; Skocpol, 1985, p. 48; Therborn, 1978, p. 37.

3. For example, Bright and Harding, 1984; Gulalp, 1987; Przeworski, 1980, p. 145; Skocpol, 1985, p. 27; Therborn, 1986.

4. In Walzer's (1970, p. 216) nice phrase, state bureaucrats "are citizens in lieu of the rest of us; the common good is, so to speak, their speciality." Also, see Eckstein, 1979, pp. 16-17.

5. Badie and Birnbaum, 1983, pp. 135-136; O'Donnell, 1979; Offe, 1984a.

6. Nettl, 1968; Anderson, 1987, p. 14; Azarya and Chazan, 1987; Young, 1984.

7. When combined, these three dimensions form a six-cell matrix with a depth dimension on the stateness axis. Each cell presents a type of state determined by degree of control or autonomy, by type of organizational technology which dominates, and by the level of stateness achieved. Changes in the state are movements across the dimensions of the matrix.

The three dimensions are continua. The division of the autonomy and organizational technology dimensions into three values is not meant to suggest either clear breaks between the values or that only three values exist. In the real life of states, organizational technologies often are intermixed within one state agency or differ from one state agency to another (e.g., Ergas, 1987).

The three dimensions can be articulated in different ways. For example, unity of the state is more likely if mass/cadre or bureaucratic organizational technologies are used. Patrimonial forms of organizing tend to split the state into factions.

8. Autonomy must mean something. It cannot be mere oratory to get past a theoretical difficulty (Thompson, 1978), nor beg the "critical questions, which soon arise: how relative is state autonomy and how autonomous is a relatively autonomous state" (Therborn, 1986, p. 208). The question of autonomy can be phrased as autonomous for what and from what? The state is autonomous so it can manage. It is autonomous from economic, social, political, and ideological anchors in society. The state can be autonomous from all societal anchors, but least so from cultural norms. As MacKinnon (1983, pp. 644, 658) argues, the (capitalist) state has never been free from (or autonomous from) sexist conceptions of interests.

9. The ultimately coercive nature of the state is but a logical syllogism which is not always made concrete in the historical experience of states. The notion that the state rests on coercion, immediately or ultimately, is based on experience (we can observe state terror and random police

violence), yet the persuasiveness of the image rests not on generalizations from such data but on an implicit syllogism: if the state cannot persuade, entice, motivate, manipulate, mislead, or mystify to gain compliance, what else is left as a means to achieve obedience? The threat or use of force remains the final motivation for social action when other motivations have ceased to work. The coercive nature of the state is merely this syllogism writ large again and again, and, being a sensible syllogism, seems accurate.

7

State-Making and State-Breaking

The Origins and Paradoxes of the Contemporary Taiwanese State

STEVE CHAN

England, it is true, in causing a social revolution in Hindostan, was actuated by the vilest interests, and was stupid in her manner of enforcing them. But that is not the question. The question is, can mankind fulfill its destiny without a fundamental revolution in the social state of Asia? If not, whatever may have been the crimes of England, she was the unconscious tool of history in bringing about the revolution. (Marx quoted in Moulder, 1977, p. 16)

What was it that enabled Japan to take a course so radically different from that of all the other countries in the now underdeveloped world? . . . The answer to this question . . . comes down to the fact that Japan is the only country in Asia (and in Africa and in Latin America) that escaped being turned into a colony or dependency of Western European or American capitalism, that had a chance of independent national development. (Baran, 1957, p. 158)

It is by now almost standard practice to invoke the role of a strong state in explaining the economic and commercial successes of Japan and the "four little tigers" of East Asia (i.e., Hong Kong, Singapore, South Korea, and Taiwan). This chapter addresses those historical legacies that have been crucial in shaping the *structure* of the contemporary Taiwanese state. I set aside the treatment of this state as an *agent* (i.e., its policy conduct) for another time and place.

The rationale for focusing on the Taiwanese case can be briefly stated. This island nation has featured an impressive record of GNP growth, averaging about 9% annually in the past 35 years. Real per capita income during this period increased 7.6 times. Few, if any, country can match this record of *sustained* rapid growth. This growth has been fueled by a very successful export drive, which has enabled Taiwan to compile the second largest (after Japan) foreign reserve in the world.

Taiwan's economic and commercial accomplishments have been accompanied by a record of political stability, social equity, and improving physical quality of life index (PQLI). Its income distribution is about as equal as those of Norway and Sweden. And on some dimensions of PQLI, such as infant mortality, it has even outperformed the United States. As such, Taiwan's experience sets it apart from others featuring either a stagnant economy, or economic growth accompanied by acute instability or inequality (e.g., Iran and Brazil, respectively). Indeed, some have described Taiwan's *simultaneous* achievement of rapid growth, political stability, and social equity as a miracle (e.g., Gold, 1986). Prevailing Western theorizing suggests the opposite expectation: that rapid growth tends to undermine stability as well as equality (e.g., Kuznets, 1955; M. Olson, 1963).

In short, then, the Taiwanese experience represents a "deviant" case to cross-national norms of policy performance, and poses an enigma or challenge to classic theories of modernization and dependency (e.g., Amsden, 1985, 1979; Barrett & Whyte, 1982; Chan, 1988; C. Clark, 1987; Crane, 1982). And for proponents of the Kuhnian (1970) version of scientific progress, anomalies offer a necessary and useful stimulus to revise old theories or seek new ones.

In the recent past, dissatisfaction with classic modernization and dependency explanations has led a number of scholars to emphasize the role of the state in Taiwan's development. There has, however, been a relative lack of attention to the historical context in which the Taiwanese state developed, especially the continuities and legacies from a more distant (i.e., pre-1949) past. This shortcoming is accompanied by a tendency to focus on the more transient policy conduct of the Taiwanese state rather than its deeper and more enduring structural properties. Finally, whereas much has been made of the *domestic* strength and autonomy of the Taiwanese state, less effort has been made in addressing how external influences have contributed to this outcome. As I will try to show, the Taiwanese state has been the exact opposite of the American state with its paradox of internal weakness and external strength (Krasner, 1983). In Taiwan, exogenous forces have tended to shape the endogenous conditions.

The discussion below focuses on how imperial China, colonial Japan, and liberal anticommunist America have left their respective marks on the development of the Taiwanese state. I treat with broad strokes the pertinent historical legacies, and leave the detailed documentation to several comprehensive studies on the history of Taiwan's political economy that already exist (e.g., Galenson, 1979; Ho, 1978; Hsiung, 1981).

Imperial China

China left feudalism long before Europe and Japan. Yet neither an autonomous state nor a strong bourgeoisie emerged in prerevolutionary China. Economic take-off in the Rostovian (1960) sense did not take place until the 1950s, long after Western Europe, North America, and Japan. Why? The answer has to do with the mode of traditional production, the extraction and consumption of surplus, and the impact of foreign penetration during the 19th century.

In imperial China, agriculture was the dominant mode of production. To be specific, the Chinese emphasized rice cultivation. Several implications follow from this emphasis. Rice cultivation is labor-*intensive*. It contrasts with the *extensive* agriculture practiced in the West with its emphasis on grain and livestock. Whereas surplus from the intensive mode of Chinese agriculture was derived from additions of *labor* input, that from the extensive Western mode was expressed in *territorial* expansion. Thus Wallerstein (1974, p. 57) remarks that "China had in fact been expanding, but internally, extending its rice production within its frontiers. Europe's 'internal Americas' in the 15th century were quickly exhausted, given an agronomy that depended on more space."

The European need for more space stimulated *lateral expansion* with its concomitants of imperialism, war, and foreign rivalry (Choucri & North, 1975). In their turn, war-making and war-financing promoted the making of the state and of the bourgeoisie (e.g., Rasler & Thompson, 1985; Tilly, 1985). In contrast, traditional China existed in more or less "splendid isolation." To be sure, there were wars with the "barbarians" from the north and the west. But the traditional Chinese international system hardly resembled the European system of competing sovereign powers with roughly equal capabilities. China was clearly the preeminent power in its "universe," and exercised informal influence rather than direct control over its much weaker neighbors in the form of a tributary system. In Wallersteinian terms, it was a self-satisfied "world empire" with little interest in foreign intercourse. Different dynasties repeatedly banned foreign trade and emigration in sharp contrast to the European practice of encouraging overseas exploration, commerce, and settlement in the colonies.

Traditional China was a collection of relatively self-sufficient village communities. To be sure, there was internal commerce and large cities grew up in the path of trade routes. But given the continental size of China, its internal trade would often be equivalent to external trade in Europe. More importantly, political and economic power had always been tied to the land or, rather, the ownership of land (more on this point later). The towns tended to be marketplaces, and especially administrative outposts of the state. They never developed into the centers of bourgeois power as in early modern Germany, France, and England.

Rice cultivation requires abundant water supply in addition to labor. As earlier observers of the "Asiatic" mode of production, including Marx and Engels, had remarked, the development and maintenance of an extensive irrigation system did give rise to a centralized state bureaucracy in China, long before anything worthy of this description took place in Europe. Yet this bureaucracy did not facilitate a strong and autonomous state, nor did it promote capitalist development. Why?

The imperial bureaucracy offered the ladder of social mobility in traditional China (Ho, 1962). Office-holding, or the status as a *mandarin,* can be obtained by successfully undertaking the competitive examination administered by the state. This examination was open to everyone since the Ming dynasty, when bans against certain merchant and artisan classes were lifted. Thus imperial China had an open system of mobility, so that even the poorest peasant boy could aspire to become a *mandarin* through the mastery of Confucian texts. In contrast, Japan had a closed system; the *samurai* status was hereditary and, short of adoption, it was usually beyond the reach of a commoner. Moreover, in imperial China (as in France and Spain), the venality of office permitted wealthy commoners to purchase nobility titles from the crown (which was always looking for ways to increase revenue). These titles, however, were usually not inheritable, so that the purchaser's descendants would have to repurchase these titles if they wanted to maintain their family's social position.

In imperial China as in other traditional agrarian societies, land ownership provided another status symbol. Successful merchants invested in land in order to join the gentry class. They also invested in the education of their male offspring with the hope of joining the officialdom. On the other hand, land belonged to the *daimyos* (lords) in traditional Japan. It was subject to confiscation as a private property.

It should not be difficult to infer from the preceding two paragraphs the reasons why the imperial Chinese state lacked autonomy, and was unable as well as unwilling, to paraphrase Rostow, to explore the impulses of capitalist expansion. Factors related to *elite fusion, mobility incentives,* and *capital accumulation* were responsible for these outcomes. Successful Chinese merchants wanted to buy their way out of the commercial class, which was assigned by the Confucian ideology to near the bottom of the social hierarchy. They were not motivated to plow their profits back to business pursuits, but aspired instead to becoming members of the officialdom, the gentry, and the rural *rentier* class. There was, consequently, a constant flight of capital and entrepreneurial talent from business to the economically less productive but socially more prestigious investments in land, titles, and classical education. In contrast, Japanese merchants, caught in a closed social system, "through no virtue of their own . . . were forced to think in terms of buying and selling and production and investment" (Levy, 1953-1954, p. 187). Other authors (e.g., Holt & Turner, 1966; B. Moore, 1966) have commented that the widespread venality of office also had hampered capital accumulation in France in comparison with England. One might further note that in Japan and England, the custom of *primogeniture* helped to preserve family wealth, whereas in China and France the division of inheritance among all heirs again had the effect of dissipating capital over several generations.

Traditional Chinese mobility patterns also contributed to a fusion of the Confucian literati, the rural gentry, the upwardly mobile merchants, and the imperial officialdom in one "grand coalition." One consequence of this fusion was that the imperial Chinese state was deeply penetrated by and under the influence of the landlord class. The development of a national bourgeoisie along the lines of the Western European experience was stunted. Imperial China did not undergo the sort of rivalry between the crown and the burghers (or the rivalry between the state and the church) that was characteristic of the emergence of European *etatism* and capitalism. There was nothing comparable to the Western European legacy of opposition against royal absolutism. Instead, a system of "Oriental despotism" prevailed (Wittfogel, 1957).

The "grand coalition" also expressed itself through the propagation and permeation of Confucianism. It became the dominant ideology of the state bureaucracy. Its *weltanschauung* provided the justification for the traditional order with the emperor and landlord class at its apex. Whereas (unlike the Tokugawa shugonate) the imperial Chinese state enjoyed rather *extensive* geographic *scope* in its administrative coverage (as exemplified by the organizational apparatus for irrigation maintenance and tax collection), it lacked the *depth* of political penetration and the *intensity* of feudal control shown by the Japanese *daimyos*. Moreover, the imperial Chinese bureaucracy was a far cry from the Weberian notion of a salaried and professional administrative class operating under formal regulations and accountable to a central authority. The Chinese *mandarinate* was expected to operate according to the rule of virtuous men (i.e., personal authority and leadership) rather than the rule of impersonal rules and laws. Most officials could not depend on the state treasury for their living expenses, and instead had to resort to their own extractions from local sources. The maintenance of sociopolitical order relied heavily upon the authority of the local gentry and the power of social sanctions. Drawing upon a distinction made by Chalmers Johnson (1981) in a different context, the Chinese ruling elite and especially the court in Beijing did less *ruling* than *reigning*.

In short, I argue that far from being an autonomous and strong actor, the state in imperial China was a captive of the dominant gentry class with its Confucian ideology. There is, however, one more critical piece to the puzzle of a weak Chinese state and its failure to undertake industrialization. Following Baran's (1957) argument cited at the beginning of this chapter, Moulder (1977) has persuasively shown that endogenous factors alone cannot satisfactorily explain the political and economic disarray of prerevolutionary China in comparison with Japan's accomplishments after the Meiji Restoration (1868-1869). In order to account for these two countries' divergent experiences, one must look at the critical difference in the degree to which they had been incorporated into the capitalist world-system during the 19th century. The (perceived) Chinese market, then as now, was a powerful magnet that attracted European traders, investors, and missionaries. China had the particular misfortune of producing a staple commodity desired by Britain. The export of Chinese tea to Britain aroused British concern with specie outflow. London tried to plug and then reverse this drain through massive exports of Indian opium to China. China thus became a critical link in the British imperial system that facilitated the extraction and transfer of Indian surplus.

Beijing's efforts to stop the illicit drug trade led to the infamous Opium War of 1840-1842 ("just say no" was just not enough). Chinese defeat in this war led to the Treaty of Nanking with its stipulations of loss of territories (Hong Kong), the opening of more treaty ports, the payment of vast indemnities, and the abolition of Chinese state and commercial monopolies in the name of free trade. This pattern of defeat in foreign wars and concessions to foreign demands (political, military, economic, and missionary) was repeated many times. China quite literally lost its sovereignty in the collection of customs, the imposition of tariffs, and the issuance of banknotes— powers that were taken over by foreign agents. It also lost legal and political jurisdiction in the foreign "leased" areas due to treaty provisions requiring extraterritoriality. As Moulder (1977) has shown, in contrast to Japan, Ch'ing

China was forced to grant large concessions in mining, railroads, shipping, and banking to foreign investors, so that autonomous development became quite impossible. The relentless foreign encroachments were accompanied by severe internal instabilities, especially the devastating Taiping Rebellion (1854-1861). The Ch'ing state crumbled under their combined effects.

Japan, of course, was not able to entirely escape foreign encroachments (it too lost tariff autonomy, for example). Nevertheless, as Baran (1957) and Moulder (1977) have shown, it enjoyed a less constrained position than China in the 19th-century world-system. Europeans were initially preoccupied with the bigger "prizes" of India, Indonesia, and China, and paid scant attention to "puny" Japan. Later on, rivalry among the imperialist powers gave Japan some room to maneuver and a "breathing space" (Norman, 1940, p. 46) to put its house in order. During the critical period between the 1850s and the 1880s, the Japanese undertook a program of industrial and military modernization in which the state played a major and direct role (e.g., Lockwood, 1965). By the end of this period, Japan had developed a sufficiently strong military to deter European encroachments by making such efforts relatively costly. And, as Moulder (1977, p. 93) remarks, "fortunately for Japan, Great Britain was looking for such a partner in Asia by the mid-1890s, and Japan, rather than being conquered, as it might have been, was bolstered."

Indeed, by that time, Japan had started to launch its own imperialist expansion. For the patient reader who might be wondering what happened to Taiwan in our discussion, that island was ceded to Japan as a result of China's defeat in the Sino-Japanese war (the Treaty of Shimonoseki, 1895). Thus, Taiwan became a Japanese colony as a direct result of the incapacities of the imperial Chinese state, exhausted and crumbling as it was under the mounting pressure of internal disintegration and external aggression. Traditional China, however, had already left an indelible mark on Taiwan.

Chinese immigrants from the coastal provinces had been settling in Taiwan on a regular basis since at least the 15th century. On the eve of Japanese takeover, the island shared the essential social and political characteristics of the rest of China. It had a small upper literati-gentry class. Classical education and investment in land provided the means of upward mobility. As on the Chinese Mainland, the state apparatus and personnel were both fused with and dominated by the literati-gentry class. The administrative organs of the state were only loosely superimposed on a society composed of relatively self-sufficient village communities. The governor-generals sent by Beijing undertook the usual sort of provisioning policies. Efforts to develop the island's infrastructure and defense capabilities were few and sporadic (Gold, 1986). The Chinese saying, "the sky is high and the emperor far away," describes well the physical, psychological, and political distance between the local state and the people, and between the local state and the court in Beijing. However, in Taiwan as in other parts of China, foreigners—first the Dutch and the Spaniards, then the British, and now the Japanese—had been ever more insistently knocking on the door, producing the familiar pattern of Ch'ing concessions in the form of treaty ports, consular representation, and war reparations.

Japanese Colonialism

Unlike the Europeans, the Japanese were latecomers in the business of colonialism. By the time they arrived on the scene, "the world has been pretty well pillaged already" in the memorable words of King Leopold of Belgium (quoted in Cumings, 1984, p. 8). There was, however, more than just a difference in timing that distinguished Japanese colonialism from European colonialism.

Japan settled for colonies that were populated by its "co-ethnics" and contiguous to its home islands. Like the other colonial powers, it was obviously primarily interested in surplus extraction. However, unlike the typical Western practice of shipping raw materials from the colonies to the metropoles for industrial processing, Tokyo brought some industries to the sources of labor and raw materials (Cumings, 1984). In doing so, Japanese colonialism helped to lay the groundwork for the subsequent industrialization of Taiwan and Korea. It is in this sense that the quotation from Marx introduced at the beginning of this chapter seems apposite.

In order to increase and extract Taiwan's agricultural surplus, Japan introduced *commercial farming*. The island was made to specialize in the export of rice and sugar to the metropole. The *sotokufu* (Japanese colonial government), however, did not try to alter but instead sought to strengthen (see below) the Taiwanese system of *small agricultural owner-cultivators*. This point needs to be stressed, because unlike the American South (cotton) or the Eastern European periphery (grain), the onset of export-oriented commercial farming did not produce a plantation culture or large rural estates—with their attendant social, political, and economic consequences (e.g., Keohane, 1983; B. Moore, 1966; Wallerstein, 1974). The institutions of slavery, serfdom, or indentured peasants did not develop in Taiwan as it did elsewhere. This island did not have a class of rural elite comparable to the American plantation owners, the Prussian *junkers,* or the Argentinean squires of *latifundias*—the very embodiments of social, economic, and political reactionary forces. Additionally, the *decentralized* nature of Taiwan's system of agricultural production facilitated industrial and technological diffusion. The rural associations and sugarcane processing plants set up by the Japanese in different districts had this important effect, even though they were introduced with the primary objective of facilitating surplus extraction and political control. Equally significant, Taiwan was thus able to escape an *enclave* pattern of development—a legacy of colonialism that has characterized much of the Third World.

In its efforts to improve the extraction of agricultural surplus, the *sotokufu* undertook an extensive cadastral survey. As Amsden (1979, p. 345) remarks, "two by-products of this inventory were the uncovering of farms that were not on the tax roll and a record of agricultural holdings that would prove of immense usefulness for the land reform effected by the government of Jiang Jie-shi [Chiang Kai-shek] half a century later." The Japanese had effected a land reform of their own on Taiwan that, in retrospect, also had far-reaching consequences. This reform altered the traditional system of absentee landlords based on an archaic hierarchy of three-tier tenancy. Under this system, *property rights* were unclear, with its attendant complications for tax collection and land transaction. Moreover, the layers of financial burdens placed on the peasant cultivator diminished *production incentives*. The significance of the Japanese reform is elaborated by Amsden (1979, p. 345) in the following passage:

> Under the reform, the tenant landlords became the legal owners of the land, directly responsible for taxes. The clarification of property rights was judged by the Japanese administration as the key prerequisite for investment in land development under non-communal farming. A flat tax on land, rather than a proportional tax on output, was also viewed as an incentive to greater production.

In brief, the Japanese colonialists laid the legal groundwork and introduced the incentive structure for *capitalist production and accumulation,* conditions that were heretofore murky, fragile, or absent on the island.

With the exception of a few prominent Taiwanese families that collaborated with the colonial administration (Gold, 1986), commercial and industrial enterprises were concentrated in Japanese hands. These enterprises were conducted on a "semiofficial" basis as they were jointly organized and operated by the *sotokufu* and the *zaibatsus* (large Japanese commercial and industrial conglomerates). Local Taiwanese participation in business ventures was quite restricted by law. Moreover, the Japanese launched some projects intended to improve the island's industrial capacity and communication infrastructure only belatedly as Tokyo began to be concerned about the threat posed by a prospective war to the island's imports and, at the same time, as the acquisition of Southeast Asian raw materials beckoned the "graduation" of the island into a Japanese "semi-periphery" specializing in the intermediate processing of such materials. Nevertheless, these Japanese efforts did prepare Taiwan better than perhaps any Asian country except Korea for subsequent industrialization. And, as will be seen shortly, the large Japanese monopoly enterprises facilitated in an indirect way the land reform of the early 1950s.

The Japanese colonial state penetrated deep and wide into the Taiwanese society. The traditional relationship between state and society under imperial Chinese rule was thus reversed. The *sotokufu* laid the groundwork for a strong state after the retrocession of Taiwan to Chinese rule. Thus, quite paradoxically, the strength and autonomy of the modern Taiwanese state could be traced to the Chinese incapacities during the 19th century that resulted in the interlude of autocratic Japanese rule. This colonial period stunted the formation and development of native classes on the island, thus leaving the field almost by default to the state. Moreover in Taiwan, as in Korea, the Japanese left behind an ubiquitous administrative and police apparatus. Chiang Kai-shek and Syngman Rhee inherited, quite directly, the structure, personnel, and bureaucratic style of the Japanese colonial state (C. Hamilton, 1983).

Fifty years of Japanese colonialism paved the way for a strong state in Taiwan by eliminating and suppressing class formation, by instituting stringent rules of social and political controls, and by placing the *sotokufu* administration at the "commanding heights" of the political economy. As well, Tokyo had kept other foreign economic interests out during its rule. Thus, significantly, when the island reverted to Chinese control at the end of World War II, "comprising little more than a bureaucracy and army, the KMT [Kuomintang] had no social base on Taiwan with demands to constrain its actions" (Gold, 1986, p. 123). One might add that defeat in the Chinese civil war had severed the KMT's ties with the landlord class, the Shanghai business community, and the foreign financial and industrial interests on the Mainland. In Taiwan, it had no roots and was thus not beholden to any entrenched interest. In short, the circumstances on Taiwan during the late 1940s and early 1950s were singularly unpropitious for the sort of triple alliance of local capital, state capital, and foreign capital discussed by Evans (1979) in the Brazilian case. It was, on the other hand, almost uniquely favorable to the establishment of a strong and autonomous state. The KMT on Taiwan did not need to enter into a "pact of domination" with any domestic group. But before I get ahead of my story, it needs to be stressed again that the transplant of the KMT regime to Taiwan was due to events *exogenous* to the island. External developments—the defeat of Japanese militarism in World War II and of the KMT on the Chinese Mainland by the Chinese Communist Party (CCP)—again played a far more important role in shaping Taiwan's fate than its internal conditions.

American Hegemony

In 1949, the Kuomintang government fled to Taiwan, with the People's Liberation Army at its heels. The Chinese state under the KMT was emphatically neither strong nor autonomous. It had been, on the one hand, harassed and undermined by war with Japan from 1937 on. Under the onslaught of the Japanese invasion army, it was forced to retreat to the Chinese hinterland, with its wartime capital in Chungking. Indeed, in the absence of Pearl Harbor, it would have had a very doubtful fate. On the other hand, the KMT state was deeply penetrated by and closely identified with the interests of the landlord class (it was also beholden to and came to depend heavily on American dole). During its tenure on the Mainland, the KMT was incapable of undertaking the necessary social, economic, and political reforms to pull China out of its domestic morass. In particular, its inability and unwillingness to implement a credible program of land reform—along with the same inability and/or unwillingness to resist Japanese encroachments—were a direct cause for the popularity of the Chinese Communist Party.

Thus, external vulnerability in the form of Japanese invasion and internal weakness in the form of Communist revolution precipitated a chain of events that eventually pushed the KMT to Taiwan. Then, just when it was seemingly destined for the garbage heap of history, the KMT state was again "saved by the bell." As in the case of Japan's attack on Pearl Harbor, the outbreak of the Korean War in 1950 came at a propitious moment. Without Truman's order for the 7th Fleet to "neutralize" the Taiwan Strait, it is quite doubtful that there would be a Taiwanese state today. The latter owed its very existence to the American intervention—that is, to its lack of strength and autonomy in external relations.

It is difficult to overemphasize the tangible and intangible role played by the United States in the post-World War II political economy of Taiwan and, its close regional counterpart, South Korea. Some enduring legacies of the American effort to bolster their conservative states (as well as that of Japan) as a bulwark against the left have been the exclusion of labor in their respective postwar politics, the low levels of their social welfare expenditures, and the exploitation of low wages as a comparative advantage in their export drives. In the name of anticommunism, U.S. support reinforced the bureaucratic authoritarianism of these states.

If Raul Prebisch and the UN Economic Commission of Latin America have had a lasting influence in orienting Latin American countries toward an import-substitution approach to economic development, then the U.S. Agency for International Development played at least a comparable role in encouraging a liberal outward-looking posture in Taiwan and South Korea (e.g., Haggard & Moon, 1983) after the initial stage of "easy" import substitution came to an end by the early 1960s. Indeed, Cumings (1984, p. 27) states flatly that "in both countries the export-led program was decided by the United States."

Massive aid gave Washington this influence over Taiwan's political economy (e.g., Gold, 1986, pp. 68-69). U.S. commodity shipments were crucial in bringing down the rampant inflation in the early years. U.S. military aid replaced lost equipment, boosted morale, and alleviated a crushing defense burden. It made possible the diversion of funds that would otherwise have gone for military purposes to desperately needed civilian projects. And U.S. economic, technical, and commercial assistance was instrumental in first stabilizing the Taiwanese economy and then in helping to launch its take-off. Some of today's largest private enterprises on Taiwan got their start with the help of seed money from AID's program for funding small business. American aid constituted half of Taiwan's gross investment during the mid-1950s, and was still as high as 20% in the mid-1960s on the eve of its termination. Moreover, U.S. aid extended to trade concessions (e.g., differential tariffs, preferential market access, easy terms for credit provision and technology transfer) that amounted to indirect subsidies. According to Jacoby (1966), in the absence of *direct* U.S. aid, Taiwan's annual GNP growth would have been cut by half, its per capita GNP would have been reduced by three-quarters, and 30 more years would have been required to reach its 1964 standard of living.

The *timing* of the American aid was as important as its *magnitude*. It arrived at a time when the KMT state was quite literally on the brink of collapse. Both directly and indirectly, U.S. support stabilized the regime, increased its confidence, and gave it a much needed "breathing space." It cannot be overemphasized that the *intangible* effects of U.S. support were as important as the *tangible* effects. In particular, at several critical junctures (e.g., the decisions to undertake land reform, currency liberalization, export expansion, opening to foreign capital) in the history of Taiwan's political economy, U.S. influence tilted the balance of power within the KMT state.

It was instrumental in promoting the rise of a foreign-educated techno-bureaucratic elite (the term is from Duvall & Freeman, 1981, 1983) over the opposition of the party old guards and military stalwarts. In a sense, the KMT was nudged by outside forces to undertake reform policies almost in spite of its own basic outlook and predispositions.

My discussion so far should not be construed to suggest that somehow American influence was the only or even the primary reason for the way in which the Taiwanese state evolved. Much of this influence was indirect and facilitative rather than direct and deterministic. Conditions internal to the island also combined to put the state at the "commanding heights." As already mentioned, the legacies of Japanese colonialism, Chinese civil war, and American influence led to the suppression of labor as a possible source of opposition to the state. The continuing exclusion of labor is a common feature of the body politics of Taiwan, South Korea, and Japan, and distinguishes them from the social and plural democracies of Western Europe and North America. Unlike Japan with its industrial conglomerates or *zaibatsus* (even in their much weakened postwar form) and South Korea with its equivalent of *chaebols,* Taiwan features a much more *decentralized* industrial structure. In comparison with the former countries, small and medium firms account for a far larger portion of Taiwan's manufacture production and export volume. Therefore, Taiwanese industrialists are in a much weaker position vis-à-vis the state, which is able to shape their behavior through a battery of policy leverages (e.g., import licenses, export quotas, tax credits, loan subsidies, tariffs, currency-exchange controls, and state purchasing programs). Moreover, monopoly state enterprises have loomed large in Taiwan's political economy. Through these enterprises the state has been able to control and allocate to private producers essential industrial inputs such as cement, steel, petroleum, electricity, and capital. Public enterprises captured 26.3% of gross domestic capital formation in 1985, and direct government expenditures accounted for another 20.4% (Council for Economic Planning and Development, 1987, p. 47).

The tradition of public enterprises has, of course, been inherited from the days of Japanese rule. Significantly, the Japanese monopolies had served another important function in the rise of a strong and autonomous Taiwanese state. As mentioned before, the close association with, and the dominance by, rural landed interests prevented the KMT from undertaking any meaningful land reform on the Mainland. This was one basic reason of its defeat in the civil war. On Taiwan, however, the KMT was freed from rural vested interests. Many large Taiwanese landlords had also been tainted by their previous collaboration with the Japanese, thereby making their properties popular targets for expropriation. On top of these considerations, the Americans insisted on land reform as a condition for continued aid. As a result, the KMT undertook a three-stage program of lowering rents and redistributing land. The confiscated Japanese properties provided the means of compensating the landlords, who were paid off partly in the form of bonds and stocks of Japanese industrial monopolies.

Whereas many observers have commented on the positive effects of Taiwan's land reform in enhancing agricultural productivity, it also has had far-reaching political consequences in strengthening the dominance of the state. Intentionally or unintentionally, the land reform removed the native landlord class as a possible source of challenge to the KMT state. By paying off the landlords in industrial bonds and stocks, and by subsequently converting the public enterprises in question into private corporations, the state helped to transform the rural *rentiers* into industrial capitalists. At the same time, the land reform altered the traditional pattern of *capital consumption and accumulation*. As C. Hamilton (1983, p. 50) remarks,

> the essential point is that after the land reforms it was no longer profitable or safe to invest in land, and there began a shift into industry and commerce (which continued into the 1960) the upshot of which was to leave the social and economic position of the landlord class seriously weakened.

Yet another accomplishment of the land reform has been to change peasants into owners of the land that they tilled. Today, over 80% of Taiwan's farmers are owner-cultivators, and another 10% are part owners (Amsden, 1985, p. 85). Through the land reform, the KMT had thus preempted another source of possible challenge to the state. It successfully defused the danger of agrarian discontent and uprising that had been its undoing on the Mainland. It moreover moved effectively to extract the surplus of rural production and to transfer it to the urban and industrial sectors.

While, as shown above, the Taiwanese state and economy have been heavily dependent on the U.S., Washington was more concerned with the intangible rather than the tangible payoffs of its hegemony. Its primary goals were to maintain Taiwan as an anticommunist island bastion, as a showcase for "democracy and free enterprise," and as a political symbol to deflect any domestic right-wing attack on the White House or the State Department for "being soft on communism." Thus, contrary to the "vile interests" and "stupid enforcement" remarked by Marx in England's colonial policies toward India, the U.S. was *self-deterred* from taking actions that might otherwise undermine the Taiwanese state and economy. In fact, American aid and influence provided a protective shield—in the words of one analyst (Gold, 1986), a cocoon—against adverse foreign economic influences.

To be sure, in the 1950s and even in the early 1960s Taiwan was hardly an attractive investment site. Its political and economic uncertainties deterred foreign investors. It certainly lacked the lure of a large domestic market in comparison with, say, Mexico and Brazil. However, by the time foreign investors appeared, both state and local capital had become sufficiently strong to resist industrial denationalization and to drive a more favorable bargain. Indeed, Taiwan has been more successful in dealing with foreign multinationals than Singapore and South Korea, not to mention most other developing countries (e.g., see Huang, 1989). Foreign investors were lured to the so-called Export-Processing Zones. They were induced to agree to various requirements regarding joint ownership, local content, export quota, and technology transfer. Almost all of the foreign investments have been in the manufacturing sector and increasingly in the so-called knowledge-intensive sector. Thus, Taiwan has not had large foreign investments in the agricultural and mineral sectors, a phenomenon that has resulted in distorted growth, social inequity, and reactionary politics in many developing countries.

As alluded earlier, foreign investments arrived *after*—not *before*—Taiwan's economy had started to experience rapid growth, and *after* its bureaucracy had developed sufficiently to manage and regulate multinational corporations. Furthermore, Taiwan has had very high rates of *domestic savings,* which have amounted to between one-fourth to one-third of gross domestic product. In other words, its dependence on foreign capital has been much less than that of many other developing countries. At its peak in the early 1970s foreign direct investment did not exceed 10% of gross domestic capital formation. With the exception of the U.S. aid prior to the mid-1960s, indigenous capital—both state and private—has in the aggregate tended to dominate over foreign capital (although, to be sure, there are specific sectors, such as the electronics industries, where foreign capital looms prominently).

It is also important to note that unlike some other countries such as Mexico, Brazil, and South Korea, Taiwan has not resorted to foreign borrowing as a means of financing its development. As a result, the Taiwanese state has been more autonomous relative to the international lending institutions. Its debt burden as a percentage of its export value has been rather low (about 5% to 10%). Yet another reason for Taiwan's ability to maintain a more autonomous position relative to international capital has been the fact that much of its foreign investment has come from overseas Chinese. As of 1986, the latter source accounted for 1,827 cases out of a total 3,757 approved cases of foreign investment, or about one-fifth of the total value of foreign investment

($1.2 billion out of a total of $5.9 billion, Council for Economic Planning and Development, 1987, p. 268).

In short, then, the Taiwanese state has been strong and autonomous as a result of a confluence of endogenous and exogenous structural factors. Among these factors are massive tangible and intangible subsidies from a foreign sponsor, stunted bourgeois and proletarian class formation due to colonial extraction and repression, the existence of many small- and medium-size firms in a decentralized economic system in which the state commands large public enterprises and important administrative tools, and the diffusion of possible agrarian challenges to the state from both the haves and the have-nots. Finally, the state was able to hold multinational corporations at bay during its more vulnerable years, and was subsequently able to entice and regulate foreign investments on terms that have been more favorable to it than in most other developing countries.

Conclusion

The preceding discussion has been guided by two propositions. First, the contemporary Taiwanese state has been very much a product of history. It did not suddenly materialize overnight. Rather, its structure is deeply embedded in the successive legacies left by imperial China, colonial Japan, and hegemonical America. It would not simply be "ahistorical" to ignore these legacies: it would be to miss the basic forces that have shaped the Taiwanese state.

Second, it would be a serious error to treat the Taiwanese state or, for that matter, any other state as an isolated entity, somehow insulated from outside forces. States are integral parts of a global system, whereby they tend to influence one another. Accordingly, the history of the Taiwanese state cannot be understood through an exclusive concern with endogenous factors. Exogenous events have been critical in the formation and character of this state.

In conclusion, it may be worthwhile to reflect on several paradoxes. Whereas recent Western scholarship has pointed to Taiwan as an example of a strong state, this essay has tried to argue that this supposed strength has been a result of a series of past Chinese weaknesses that resulted in Western encroachments, Japanese colonialism, and a devastating civil war. Put in the context of Olson's (1982) well-known theory, domestic upheavals and foreign occupation have helped to destroy and weaken existing distributional coalitions and to elevate the state's power and autonomy relative to society. This phenomenon seems to apply not only to Taiwan, but also to China, Japan, and the two Koreas (Chan, 1987).

The Taiwanese state holds a weak hand in its external relations. Indeed, it has tried to use real or imagined external vulnerabilities (e.g., foreign protectionism, diplomatic isolation, and communist threat) as a justification for continuing its autonomy relative to society—that is, in attempting to hold rising social pressures at bay (such as pressures to further liberalize the state's control of political activities, press publications, commercial undertakings, and foreign travel).

It is, of course, true that Taiwan is heavily dependent on external trade and raw materials. In particular, much of its commercial relations has been concentrated on the U.S. and Japan (with the American market accounting for almost half of all Taiwanese exports). Indeed, it is only a slight exaggeration to say that Taiwan has pursued a basic economic strategy of "coattail" growth, "hitching" its export-oriented industries to the pocketbooks of American consumers. In other words, it has actively sought to *incorporate and integrate* itself into the capitalist world-system—economically, politically, militarily, and ideologically. Other dependent countries may be concerned with the danger that such incorporation and integration would undermine national autonomy. In contrast, Taiwan fears and worries about the possibility of being "shut out," "cast adrift," and "abandoned" by its chief export market, political sponsor, and military protector—the United States.

This observation in turn brings us to yet another paradox. Waning U.S. zeal for the Cold War, *rapprochement* with Beijing, and increasing global protectionism threaten to disrupt the external props for a strong and autonomous Taiwanese state. It is quite beyond the latter's ability to perpetuate those conducive conditions that during the 1950s and 1960s had helped its commercial ascent and political survival—namely, the containment doctrine, the China lobby, General MacArthur and Senator (Joe) McCarthy, hot wars in Korea and Vietnam, a booming world economy, and a general trend of trade liberalization. The perception of Taiwan in Washington has changed from that of a junior partner and dependent client in the global struggle against communism to one of a formidable commercial competitor that is taking away American money and jobs. The pressure on Taiwan to "graduate" mounts. The island's manufacturers are increasingly "squeezed by the international product cycles between 'high-tech' Japan and the United States from above and industrializing states with lower-cost labor (including the PRC [i.e., China]) from below" (C. Clark, 1987, p. 342). To put it mildly, Taiwan's incorporation into the capitalist world-system presents a *double-edged sword*.

In a very real sense, the Taiwanese state is becoming a victim of its own successes—not only in the international area, but in the domestic arena as well. From its beginnings as a garrison state presiding over a relatively backward agrarian society, it has increasingly transformed itself into a technocratic bureaucracy. The professed goal of the KMT state of the 1950s—with its domineering military and police components—to "retake" the Mainland appears today more illusory than ever. Instead, the state is being impelled by the forces of history and by its own past successes to justify its performance on the basis of further economic growth, political liberalization, and the realization of *la dolce vita* for the masses. There has been a series of political and economic reforms in recent years. They include the lifting of martial law, the legalization of opposition parties, the liberalization of regulations regarding currency exchange and press control, and the relaxation of the ban against travel to China. The state is no longer in a position of "commanding heights" relative to society; its autonomy and strength have declined. The state is being transformed by society.

8

Change and Continuity in the British Colonial State in Africa

Integrating Theoretical Perspectives

JAMES R. SCARRITT
SHAHEEN MOZAFFAR

In this chapter, we outline a theoretical framework we believe is especially useful for analyzing the historically distinct type of state-society relations fostered by the British colonial state in Africa. This framework integrates key concepts and hypotheses from each of the major theoretical perspectives reviewed in the first chapter of this book. We then apply this framework to the British colonial states and societies in Nigeria and Northern Rhodesia as they evolved through three analytically distinct but temporally continuous phases of colonial rule: construction, institutionalization, and decolonization (Young, 1988, pp. 41-56). We show how and why the pattern of pragmatic policy responses to conflicting historical pressures emanating from both Europe and Africa in each phase foreclosed options and shaped developments in the next. We contend that the overall outcome of this process in both colonies was the ad hoc development of the colonial state and state-society relations resulting in the sacrifice of long-term accumulation for short-run legitimacy, control, and state revenue. This outcome would be difficult to conceptualize, much less predict, without an inclusive theoretical framework. Since Nigeria and Northern Rhodesia exemplify the two major types of British colonial state in Africa—non-settler and settler respectively—they provide a convenient "different systems" design which allows cautious, limited generalization of our findings to all British African colonies.

149

British colonial states were imposed on Africa to advance the interests of European capital, and they continued to do so throughout their existence. But, on the ground, colonial officials were also confronted with the need to maintain both legitimacy and, more importantly, control at minimum cost, as well as to secure sufficient state revenues to cover this cost. Malintegration in colonial societies, itself largely a product of colonial rule, combined with the structural and procedural incoherence within the colonial state to render the simultaneous realization of these conflicting goals extremely problematic. When forced to choose, as they often were, colonial officials usually sacrificed the interests of capital to attain the administrative goals of the state. Each time such a policy choice was made, it established the institutional parameters for subsequent decisions that served to further vitiate the integration of colonial society and the colonial state.

An Inclusive Theoretical Framework

Understanding the nature of the tension among accumulation, legitimacy and control, and the contribution of incoherence within the state to the creation and management of this tension, necessitates integrating these phenomena within an inclusive framework.[1] This framework locates societies (the major concrete unit of analysis) within an international system comprised of a capitalist world-economy and a system of sovereign states. The international system establishes parameters within which the internal components of societies—state, economy, culture, and stratification—interact, but it does not determine the nature of this interaction, which can take a variety of forms. Pressures from the system of sovereign states are at least partially in conflict with those emanating from the world economy.

Following Benjamin and Duvall (1985, pp. 23-28, 36-41), we define a state as both the institutional-legal order and the organizing structure of government agencies which animates that order. The institutional-legal order establishes the broad parameters of sociopolitical relations by defining basic property rights or rules in society, drawing boundaries between public and private realms, and resolving tensions among freedom, equality, order, and justice. Organizational structure consists of the network of public agencies and the rules of the game which link these agencies into a coherent whole. Attention is directed here not simply to the structural position occupied by individual agencies in the governmental apparatus but, more importantly, to their patterned relationships which emerge out of the ways in which each agency performs its assigned task. Organizational structure is animated by the social composition of the personnel staffing public agencies; the degree to which these agencies penetrate society; and the extent to which they are facilitated or constrained by the institutional order and, in turn, enhance or diminish its coherence.

These processes emphasize the management of tension between two contradictory internal structural imperatives of the state: organizational certainty and operational flexibility. Three institutional strategies exist for managing these contradictory imperatives: centralization, involving concentration of both the formulation of broad policy directives and the implementation of specific policy programs at the top level of the state apparatus; decentralization, involving delegation of both these powers to the bottom; and deconcentration, involving retention of discretion over policy formulation at the top and delegation of responsibility for policy implementation to the bottom (Graham, 1980). We will show that British colonial officials faced severe difficulties in imposing the European-inspired institutional-legal order and organizational structure of the colonial state on African societies. They attempted to resolve these difficulties by incorporating indigenous principles of rule and authority into the colonial institutional-legal order, and by constructing an organizational structure that simultaneously reflected an ideology of decentralization and embodied primarily centralized procedures mixed with significant elements of deconcentration.

The relationship between the state and other components of society involves three interconnected but contradictory processes—accumulation, control, and legitimacy—which constitute the external functional imperatives of the state (compare with Young, 1988, pp. 31-32). The management of the tensions inherent in these contradictory imperatives animates state-society relations through a dynamic exchange of policies affecting the economy and culture and meeting the demands of some classes and groups but denying the demands of others, for revenue (material resources), compliance, and legitimacy provided to the state.

The economy, embodying the social organization of available factors of production and their utilization in terms of a particular type and level of technology, is the primary source of accumulation for the state. Accumulation is necessary because the state needs revenues to finance its activities (Bates, 1981, pp. 12-19; North, 1979; O'Connor, 1973). State policies, therefore, aim to create and maintain the systemic conditions which facilitate continuous accumulation. Yet accumulation generates conflicts over the distribution of payments and benefits which threaten the stable flow of state revenues unless adequate attention is paid to the imperatives of control and legitimacy.

While states traditionally possess a comparative advantage in the exercise of coercive control (North, 1979), sustained use of coercion is both costly and counterproductive. Control is most productively exercised, therefore, when it is legitimized by the prevailing values and norms of the society. A society's stratification system distributes wealth, power, and influence—the circulating media of politics—usually, though not inevitably, in an asymmetrical manner. The pattern of cultural symbols, norms, and values cumulates into a more or less coherent ideology which prescribes the normative parameters of social relations and legitimizes (or provides alternatives to) the existing stratification system (Mullins, 1972, p. 510).

The stratification system and economic structure combine to differentiate categories of people vertically with regard to shared positions in media distribution (e.g., classes). Alternatively, the stratification system and cultural patterns combine to differentiate categories of people horizontally with regard to shared identities (e.g., ethnicity). Class and ethnicity, however, are dynamic categories whose individual and combined political salience vary in relationship to fluctuations in state policies and state power.

State legitimacy is thus most fully acquired when control is both grounded in a *quid pro quo* exchange of state policies providing services (welfare, protection, and justice) for revenue and compliance provided by fluctuating combinations of classes and ethnic groups, and rationalized in terms of the underlying cultural norms, values, and symbols. Obtaining legitimacy and compliance from those classes and ethnic groups that provide the largest amounts of accumulation (and often state revenue) and from which the largest numbers of state personnel are drawn is especially important for the state.

Change in the structure and policies of the state is empirically specified by the historically varied interaction among agents within the state, economic, stratification, and cultural structures, and the international environment. Conflicts and contradictions within society are never fully resolved; rather, the change that actually occurs is likely to be the minimum necessary to maintain workable compatibility among its components and agents within them. For example, the British colonial state sought to impose its alien organizing structure and much of its alien institutional-legal order on African societies by combining the legitimacy of their traditional political leaders with authoritarian and essentially European forms of accumulation and control through limited deconcentration. Because it failed to achieve workable compatibility among these elements, it continued to change until it was replaced by another type of state.

To explain the particular patterns of change in Nigeria and Northern Rhodesia, we will explore four interrelated issues: (a) the ways in which colonial officials relied on, modified, and were constrained by the social structure of indigenous societies, resident Europeans, and multinational firms in managing the state's external functional imperatives of accumulation, control, and legitimacy; (b) the ways in which such reliance and organization were linked to officials' management of the state's internal structural imperatives of organizational certainty and operational flexibility; (c) the ways in which the management of both sets of imperatives impacted on indigenous and European culture, stratification, economy, and polity; and (d) the ways in which the management of both sets of imperatives impacted the overall coherence of the colonial state.

Constructing the Colonial State

The construction of the British colonial state in Africa was a singularly incremental process, shaped by the forces described above and the attendant policy responses of British officials to these forces. Political and economic changes in the international system in the late 19th century provided the initial impetus for the British colonization of Nigeria and Northern Rhodesia. But the impact of these changes on the construction and the emergent form and dynamics of the colonial state was mediated by three interrelated factors: (a) the financial cost of colonial administration and the resulting political pact between metropolitan supporters and opponents of African occupation; (b) the varied configurations of indigenous and resident European sociopolitical structures and their correspondingly varied responses to the imposition of alien rule; and (c) the administrative style of British policymakers and their concomitantly pragmatic response to the dilemma of coping with the contradictory internal and external state imperatives that they faced.

Beginning about the 1870s, changes in the European state system associated with the rise of France and Germany as major industrial and imperial powers, and changes in the international economy associated with the onset of a global recession and sharp drop in commodity prices, threatened Britain's "informal empire." This empire had been sustained, since the beginning of the century, by a free-trade regime backed by British naval supremacy. As the European economic and diplomatic rivalry intensified in Africa, the Berlin Conference (1884-1885) met to defuse the escalating conflict by establishing a *modus vivendi* for the European partition of Africa, the key to which was the swift accomplishment of "effective occupation" as a condition for legitimizing control of African territories (Gallagher & Robinson, 1953; Gann, 1964; Hargreaves, 1963, 1974, 1985; Robinson &

Gallagher, 1961; Wills, 1973). Effective occupation, however, dictated a greater commitment of financial resources than the British government, especially the Treasury supported by parliamentary opposition to African occupation, was willing to invest (Burton, 1966). The British government's pragmatic strategy for extending and consolidating imperial control was to rely on the limited economic and administrative instruments of "informal empire" that were already in place in Africa.

In both colonies, the early construction of a self-financing colonial administration was delegated to chartered companies. By 1890, George Goldie's Royal Niger Company (RNC) in Nigeria and Cecil Rhodes's British South Africa Company (BSAC) in Northern Rhodesia had successfully eliminated all competitors and had established monopolies over key economic activities in their respective areas. Their royal charters now authorized them to establish administrative infrastructures, make treaties with African chiefs, and levy tariffs on and raise taxes from local sources (Flint, 1960, 1974). Direct British government involvement in Northern Rhodesia remained limited to the swift acquisition of the eastern region by the British Central Africa Protectorate (under the Colonial Office) and its equally swift transfer to the BSAC for administration (Gann, 1964). In Nigeria it was confined to the opening of the profitable hinterland trade routes to ensure stable state revenues in the southeast by a Foreign Office consul and in the southwest by the governor of Lagos colony under Colonial Office jurisdiction (Anene, 1966; Dike, 1956).

The chartered companies and limited direct involvement of the British government accomplished the effective occupation mandated by the Berlin Conference, and rationalized colonial rule as the cost-effective enterprise required by the political pact between metropolitan supporters and opponents of African occupation. However, the restricted functional scope of these administrative instruments, reinforced by the reluctance of the British government to incur the financial burdens of more elaborate administration, engendered conflicting pressures and patterns of development which served to undermine the systematic construction of a coherent state. Company rule, because it necessarily stressed accumulation over control and legitimacy, antagonized indigenous groups and, more seriously, undermined their established patterns of social relations. The imposition of mandatory taxation, for instance, forced African males into wage labor at extremely low wages; but since taxation was insufficient to meet the growing demand for labor, it was supplemented by conscription (Macpherson, 1981, pp. 105-190). The responsibility for tax collection and labor conscription fell on local chiefs and village headmen, who, because they were usually supported with armed force by colonial officials, were now viewed by their own people as agents of colonial rule, and thus lost their traditional legitimacy. In Northern Rhodesia, moreover, the BSAC's land titles, granted under the royal charter, as well as the growing demand for labor by the multinational copper mining companies, clashed with the European settlers' demands for land and labor for agriculture and cattle raising. Further yet, expansion of the settler population increased demands for roads, medical facilities, and education, demands which the BSAC, caught between its financial obligations to its shareholders and its chartered administrative responsibilities to the imperial government, was unable to meet. A state that was capitalist in the literal sense of being administered by a capitalist firm was unwilling or unable to foster the interests of other capitalists. And in Nigeria, the simultaneous development of company rule, consular rule, and colony rule not only created jurisdictional conflicts between the RNC, the Foreign Office, and the Colonial Office, but also produced inconsistent administrative structures and procedures and contradictory policies.

These various contradictions of the company-colonial state, coupled with the financial losses suffered by the chartered companies, provided the major incentive for the consolidation of the disparate administrations in both Nigeria and Northern Rhodesia under the Colonial Office. Even so, the subsequent elaboration of the colonial state's institutional-legal order and accompanying governmental structure was strongly influenced by the practices of company rule. British officials, lacking sufficient funds and personnel, responded pragmatically to the dilemma of organizing the diverse indigenous polities within a coherent institutional-legal order and a systematic governmental structure in order to maintain control at minimum cost and promote accumulation to generate state revenues and satisfy the demands of capital. Thus British law was introduced to ensure minimum standards of British justice and facilitate European capital accumulation. At the same time, however, traditional African law (officially designated as customary law) was deliberately retained for defining African property rights and adjudicating inter-African disputes. Because of this legal dualism and the fact that indigenous polities varied markedly in the nature and scope of customary law, ranging from the codified prescriptions of Islamic jurisprudence in the Hausa-Fulani emirates of northern Nigeria to the highly diffuse procedures of acephalous communities found in both colonies, the colonial state's institutional-legal order embodied conflicting definitions of legitimate authority and rules of conflict management.

If the emergent institutional-legal order embodied ambiguous and conflicting principles, the evolving governmental structure through which those principles were to be operationalized was equally bifurcated. The colonial bureaucracy consisted of a British superstructure supported by a system of local native administrations. The superstructure, staffed entirely by British personnel, consisted of the governor and lieutenant-governor, the central secretariat staff, and field officers or the Provincial Administration, the police, and the army. A Legislative Council (Legco) afforded highly circumscribed representation to Europeans and to very select Africans. In Northern Rhodesia, because of its settler population, Europeans exercised greater influence in the Legco. In Nigeria, the Legco's jurisdiction extended only to the Colony and the Southern Protectorate; the Northern Protectorate had only advisory representation through British officials posted in that region.

This governmental edifice was supported at the base in both colonies by a system of indirect rule organized around numerous local administrative units called Native Authorities. To facilitate tax assessment and collection (the accumulation imperative), and mediate the coercive superiority of the alien superstructure (the control and legitimacy imperatives), the Native Authorities were staffed by African personnel, possessed their own treasuries, and exercised delegated administrative and judicial powers under the supervision of British field officers. Indirect rule was an attempt to replace the limited deconcentration found in the use made of African chiefs under company rule with elements of decentralization, without sacrificing organizational certainty. This partial decentralization was undermined by the almost universal unwillingness of colonial officials to allow the Native Authorities to formulate policy outside prescribed narrow boundaries.

This system worked best where precolonial polities were centralized with well-established administrative and judicial structures and a tax system, as in the Hausa-Fulani emirates of northern Nigeria and the Lozi kingdom in southwestern Northern Rhodesia. Attempts to introduce indirect rule elsewhere, however, proved to be more problematic, as these areas lacked the requisite hierarchical structures and a tradition of mandatory taxation. In these mostly acephalous areas, the British embarked on a ceaseless quest for nonexistent chiefs, installing individuals with powers that violated traditional precepts of legitimate authority, or resurrecting local chiefs and hereditary rulers whose powers were already declining in the face of socioeconomic change. These various transmutations of indirect rule, while pragmatically dictated by the need to balance the contradictory imperatives of accumulation, control, and legitimacy, only served to reinforce both the disjunctions between the colonial state's institutional-legal order and its governmental structure and the accompanying disparities between the state and indigenous social structures.

While the pattern of structural and procedural bifurcation in the colonial state was similar in both Nigeria and Northern Rhodesia, the accompanying social structural disparities reflected the particularities of each territory. In Nigeria, political disparities overlapped with ethno-regional and economic differences among indigenous polities. In Northern Rhodesia, where socio-economic change was concentrated in towns to which people from most ethnic groups migrated, the most important of these disparities paralleled the racial-class cleavage between European settlers and indigenous Africans. In both territories, the contradictory imperatives of accumulation, control, and legitimacy defined the context in which conflicting global and local pressures combined with British administrative ethos and practice to shape the ad hoc construction of the colonial state.

Institutionalizing the Colonial State

The institutionalization of the colonial state, aimed at reducing the various diversities noted above, entailed a combined attempt to: (a) ground colonial domination in a more systematic and (in the context of its time) "progressive" ideology in order to assuage metropolitan sensibilities, (b) systematize the institutional-legal principles of the state, and (c) rationalize, deepen, and professionalize the governmental structure in order to produce coherent policies for operationalizing those principles within the constraints of state revenue. State institutionalization also distracted attention from the task of supporting private capital accumulation. Articulating a systematic ideology involved specifying the purpose of colonial rule. Christianity, commerce, and civilization, the ideological trinity which had initially justified the European colonization of Africa, even while changing indigenous societies in signifi-cant ways, had also induced social instability, provoking ironically similar responses from two otherwise opposed quarters. British social critics strongly condemned the notion, advanced by missionaries, that Africans had no history and possessed nothing in local culture worth preserving. They advo-cated instead that African peoples must be allowed to develop at a pace and along lines defined by their respective traditions, but under European tute-lage. For colonial administrators, social dislocations engendered by socio-economic change posed problems of control and stability. Their response characteristically emphasized the management of change along lines consis-tent with their own bureaucratic orientation. For both social critics and colonial officials, colonial rule implied a trust which Europeans exercised by providing good government for Africans to develop according to indigenous tradition and history. Trusteeship, good government, and development thus emerged as the new legitimating ideology underpinning the legal order and structure of the colonial state.

Formulating and implementing policies consistent with the new ideology required unifying and rationalizing the disparate bureaucratic machinery that had evolved during the ad hoc construction of the colonial state. The process of state institutionalization in Nigeria and Northern Rhodesia was affected by the specific configuration of social, economic, and political factors in each colony, but the general trajectory was similar in that it was shaped by past patterns of development.

In Northern Rhodesia, the presence of European settlers engendered political conflict between them and colonial officials. Hampered by inadequate infrastructural support for their economic activities, and burdened by taxes imposed on them for the first time during the last days of company rule, European settlers moved quickly after the end of that rule to demand extension and improvement in their share of land, wages, prices, social services, and taxation vis-à-vis the Africans. In particular, they pushed for amalgamation with Southern Rhodesia, which would have given the enlarged European population in the combined territory almost unlimited power over the African population. Colonial officials, however, reflecting the new ideological orientation of trusteeship, and characteristically more concerned with legitimacy and control than with settler capitalist accumulation, favored the paramountcy of African interests. The resulting compromise emphasized the simultaneous development of both European and African interests, thereby ensuring the continued bifurcation, instead of the integration, of the state apparatus. At the center, amalgamation did not take place, but Europeans secured expanded representation in the Legco, being outnumbered only slightly by colonial officials and Africans taken together until 1962 (Helgerson, 1971, pp. 15-37; Mulford, 1964, pp. 1-18). The devolution of powers to Legco enhanced European influence over policy, enabling them to obtain the substantial advantages that they demanded with regard to accumulation.

At the local level, colonial officials, in keeping with the notion of guided development of Africans embodied in the ideology of trusteeship, proceeded to organize and strengthen the administrative machinery and personnel they inherited from the BSAC into a system of indirect rule as described above (Gann, 1964, pp. 226-250, 261-284). This system involved territorial fragmentation because it was applied only to Africans, and usually only in African and not in European areas of the country, and because it encompassed the partially successful attempt to keep the Lozi kingdom with its province-wide

Barotse Native Government administratively separate from the rest of the colony.

While Nigeria lacked a European settler presence, the growing diversity between the conservative north and the more modernized south (comprising the Colony and the Southern Protectorate), which had emerged during the construction phase, continued to shape the institutionalization of the colonial state. Thus, when Legco membership was expanded to include four Nigerians elected on a limited franchise, its jurisdiction remained restricted, as before, to the Colony and the Southern Protectorate. The Northern Protectorate continued to be represented in the Legco by British officials from that region. No northern Nigerian attended its proceedings until 1948 when an all-Nigerian Council was created as part of the decolonization arrangements. Furthermore, colonial policies regarding land, education, and taxation continued to diverge markedly for the two regions, which only intensified their political, economic, class, and cultural differences (J. S. Coleman, 1960).

Concurrent with these developments institutional conflict emerged within the colonial state. This conflict was associated with the attempt to reform the indirect rule system and streamline the state's administrative structure in a manner providing for effective decentralization. In the construction phase, as we have seen, the centralized Muslim emirates of northern Nigeria had provided colonial officials, confronted with insufficient funds and personnel, a convenient and cost-effective way to balance the contradictory imperatives of accumulation, control, and legitimacy. Administrative pragmatism, however, was transmuted into theoretical rationalization, whereby indirect rule was elevated, primarily by northern British officials led by Frederick Lugard, into a systematic theory of colonial administration (Heussler, 1968; Nicholson, 1969). This theory viewed indirect rule as implying separate and mutually exclusive regional and local administrations (Native Authorities), only loosely linked to a nominal center. Central officials, however, given their organizational position in the state apparatus, held that indirect rule implied only deconcentration—(i.e., delegation of powers to and supervision of local units by the center through a set of overarching and rationalized bureaucratic procedures). When the indirect rule ideology was imported wholesale into Northern Rhodesia in 1930, and was subsequently expanded into the urban areas in the form of Urban Native Courts and Tribal Elders, the same conflicts between central (Secretariat) and local (Provincial Administration) officials arose there as well.

This organizational conflict within the colonial administrative apparatus, combined with changes in the state's domestic and global environments, shaped the pattern of state institutionalization in both Nigeria and Northern Rhodesia. Generally, the attempted reforms introduced some semblance of rationality in the erstwhile chaotic system of indirect rule and made Native Authorities relatively effective instruments for maintaining control and generating tax revenues. Native Authorities—whether single chief or chief-in-council—were now based on some degree of popular consent. They also acquired delegated executive, judicial, and financial powers with discretion, limited by the "advice and supervision" of British field officers, to implement central policy directives according to local conditions. Finally, their streamlined financial responsibilities enabled them to improve tax assessment and collection, and to retain a stipulated percentage of the proceeds to pay for local staff salaries and development projects.

Yet, the very logic which impelled the reorganization of the indirect rule system militated against the systematic integration of the Native Authorities into the colonial bureaucracy or the delegation of more power to them, and hence against the institutional coherence of the colonial state in accordance with an officially articulated decentralized model. First, the logic of reorganization viewed Native Authorities as institutional mechanisms for managing socioeconomic change, but this view ignored the very real possibility that Native Authorities could just as well become the agents, rather than the managers, of change. Thus Native Authorities became the crucibles in which hundreds of Africans served as clerks, interpreters, and messengers, acquiring important political and administrative skills which they employed successfully in support of the anticolonial nationalist struggle. Second, and conversely, Native Authorities could also become not managers or agents of change, but obstacles to change. Since British officials, concerned with obtaining legitimacy and control inexpensively, emphasized traditional criteria of legitimacy for heading Native Authorities, albeit modified to meet colonial administrative needs, traditional rulers viewed and used Native Authorities for preserving their own power and influence.

A natural corollary of this contradiction was the growing opposition of the indigenous Western-educated class to the Native Authorities, which manifested itself in several ways. Initially, members of this class vocally attacked Native Authorities as obstacles to change, that is, to the advancement of their own political and economic interests. Subsequently, especially in the more modernized areas of Nigeria, some of them used their ethnic and lineage connections to get elected to the Native Authorities, from where they launched a vigorous attack on the power of the traditional rulers. The inclusion of the Western-educated class in the Native Authorities was initially encouraged by colonial officials as a way to neutralize their opposition, but the intensity of their criticisms forced these officials to uphold the authority of traditional rulers, which only bolstered the position of the educated class. Thus, even as they were being institutionalized, the Native Authorities were becoming crucial instruments of class formation and arenas of class conflict.

These various contradictory logics underpinning the indirect rule system were never adequately resolved for several reasons. First, the fundamental differences between the decentralist and centralist views of colonial administration and the place of Native Authorities in it were never bridged. The attempted reforms had produced only minimal organizational coherence which linked central policy directives to localized implementation by Native Authorities under the supervision of British field officers. What emerged was a dual administrative edifice in which Native Authorities remained tenuous adjuncts without being totally integrated into the colonial bureaucracy. The structure of the colonial bureaucracy itself also remained bifurcated. The specialized departments provided technical and professional services to the entire country, but the majority of their personnel worked in departmental headquarters. The Provincial Administration dealt primarily with Africans, and the vast majority of its personnel worked in the provinces. These forms of structural ambiguity would subsequently shape political and institutional arrangements in the decolonization phase.

The second reason why the contradictory logics were never resolved was that there was insufficient time for long-term institutionalization to take effect, that is, for repetitious interaction to cohere into routinized procedures (Krasner, 1988). The reorganization of the indirect rule system entailed the reconstruction of old structures along new procedures. And time was a crucial variable restricting the routinization of these new procedures. For example, the reform of the Native Authorities coincided with the onset of the depression and attendant retrenchment of human and financial resources in the colonies. This was immediately followed by the outbreak of the Second World War, which engendered more intensified extraction of resources—especially production of cash crops in Nigeria and taxes in both colonies—for which the Native Authorities, being "close to the people" according to official parlance, were mainly responsible. Intensified accumulation, however, also engendered local opposition in both colonies and political instability in Nigeria, closely linked to and stimulated by the growing nationalist movement. In the short-run, the full impact of the nationalist movement was neutralized, as nationalist leaders either were imprisoned, their agitation curbed by emergency decrees, or withdrew their demands pending the end of the war. In the long-run, however, the war set in motion new political pressures which neither the Native Authorities, because they were unsuited for the task, nor the colonial state, because the global and domestic social and political conditions sustaining it had fundamentally changed, could manage.

Decolonizing the Colonial State

Changes in the post-World War II international system induced a major reconsideration of British imperial policy, providing the impetus for decolonization. But the actual process of decolonization on the ground was shaped by the interaction of the larger global forces with social, economic, and political changes in Nigeria and Northern Rhodesia, and the nature and dynamics of the colonial state. The postwar reconsideration of imperial policy was induced by British military and economic decline which rendered seaborne empires expensive and irrelevant; by the obsolescence of the "colonial idea" which was attacked by both superpowers; and by the growing nationalist movements which, fueled by the quickened pace of self-government in Ceylon and India, were fast becoming a potentially unmanageable force in the colonies (Lee & Petter, 1982).

In both Nigeria and Northern Rhodesia, the war and postwar world reconstruction expanded economic and political opportunities for Africans. The exigencies of war and reconstruction increased commodity exports, and also introduced secondary and tertiary industries. As a result, the economy became more differentiated and the domestic consumer market expanded as the number of Africans in paid employment increased and their wages improved. Economic and class differentiation emerged not only between urban and rural dwellers, but also among urban dwellers. Colonial officials, under the influence of a sympathetic Labor government in London and continuing their attempt to balance the state's external imperatives of accumulation, control, and legitimacy, encouraged African workers to organize labor unions. Educated Africans were given circumscribed representation in the Legislative and, for the first time, in the Executive Councils. In Northern Rhodesia, where settler domination precluded more meaningful African representation in the central government, Native Authority officials and members of the educated class, drawn mostly from the urban areas, were organized into advisory Provincial Councils and a territory-wide African Representative Council. Class and racial differences overlapped. In Nigeria, reflecting past patterns of development, class and ethno-regional cleavages overlapped, as the Ibos and the Yorubas in the south advanced more rapidly than the conservative Hausa-Fulanis in the north in education, business, and the professions. This combination of class formation and racial-ethnic cleavages intensified the conflicting pressures for and against political change from educated Africans, Native Authorities, and European settler and multinational capital.

Colonial policies typically embodied pragmatic attempts to balance these contradictory pressures. In Northern Rhodesia, the white settlers were successful in persuading the British government to establish a federation with Southern Rhodesia (and, at British insistence, Nyasaland), and pushed for self-governing status for it to forestall growing African economic and political power and to free themselves from the control of what they considered to be an unsympathetic Colonial Office. Colonial officials, under increasing pressure from the international community and from both the imperial government and metropolitan public opinion to prevent the transfer of power to a privileged racial minority, continued to favor the existing federal scheme. According to them, it brought the economic advantages of a large political unit and simultaneously protected African interests. Inevitably, however, the Federation, by bifurcating political and administrative powers between the Federal government dominated by the Europeans and the constituent territorial governments responsible for African affairs, failed to reconcile these conflicting objectives. European settlers, assisted by the self-governing status of Southern Rhodesia within the Federation, consolidated and enhanced their political power; their control of the overfunded federal bureaucracy enabled them to channel scarce resources away from the territorial administrations, which only aggravated the existing socioeconomic differences between settlers and Africans and radicalized African nationalist sentiments (Dresang, 1975).

In Nigeria, ethno-regional conflicts rooted in the North's socioeconomic disadvantage and larger population and the South's more rapid economic and educational development and smaller population combined with the concern of British officials with maintaining an economically viable political unit to shape decolonization institutional arrangements. Thus, the federal system which was negotiated allocated central representation on the basis of population, mollifying Hausa-Fulani apprehension at being dominated by the southerners. At the same time, however, the state's organizational procedures centralized financial and taxing authority but decentralized administrative powers, making the two southern regions, which produced most of the country's economic wealth, dependent on the northern-dominated central government for development funds (Rothchild, 1970, pp. 520-522).

In both Nigeria and Northern Rhodesia, then, the pragmatic attempt of colonial officials to manage the state's contradictory internal and external imperatives produced a common federal solution. But the specific sociopolitical configuration of each colony engendered different pressures, leading to separate outcomes for the two federations. In Nigeria, the prevalence of ethno-regional disparities, reflected in the formation and persistence of three African nationalist movements, served to legitimize, albeit precariously, the federal scheme which was carefully negotiated to balance power among the movements, but also to make its operation highly conflictual. In Northern Rhodesia, the conflict between white settlers and African nationalists, with its attendant racial antagonism, overshadowed the purely tactical differences between the two nationalist movements and led to the Federation's dissolution. In both colonies, however, nationalist pressures succeeded in obtaining independence.

Summary and Conclusion

In this chapter, we have employed an inclusive framework, which integrates concepts from all the major theoretical perspectives reviewed in the first chapter, to examine the pattern of change in the British colonial states of Nigeria and Northern Rhodesia. We focused on three analytically distinct but temporally continuous phases of state change to show how the combination of (1) a changing global environment, (2) the need to establish a coherent institutional-legal order and organizational apparatus and (3) the need to simultaneously balance the contradictory imperatives of accumulation, control, and legitimacy engendered conflicting pressures which structured the form, dynamics, and policies of the colonial state. While these pressures manifested themselves in different ways in each colony, the pattern of state change in both was similar, with institutional developments and attendant socioeconomic changes in one phase effectively foreclosing policy options and shaping the development of the colonial state in the next.

In the construction phase, British officials attempted to establish a cost-effective administration and simultaneously achieve a working balance among accumulation, control, and legitimacy by initially employing chartered companies and then relying on indigenous African rulers. Chartered companies, however, not only failed to balance their contradictory obligations to their shareholders and to the imperial government, they also undermined imperial control by emphasizing accumulation over legitimacy. But when the imperial government took over the colonial administration and sought to promote accumulation and control through indigenous African rulers, it vested them with new powers which violated traditional precepts of authority and thereby threatened the legitimacy of the colonial state. It also provoked the hostility of white settlers in Northern Rhodesia, while the uneven impact of modernization associated with colonial policies produced ethno-regional differences in Nigeria. The combination of company rule and imperial administration coupled with the system of indirect rule, moreover, fostered incoherent state structures and procedures.

These earlier uneven developments in the colonial state and in its relationship with indigenous social structures served to vitiate the subsequent attempts to institutionalize more coherent state structures and procedures and more systematic state-society relations. Native Administrations, the instruments of indirect rule, remained tenuous adjuncts that were not totally integrated into the colonial bureaucracy; racial and class differences overlapped in Northern Rhodesia; and class and ethno-regional cleavages reinforced each other in Nigeria. Rapid decolonization occurred in both colonies, then, because it restored minimum working compatibility among the various contradictory imperatives, especially after the educated political-administrative class of Africans, despite its internal differences (sharp as these were in Nigeria), was able to undermine the legitimacy of the colonial state and its indirect rule appendages and make continued colonial control too expensive in terms of the available state revenues.

More generally, the incremental development of the colonial state described above cumulated into a "fatal dualism" (J. S. Coleman, 1960) which became vested in the successor postcolonial states. First, the independence bargain struck between the departing British officials and the African nationalist leaders retained the authoritarian structures and bureaucratic procedures of the colonial state, embodied in the principles of administrative-legislative dyarchy and executive supremacy. Simultaneously, the bargain grafted onto these structures and procedures a fully legal-rational order rooted in the entrepreneurial procedures of democratic politics. Thus, the institutional-legal order and organizing administrative apparatus of the successor postcolonial states were profoundly at odds with each other, while contradictions within the latter remained.

Second, colonial rule fostered the emergence of a nascent indigenous dominant class whose structural roots were embedded not in the socioeconomic foundations of African societies, but in the relations of power centered around the bureaucratic procedures of the colonial state and the mobilizing procedures of the nationalist movements. The political dominance of European settlers prevented Africans from accumulating significant amounts of capital in Northern Rhodesia. And in Nigeria, the European merchant houses' monopoly over the agricultural marketing boards similarly prevented the emergent dominant class in the south, itself the beneficiary of the colonial state's mercantilist policies, from advancing its economic interests. In Nigeria also, the general socioeconomic underdevelopment of the north limited emerging class differentiation along capitalist economic lines in that region. Economic, racial, and ethnic cleavages fostered by the colonial state thus combined to animate and structure the nationalist movements in both colonies. Led by Africans from the emerging dominant classes, these movements served to strengthen the power of these groups vis-à-vis the indigenous popular classes and to legitimize their political position vis-à-vis the colonial rulers.

In both colonies, then, the dramatic changes that occurred in the colonial state's external functional imperatives during decolonization overwhelmed the years of effort devoted to institutionalizing an integrated decentralized governmental apparatus, and prompted acceptance of a minimalist solution to the problem of furthering capital accumulation. While the independence bargain guaranteed the position of multinational capital in the erstwhile colonies, at least in the short run, it placed resident European capital at risk and brought to power an indigenous elite group that was weakly prepared to foster capital accumulation without substantial state intervention. After independence, therefore, the successor African rulers were confronted with choice between retaining inherited bureaucratic structures and institutionalizing untested democratic procedures, and between fostering acquisitive capital appropriation and productive capital accumulation. That the choices they made were structured by the institutional logic of the colonial state and dictated by the political rationality of their own class consolidation, albeit at odds with the wishes of the former colonial power, is not surprising. But that story is beyond the scope of this chapter.

Note

1. The framework combines theoretical elements presented in Scarritt (1986) and Mozaffar (1987), where their logical underpinnings and analytic utility also are elucidated.

PART IV

Changes in State Policy

9

The Transformation of
Interests and the State

DAVID LEVINE

What demands, if any, does the theory of the state make on our conception of private interests? Does the ability of the state to accomplish goals appropriate to it require that private interests have a specific form or content? In this chapter, I explore some of the implications of answering these questions in the affirmative. In doing so, I emphasize the necessity of a dynamic interpretation of private interests and their relation to the state. I will term this dynamic the transformation of interests although I recognize that this may seem to place the dynamic exclusively on the side of private interests. Since the process involves the state—its structure, goals, and sense of itself—we will also need to consider implications of the transformation of interests for state change.

A static view of interests characterizes society-centered approaches to the relationship between private interests and the state. Often under the influence of economic theory, these approaches link the interpretation of interests as preference orderings to a procedural interpretation of the state. The interpretation of interests as preferences emphasizes their connection to the subjective mental states of individuals. Such interests remain the same whether motivating individuals in the private sphere or in the state. Individuals do not modify or rethink their interests as a result of political participation. James Buchanan and Gordon Tullock present a clear and uncompromising state-

AUTHOR'S NOTE: I am indebted to Naeem Inayatullah for discussion of the issues treated here and to Gregg Kvistad, Robert Urquhart, and the editors of this volume for their criticisms of an earlier draft.

ment of this approach (1962, p. 20). Indeed, they consider it puzzling that anyone would be tempted to think otherwise.

Utilitarian theories best exemplify the society-centered approach. Economic theories of the state (e.g., public choice theory) demand that preferences of individuals determine state action. Within these theories, the ideal state does not act on its own initiative in accordance with its own (possibly the public or national) interest. Pluralist theories, though less normative in aim than public choice theories, similarly argue that state organization responds to private interests (of groups rather than individuals). The term society-centered, when used in this connection, refers to interpretations that place the initiative for state action outside the state, in society. The term society as used here refers more specifically to civil society: the system of private relations between agents motivated by private interests.

Certain versions of Marxian theory also are society-centered in this sense (although others, as we will see further on, attempt to modify the society-centered way of thinking). For the narrower versions of Marxian theory, classes emergent within civil society treat the state as a mechanism through which to satisfy economic or material interest. Even the more complex versions of Marxian theory argue for a class-dominated state and thus employ a society-centered method.

In society-centered approaches, the state responds to interests formed independently and assumed to be given. While interests can change in the society-centered world, change does not result from interaction between private agents and the state. In this sense, the society-centered approach employs a static notion of interests.

Society-centered theories interpret the state, ideally at least, as a set of procedures for aggregating, sifting, ranking, or otherwise organizing and reorganizing private interests. Such theories assume that interests remain constant as they bring their influence to bear on the state. By contrast, state-centered approaches can make real and substantial claims on interests. They must do so when they argue that the state has ends irreducible to those of private agents.[1] The state, if it is to pursue its own ends, must act on or restrict private interest. This excludes the one-directional influence of society on the state favored by society-centered approaches. As Peter Katzenstein points out, while private interests may influence the state, "interest groups are not autonomous agents exerting the pressure which shapes policy but subsidiary agents of the state" (1978, p. 18).

One way of understanding this relationship emphasizes what Peter Gourevitch terms mediating factors: mechanisms of representation, the organization of the state, and ideology (1986, p. 21). These factors adapt or transform interests making them appropriate to ends and activities of the state. Interests may still influence state decisions, but only through these mediating factors. In his case study of the regulatory apparatus of the state, Stephen Skowronek draws a much stronger conclusion: "The key to understanding the early regulatory effort is not to be found in the interests themselves but in the structure of the institutions they sought to influence" (1982, p. 131).

As suggestive as the historical studies of Katzenstein, Gourevitch, Skowronek, and others (Evans et al., 1985; Krasner, 1978) are, their claims against the static view of the state-society relationship fall short in important ways. First, we can interpret arguments such as Skowronek's as chronicling the failure of the state to live up to the ideal proposed by society-centered approaches. This failure does not invalidate the theories although it does cast doubt on their relevance for historical studies. This raises the question: Do these historical studies point toward an alternative theory, or do they, as Evans and colleagues suggest (1985, p. 363), question the desirability and even possibility of theorizing in this area?

Second, the emphasis in these studies is on the organization of the state. Because of this, even if they require a distinct interpretation of interests, they do not attempt to reconceptualize interests in a way that might challenge the static view. This is especially the case when intermediate organizations and the structure of the state are understood to channel, organize, or frustrate rather than transform interests. This second failure is also, in a sense, one of theory. The historical studies do not provide a language or conceptual apparatus that could articulate a distinct idea of the state-society relationship and thus challenge the language of the static interpretation (which is, after all, well-developed and in some areas hegemonic).

Thus, while state-centered approaches suggest a break with the static interpretation of interests, they stop short of articulating an alternative. This failing results primarily from the hegemony of utilitarian language and method in the interpretation of the private sphere. State-centered theorists tend to accept that language and method, circumventing some of its implications by focusing on historical-organizational rather than theoretical issues. They, in effect, abandon the theoretical ground to the society-centered approaches.

In the following, I explore the implications of thinking about private interests as bearing a more organic, dynamic, and interactive relation to the state. After considering some of the ways society-centered theories approach this more organic relation, I present the rudiments of a conceptual framework for thinking about interests dynamically.

Real and Subjective Interests

A notion of the transformation of interests exists implicit in traditional interpretations, and I will take this notion for my starting point. This notion emphasizes the transition from "subjective" to "real" interests (Balbus, 1971; Connolly, 1983; Lukes, 1974) and from false to true (or class) consciousness (Lukacs, 1971). In this view, private agents have subjective interests governed by their particular circumstances and by the knowledge or understanding made available to them in those circumstances. Lack of adequate knowledge can make agents' judgments of their own interests incorrect. Pursuit of what agents perceive to be their interest (i.e., pursuit of subjective interest) will impede the satisfaction of their "real" interests. Within the limits of the agent's private perspective and private circumstance, pursuit of self-interest will be self-defeating.

Political institutions (including but not limited to the state) can involve themselves in the movement from subjective to real interests.[2] They do so by providing agents with the information about and understanding of their private condition required for them to determine what is in their real interest.

The relation of subjective to real interest has been a special concern of Marxian theory. While essentially a society-centered theory—more so than any other within that broad classification—the Marxian theory grapples explicity with the possibility that the state may enter into the process that forms private interest.[3] Clearly, for the state to do so it must be more than a creature of private interest.

The Marxist interpretation of the state consists of a series of variations on a central theme: the necessity that social order be maintained where the circumstances of persons in civil society set them into fundamental opposition. When the state addresses its attention to the problem of order rather than interest, it may need to influence or even transform interests. In other words, the state may need to educate interests if they threaten to conflict with the demands of order. This possibility applies as much to those who stand to benefit as to those who do not.

To preserve order, the state must educate citizens (both capitalists and workers) in the virtues and requirements of the form of social-economic organization which it represents and defends. In doing so, the state aims to instill a commitment to or interest in a particular ideal of order (capitalism) that takes precedence over private interests. The political interest in order may advance the material interest the agent has emanating out of his position in civil society, or it may conflict with that interest. In either case, political interest differs from interest emerging in civil society. Thus, Marxist theory formulated in this way incorporates an important process by which the state shapes interests and develops an interactive relationship with the private sphere.

The idea of the transformation of interests makes sense when the political education of persons acts on their sense of themselves and their place in the world. Introduction of a notion of "real" interest represents a kind of half-way house in the development of a dynamic approach to the relationship between private interest and the state. We can, after all, continue to interpret real interests in an essentially static way. We do so when we emphasize the information that individuals gain in distinguishing real from subjective interest. When private circumstances do not provide that information, real and subjective interests differ. While this difference is important, the movement from subjective to real interest, because it leaves the underlying ends of agents unaffected, falls short of capturing the full implications of a dynamic notion of interests. Society-centered theories emphasize change in knowledge concerning the social conditions within which private agents pursue their ends rather than change in the ends themselves. While important, this sense of the transformation of interests retains some limitations of the static approach. We can see this more clearly if we draw a distinction between wants (or desires) and interests.

The static interpretation treats wants (or desires) as primitive (given) data originating in material need or the individual's private mental life. Our interests project our wants outward into the world. Interests depend on our wants and on the environment in which we attempt to satisfy them. Thus, when the environment changes, interests may change even though wants do not. The interests that arise from my wanting to be wealthy will vary depending on my circumstances and on the world I live in. Wanting to be wealthy may at first lead me to support laissez faire, free-market oriented candidates for public office. But, after learning more about what is required for my business to thrive, I may decide to support parties whose platforms include protectionist measures and industrial policy. Similarly, I may at one time support free-market policies because I believe they will increase demand and employment which will lead to higher wages and greater job security. A different understanding of how markets work may lead me to revise my views and decide that job security will be better served by government intervention. My interest changes although my underlying need does not.

This is the idea of transformation of interests implicit in the traditional view. As useful as this idea may be, it depends on a static notion of wants. Such wants provide the analysis with a fixed point. As such, they stand outside of the relation of state to private interest. In some ways, keeping wants out of the reach of the state is appealing since it seems to protect the autonomy of persons. But the idea that wants are immune to social and political interaction also distorts our understanding of the relationship between persons and political institutions. A fuller notion of the dynamics of interests requires us to move away from the static idea of wants.

The Social Determination of Wants

As I indicate above, the traditional view of interests and the interpretations of the state connected to it depend heavily on a way of thinking about wants. This interpretation sets out from a crucial premise: that individuals know what they want. This knowing is taken to imply an ability, given appropriate information, to determine which objects will best satisfy wants. This determination provides a basis for explaining the interactions among persons and between persons and institutions. Individuals may fail to satisfy their wants either because they do not have access to the appropriate goods or because they have inadequate information concerning the properties of those goods. Wants may change, but not as a part of the process through which we acquire the things that satisfy them. This is the sense in which wants are static. Relations with persons (e.g., exchange) and institutions may assist (or impede) us in satisfying wants, but they do not encourage or require us to reconsider, better understand, or otherwise transform our wants.

Static wants may be consistent with the ends of the state, but they need not be. We can come fairly close to assuring consistency by making the state's ends the satisfaction of private wants. The procedural interpretation of the state denies that the state has ends of its own and therefore eliminates the primary basis for conflict between private interests and the state.[4] If we move away from procedural interpretations of the state but retain the static view of wants, we increase the likelihood of conflict between private interests and the state. Thus, the conception of wants typical of society-centered theories constitutes an impediment to the interpretation of the state as something other than a creature of private interest. To develop such an interpretation will require us to rethink wants, interests, and the relationship between them.

An alternative interpretation of wants treats knowing what we want as a complicated matter involving much more than information. It involves exploring and experiencing ourselves in the world, in relations with other persons, and with social institutions. In this interpretation, we do not know what we want prior to such relations. Indeed, this interpretation directly challenges the basic premise of the static view that individuals know what they want and that such knowledge is the starting point for understanding political and economic processes and institutions.

The alternative approach treats the self more as a potential than as a full-fledged locus of wants (or of choice). Knowing your wants means knowing yourself and knowing yourself is better understood as a process than as a fixed state. This process involves the pursuit of social connection and of the meaning found only within such a connection. I have explored this idea of self-seeking in greater detail elsewhere (Levine, 1988a). Here, I restrict myself to a brief summary of relevant conclusions.

We define our wants in social relations through which those wants emerge, change, and develop. Our interests in the world arise out of our wants but they also arise out of our effort to better define ourselves and what we want. Thus interests are not simple functions of wants. We are interested in involving ourselves in activities that might define what we want. In society-centered approaches, interests follow wants. But, as suggested here, wants may also follow interests. They do so when private interest is an interest in developing and exploring an idea of the self. Pursuit of private interest brings about the discovery of the wants appropriate to the individual's sense of self.

Consider the interest in acquiring an education. An instrumental interpretation of education works well with the traditional way of thinking about interests. The instrumental interpretation treats education as an instrument we employ to assist us in satisfying our wants rather than as a part of the process of defining, determining, and creating wants. Narrowly vocational and professional education emphasizes acquisition of skills needed to accomplish well-defined goals. Pursuit of such an education suits individuals with a well-formed, or possibly inflexible, sense of self. For individuals whose sense of self is less well-formed, or possibly more flexible, professional education will not serve their interests since it contributes little to the process of discovering wants.

Those who experience themselves as possessing a capacity for development, experience their interest as an interest in the process of development. Less predetermined educational structures satisfy their interest better than do the more structured and narrowly goal-oriented. Nonprofessional interest in education exemplifies how interest can precede wants and exist where wants are ill-defined. When the state involves itself in non-vocational education, it assumes an interest in the process by which persons develop their identities.

In important part, our private interest is an interest in making sense of the world and of our place in it. Consider, for example, our interest in consumption. The static view treats that interest in a purely instrumental way: it relates a given want to an object having the qualities capable of satisfying that want. The satisfaction of the want only affects the individual's happiness and in a very limited sense; it does not affect the individual's sense of himself and his place in the world. By contrast, in the dynamic view, the act of consumption involves the individual in his world and in an effort to understand himself in and act upon that world. In the words of Mary Douglas and Baron Isherwood, "the essential function of consumption is its capacity to make sense" (1979, p. 62). Making sense of the world involves us in the pursuit of meaning and thus of ideas that make who we are and what we do coherent and comprehensible to us and to others.

The idea that consumption is about making sense of the world may strike those who inhabit more traditional modes of thinking about consumption as odd even to the point of perversity. Obviously, preference-ordering notions of the relation of desire to object employ a simpler, more direct, interpretation of consumption, while the one posed here makes consumption more complex and problematic.

The interpretation of consumption suggested here introduces an additional term into the relationship between wants and object. This additional term is the person's sense of himself and his place in the world. This sense of self consists of more or less well-articulated, more or less conscious, ideas. Thus, the interpretation advanced here places ideas of self into the relationship between want and its satisfaction. Wants incorporate ideas, thus the need to make sense. Wants and consumption have meaning, more or less well-known, both for consumer and for society. Forming and satisfying wants, then, involves the search for and conveying of meaning, making sense of the individual and his place in the world.

Consider consumption of automobiles. Wanting an automobile is part of the complex relationship between consumer and society, between the consumer's sense of himself and society's sense of itself. Thus, a society that incorporates the appropriate notions of individual autonomy, private property, and private rather than collective life will encourage use of automobiles above other forms of transportation. A state that embodies or represents these ideas society has of itself will do what it can to enable (if not require) citizens to own and use cars. Individuals will incorporate use of automobiles into their ways of life, and will develop ways of life requiring their use.

While the effort to make sense of the world involves us in a social order, it need not require us to abandon a sense of ourselves as separate and independent agents with private interests. Making sense of ourselves demands that what we do and what we want have social meaning; it does not demand that the social meaning be the same for different persons. Private interest has a social destination in establishing a socially meaningful sense of self; but meaningful need not imply communal.[5]

The satisfaction of private wants is a learning process. The education needed for us to succeed in satisfying our wants has as much to do with finding out who we are and what we want as it has to do with finding out the technical or physical properties of objects that might satisfy our wants. If the state involves itself in the satisfaction of wants, it must involve itself in this process. It can assist or impede the individual in his effort to make sense of the world. Having involved itself, positively or negatively, in the work of making sense of the world, the state can facilitate or impede the satisfaction of wants defined as a result of that work.

If we incorporate this notion of wants into our understanding of the relationship between private interests and the state, we cannot accept procedural or instrumental views of the state. What kind of state can involve itself in the process of the transformation of interests?

The State and the Transformation of Interests

Procedural theories of the state focus attention almost exclusively on one aspect of state activity: decision making. For such theories, the state is exclusively or essentially a decision-making mechanism. This narrow focus on decision making leaves out of account an activity which, while irrelevant to the static view of interests, is of vital importance in a dynamic approach. This activity is the work of making sense of the world.

The organization of the state takes on special importance when, in addition to actually making decisions, it also incorporates a process that defines problems in particular ways. State structure not only decides, it also (1) embodies a set of ideas concerning the nature of the political subject and political problem, and (2) governs a deliberative process that determines the political relevance, and politically relevant form, of new ideas. In both of these ways, the state significantly affects the way society makes sense of itself. To clarify this point, I will refer briefly to two examples from historical studies of the state-society relationship.

In his study *Building a New American State,* Skowronek attempts to show how state structure embodied a notion of the balance between regional and national power. In doing so, state structure made important economic problems raised by a developing national economy difficult or impossible to solve. A way of thinking embodied in an organization determined the decisions the organization was capable of making and the actions it could take. So long as the state embodied the idea of a "locally oriented party democracy" it could not respond to the centralizing tendencies of economic development:

> The creation of more centralized, stable, and functionally specific institutional connections between state and society were impeded by the tenacity of this highly mobilized, highly competitive, and locally oriented party democracy. (Skowronek, 1982, pp. 39-40)

Skowronek explicitly attributes the locally oriented organization of the state to the way that state embodied important political ideas—in our terms, to the sense that such a state imposed on the world:

> The radical republican regimes of 1776-83 clearly embodied the revolutionary thrust against the emergent European organization of state power. Sovereignty was fixed in thirteen separate state legislatures, in which strict majoritarian principles and frequent elections left government at the mercy of fast-changing popular sentiments. These arrangements prevented any effective concentration of governing power at the national center, made a mockery of executive prerogatives, and inhibited institutional specialization. The results were destabilizing. Yet, the problems in this radical republican prescription had to be overcome without appearing to betray the revolutionary ideals it represented. (1982, p. 20)

For those who fashioned the state, imposing a certain meaning on the world had priority over satisfying private interest.

Of course, this example can be interpreted in different directions. A Marxian view might emphasize how the imposition of particular meaning on the world serves certain interests. Skowronek defines the problem of state change largely in this way, as a question of whether the government can "be changed so as to serve interests in a new way" (p. 132). This interpretation tends to link a more state-centered approach to the same (static) view of interests favored by those who take a society-centered approach.

Indeed, the claim that conflict over ideas about the world is best understood as conflict between interests outside of the state only makes sense if those interests are given (static). This way of thinking goes from interests to ideas and treats the latter as arising out of the former. The ideas we have about the world are governed by the contribution they make to our private well-being given our wants and circumstances. If these wants and circumstances have common features with those of a larger group we have class conditions that govern ideas appropriate to class interests. In any case, the causation runs in one direction: from wants and circumstances to interests to ideas about the world. While interests change with circumstances, ideas change with interests and not vice versa.

In criticizing this approach, I do not mean to deny that the sense we make of the world depends on the lives we lead in it. I only mean to emphasize that the opposite of this statement is equally true: the lives we lead in the world depend on the sense we make of it. Because this is true, our interests (and circumstances) can vary with our ideas.

By emphasizing the dynamic aspect of interest, I hope to focus attention on the way the state involves itself in the process through which agents attempt to make sense of the world. The organization of the state embodies a meaning, albeit complex and sometimes ambiguous. That organization imposes a sense of the world onto the political process. This sense of the world affects the decisions emerging from that process. We cannot, then, interpret the state as a mechanism for arriving at decisions because doing so obscures the equally important quality of the state as an organizational embodiment of a way of making sense of the world.

The state also governs a deliberative process that precedes decision making. This process is not the mere collection of and flow of information; it defines problems, accepts, rejects, formulates, and reformulates new ideas. Margaret Weir and Theda Skocpol (1985) in their study of responses to the Great Depression emphasize this aspect of the state. They attempt to demonstrate how the organization of the state affects the knowledge it acquires and uses in responding to social problems:

> In order to assess why and how new, proto-Keynesian economic ideas became, or failed to become, credible with governmental and political leaders in a position to act on them, we must ask not about the presence of individual persons or ideas in the abstract, but whether key state agencies were open or closed to the development or use of innovative perspectives. In effect, we must investigate how the normal mechanisms used by states to incorporate educated expertise served to facilitate or hamper innovations in economic policy. (1985, p. 126)

Weir and Skocpol argue that the structure of the Swedish state gave it an advantage in making use of innovative ideas due to the presence of "long-established mechanisms for bringing experts, bureaucrats, and political representatives together for sustained planning of public policies" (p. 129). In our language, the Swedish state incorporated a process for making sense of the world that governed the interpretation of the problem of the Depression and linked the definition of the problem to the decision-making apparatus in a particular way. This mechanism allowed officials to "ponder together"

(p. 132). The idea of pondering together is what I have in mind by a process for making sense.

By contrast, state structure in the United States tended to organize the decision-making process differently, involving different parties in the organization and flow of knowledge. In Weir and Skocpol's interpretation, the fragmented and decentralized political process in the U.S. stood in the way of the use of knowledge. This structure produced "a welter of federal initiatives" rather than "a coherent strategy"; it limited rather than encouraged the use of expert (i.e., social scientific) knowledge (p. 136). Thus, not only are states responsible for making sense of social problems, some state structures are better able to make sense of the world than others.

In a way, this is a striking conclusion. If we interpret the work of the state in making sense of the world along these lines, then our interpretation may have implications for judgments regarding how adequate state structures are to that end. Weir and Skocpol emphasize the capacity of the state to utilize expert judgment. They thus assume a specific relation between use of expertise and valid judgment of social problems. This assumption raises as many questions as it answers (see Levine, 1988b; Sassower, 1988). Regardless of what we think concerning the relationship between the use of expertise and forming valid judgment, however, the conclusion regarding state structure remains provocative. If an important part of what states do falls under the heading of making sense of the world, then we can judge state structure by its capacity to discover the sense the world makes. Of course, since state decisions affect the world we live in, the state can also affect the extent to which the world makes sense.

Private Interests and the State

Can we take a dynamic view of interests and still argue that the state responds to (and concerns itself with satisfying) private interests? To an important extent, interests are formed and transformed by nonpolitical relations and institutions. Even if the state does not take the results of these formative relations to be given, it cannot alter them at will in accordance with its own agenda. Were we to argue for the unimportance of societally determined interests in affecting state decisions we would argue against one of the most important ideas that has emerged in social science over the past 200 years.

The prevalence of society-centered approaches to the relation of interests to the state has deep roots in the idea that society has its own internal laws and processes. The modern idea of the world of private affairs sees societal outcomes as unintended results of private actions. Over 200 years of political and economic thought highlights the virtues of the self-ordering market and the self-governing polity. Both ideas can be linked to the demise of the active state. The first idea largely dispenses with the state in favor of the market. The second idea replaces the state with procedures for democratic decision making. Both ideas, plausibly enough, see the active state as an obstacle to economic and political liberty.

In advancing a dynamic interpretation of interests linked to a more active state, I do not mean simply to repudiate these ideas. I do intend, however, to question the notion of private interest in terms of which society-centered approaches advance their claims. My aim is not to eliminate or minimize the part played by private interest, but to begin to give private interest a more meaningful interpretation.

The dynamic approach emphasizes the reciprocal relation between private interest and the state. Private interests make demands on the state; in responding to these demands the state may serve interests. Private interests also look to the state as an institution within which to define their ends and to make sense of their needs and circumstances. By "using" the state in this way, private agents do not necessarily give up their autonomy or become agents of the state. Involvement with the state can contribute to the transformation of interests without the state imposing interests on persons.

The state provides private interests with (more or less effective) forums in which to discover their ends. Because of this, the state can try to establish itself as a place where interests change. If the state fails to do so, it fails to serve private wants. State change in response to private interests can adapt the state better (or less well) to the transformation of interests. State structures vary in their ability to work constructively with private interests. They also vary with regard to the kinds of interests they are capable of understanding and to which they can respond. When new interests emerge, the state may not have the capacity to understand or work well with them. By interpreting new interests according to patterns used for making sense of older interests, the state serves new interests poorly. This can lead to conflict that frustrates interests or undermines the integrity of state institutions.[6] Such conflict can play an important part in state change and the transformation of interests.

Concluding Remarks

In the foregoing, I have attempted no more than a sketch of an approach. I suggest some language that may convey meanings hidden or obscured in the more familiar formulations. Whether the specific language proposed succeeds or not, it highlights important limitations of prevailing interpretations of the relation of interests to the state. I advance the claim that our understanding of the state and of state change will be better served with a more dynamic concept of interest. Use of such a concept can reinforce some of the observations in recent literature concerning the importance of state structure, ideology, and intermediate organizations. An emphasis on the transformation of interests might also make the importance of these "mediating factors" more readily intelligible. Doing so is one of the primary purposes of theorizing. The theoretical dimension of alternatives to society-centered approaches has not been as sharp as it must be to successfully challenge society-centered approaches. The ideas advanced here are intended to give direction to the development of that theoretical dimension.

Notes

1. For this reason when I refer to state-centered approaches, I exclude those that define the state's interests on the basis of the preferences of its agents (office holders).

2. This clearly simplifies the argument considerably. It leaves out the important idea that political institutions can lead agents away from perceiving their true interests. Lukacs (1971) argues that true (class) consciousness is not possible for those who occupy certain class positions.

3. Within the society-centered literature, the work of Antonio Gramsci (1971) has the most to offer toward a dynamic interpretation of interests. His emphasis on the educational role of the state, on the idea of hegemony, and on the ethical phase of the state strongly suggests an interpretation along the lines advanced here.

4. We could argue that even procedural theories define ends peculiar to the state having to do with the procedures themselves. This means, in part, that agents value those procedures (see Dahl, 1956).

5. Michael Sandel has criticized dominant (utilitarian and Kantian) images of the self in favor of what he terms the "situated self." The situated self derives its identity from the communities (family, city, nation, party, etc.) in which it is "embedded" (1988, p. 115). Clearly, the interests of a situated self lead into social connection and an interest in social (understood as communal) ends. The connection between private interest and communal commitment remains problematic. A danger exists here similar to that which has cast doubt on organic views of the state (see Stepan, 1978). How do we avoid the tendency of these approaches to hypostatize the community (or state) equating it with the social identity of the person? The individual's sense of self may involve a sense of community, and of place in a community. This need not, however, make the sense of self communal.

6. But it may not. State structure and culture also affect the state's capacity to work with private interests in ways that protect their autonomy.

10

Farmers and the State
in the Progressive Era

ELIZABETH SANDERS

Studies of the progressive era highlight extremely varied social groups as the instigators of reform and state expansion (Rogers, 1982). However, the most frequently used and cited interpretation is that of corporate liberalism or some other variant of instrumentalist theory which sees the business class (or classes) as the motor of progressive era state expansion.

Gabriel Kolko (1963), for example, has argued that 1910-1914 legislation registered the triumph of big business men and bankers who sought government action to rationalize the new marketplace and control competition. In a similar vein, James Weinstein (1968) has described ostensible progressive era liberalism as the conscious creation of economic elites. Robert Wiebe (1962, 1967), although making more careful distinctions between big and small, northeastern and hinterland bankers and businessmen, nevertheless accords the business class the leadership role in a wide range of national reform arenas in this period. Martin Sklar (1988) describes the competing policy agendas of the period as variants of "corporate liberalism" embodied in presidential candidates Wilson, Taft, and Roosevelt.

Contemporary state theory, rooted both in Marx and the experience of European welfare states, rejects naked instrumentalism in favor of a more complex vision of interaction among "state managers," capitalists and the organized working class, in which state actors struggle both to maintain capital accumulation and to achieve social peace and legitimation of their own creative mediation role (and, ultimately, reelection). The degree to which state actors side with labor and act against at least the perceived short-term interests of capitalists is held to be a function of labor's political strength and, perhaps, the depth of the crisis the state confronts (Block, 1987; Offe, 1984b for example).

Such formulations, while they provide more plausible frameworks for reform periods, have not generated concrete propositions that can be tested against empirical reality. In addition, their assumptions are particularly deficient for the American case, for two reasons. First, the "state managers" to whom such theories refer are invariably executive branch officials, leaving unspecified (and usually ignored) the major role played by Congress in responding to societal interests, formulating policy, and guiding bureaucratic behavior. Neglect of the legislative process also marks the president-and-cabinet-centered accounts of the corporate liberalism school. In such accounts, corporate elites work their will through the president and high-level executives. Congressional initiation of legislation, and the transformation of executive initiatives so frequently effected in the legislature, are seldom acknowledged. At the second corner of the policy-effecting triangle (the third being the business and financial elite), stands the working class. This designation leaves out two critical sets of actors whose class position is ambiguous: farmers, and the dependent white-collar middle class. Although it is recognized by scholars of welfare state formation that farmers were critical coalition partners of industrial workers in the early development of welfare states in Scandinavia (Esping-Andersen, 1985), little attention has been paid to agrarian movements as instigators of political reform and state expansion. Where they are acknowledged, agrarian organizations are usually seen as contingent followers, rather than leaders, of reform (an exception is Lipset). Similarly, the educated dependent and professional middle classes are seldom treated by state theorists—whether of the neo-Marxist or state autonomy schools—as a category whose class interests are often served by state expansion. The role played by the public service intelligentsia in crafting statutes and building political coalitions is not well captured by notions of "brokering" or instrumentalism.[1]

In short, contemporary state theory gives too little attention to the role of diverse social movements and classes in instigating and shaping state expansion and often fails to recognize that in the American case "the state" has three distinct branches (not to mention 50 subgovernments) whose "managers" are connected to very different social and political constituencies.

The progressive era is an intriguing time to explore in a multifaceted way the nature and process of U.S. state development. It was a time of great social ferment, and while there was not one "progressive movement," there were political upheavals among farmers, workers, and the middle classes that pressed new demands on the state. Large industrial and financial capitalists in the urban core economy held a distinct set of preferences vis-à-vis the state, and "state managers"—notably the president, high executive branch officials, and federal judges—played key roles in channeling, compromising, and thwarting the various programmatic agendas of farmers and workers.

The pages below set out an account of progressive era state development that is starkly different from that of the instrumentalists. It is "society-centered" in the sense that initiative is attributed to social movements and "producer" coalitions—primarily, in this case, periphery farmers and their labor allies. Political action by large-scale capitalists is seen as principally negative and reactive, although their opposition was highly significant for policy outcomes. Although both farmers and workers anticipated significant, state-induced changes in the balance of market power and in the freedom of capitalists to make investment decisions, conduct economic transactions, and control labor, neither farmers nor workers seriously promoted large-scale socialization of production. At the same time, agrarians and industrial workers can hardly be described as sympathetic to the profit needs of investors. In highlighting the legislative process, this analysis emphasizes the role of social forces other than capitalists in promoting state-expanding reform, in an arena where diverse democratic forces are prominent; comparison with the fate of these proposals in other arenas points up the distinct orientations within the structures of the state. Finally, it will be argued that the structures of the state—in this case the territorial basis of representation, federalism, local control of voting and party nominations, and the awesome independent power of the judiciary—encouraged the formation and success of some coalitions and discouraged others within the political economy. The argument, then, is that both state structures and economic interests matter, and that both must be seen as more internally diverse categories than is usually recognized. An eclectic political economy approach is utilized which locates the driving force of late 19th- to early 20th-century U.S. national state expansion in the remote, primary production sectors of the economy. This origination of state change was the result of the regional polarization of the maturing industrial economy into a manufacturing/financial core and an extraction-based periphery, and the territorial nature of political representation that overlay economic society.

Agrarian Grievances and the Agrarian Statist Agenda, 1890-1916

The plight of the remote farmer has been described in many places. He or she was, in the late 19th century, increasingly victimized by government-induced as well as internationally influenced commodity price deflation; rising debt burdens and tightening credit; exploitation by monopolistic manufacturing trusts (affecting farm equipment, cotton bagging, and so forth) railroads, ocean shippers, warehouses, and elevators; commodity market speculation, manipulation, and fraud; and financial panics originating in the huge and powerful metropolitan banking firms. Southern farmers were particularly strapped, and inexorably rising tenancy rates in the region reflected and solidified their misery. By 1900, 36% of white and 75% of blacks were tenants or sharecroppers; most of the remaining "yeomen" were heavily and hopelessly in debt to bankers, landlords, and merchants. The average per capita income among the bottom three-quarters of the southern population ranged from $55 to $64 a year in 1880-1900 (Kousser, 1974, pp. 64-65; Saloutos, 1960, p. 237; Woodward, 1971, pp. 318-319). These were the conditions that gave rise to the Farmers' Alliance, the largest and most radical mass movement for economic and political change in American history until the civil rights movement of the 1960s. Like the latter, the Farmers' Alliance originated in the rural periphery and, while it spread into the plains states, had its most radical core in the South. At its peak it enrolled about three million members, including the allied Colored Farmers' Alliance. After solid class opposition from bankers, merchants, manufacturers, and large landlords strangled its attempt to construct a counter-economy based on cooperative buying and selling, Alliance leaders turned to politics (Goodwyn, 1978; Schwartz, 1976). The derivative Populist Party advocated government ownership of railroads, an expanded currency not tied to gold or bonds, an income tax, a "subtreasury" plan for public warehousing and credit, labor organizational rights, and the eight-hour day (Tindall, 1966, pp. 93-96). Like the Alliance, it also endorsed the central demands of industrial and railroad workers, although the populist vote among urban workers in the 1890 and 1984 elections was miniscule. Meanwhile, populists swept Kansas, Nebraska, and the Dakotas, and Alliancemen, populists, and fusionists routed regular Democrats in the South.

In 1896, William Jennings Bryan was the presidential nominee of both a "populized" Democratic Party (which had repudiated its northern conservative wing) and the Populist Party. Because he failed to convince the urban labor electorate, Bryan lost narrowly to McKinley and the northern capital-led Republican Party. For most historians, this is the end of the story of an inspired but ultimately futile agrarian uprising. As farmers of the 1870s had produced the landmark Granger regulatory laws in the states, only to see much of their program later repealed or emasculated (Buck, 1913), 1890s populism is viewed as another failed crusade. While agrarian pressure on both parties might be credited with passage of the Interstate Commerce Act and the Sherman Act, (Hoogenboom & Hoogenboom, 1976; Thorelli, 1955) railroad and antitrust regulation floundered in the succeeding decade as a result of weak enforcement and judicial hostility. When, after a decade, progressivism blossomed, its disjuncture with populism was stressed. It was held to be a more urban, middle-class phenomenon even (or perhaps one should say, particularly) in the south, where a decade of electoral disenfranchisement and resurgent racism sapped the old populist forces (Buenker, 1978; Hackney, 1969; Kirby, 1972; Mowry, 1958). How, then, is one to explain the clear links between the regulatory legislation of 1910-1916 and the older Alliance/populist program? The answer is that much of the content of that program was regional. That is, it reflected the position of the periphery agrarians in the national and international political economy—yeomen, landlords, and tenants alike. Hence the apparent (for the disjuncture argument) paradox that even as the southern electorate shrank and the Alliance-populist effort at biracial cooperation was lost, William Jennings Bryan—who had transformed himself from a narrow silver politician into a genuine populist spokesman—continued to lead a Democratic party anchored in the South and committed to economic decentralization, greatly expanded state intervention capacity, and the farmer-labor alliance. The periphery regions (see Figure 10.1) held 73% of Democratic Party House seats in 1910, 26% of Republican Party membership, and 47% of the total body. In the Senate, where the state formula magnified its representation, the periphery accounted for 57% of seats. A core-periphery rupture within Republican ranks and modest labor and middle-class support (in the context of three- or four-party races) in the North maximized Democratic strength in Congress and permitted the agrarians' statist agenda to succeed in the years from 1910 through 1916.[2]

In the following analysis, legislative support patterns are discussed in terms of regional political economy. For this analysis, congressional districts and states were divided into three categories based on per capita value-added in manufacturing for economically interdependent subregions (see Sanders, 1986a). The "agrarian" regions of the highly specialized economy of the early 20th-century U.S. are those with the lowest value-added scores. The industrial "core" regions of the historic manufacturing belt have the highest scores, with an intermediate category of "diverse" industrial-agricultural-extractive regions located in the middle west and on the Pacific coast. The three regions are displayed in Figure 10.1.

The statutes in Table 10.1 may be described as the legislative fruits of the agrarian drive, evident from at least the 1880s: (1) to establish effective public

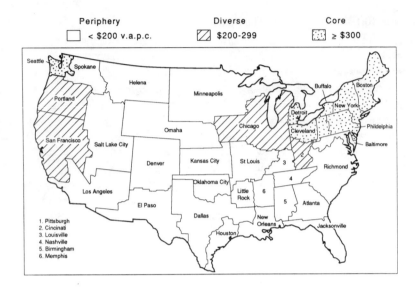

Figure 10.1. Regional Industrialization Patterns in the Early 20th Century

SOURCE: Trade area boundaries are final 1921 Federal Reserve Branch Bank Territories, from *Eighth Annual Report of the Board of Governors of the Federal Reserve*, 1921, Washington, DC, 1922, pp. 693-699. The outline map is taken from Richard F. Bensel, *Sectionalism and American Political Development*, 432. Value-added in manufacturing is taken from the 1919 Census of Manufactures, state-county tables, and aggregated into trade areas, then divided by trade area population to get per capita (v.a.p.c.) figures.

control over the trust-dominated banking, transportation, storage and grading, and manufacturing network in which farmers had become enmeshed, to their increasing disadvantage; (2) to shift the burden of government financing from consumers and, particularly, from the agrarian regions, to the wealthy; and (3) to establish unprecedented roles for the national government in funding agricultural and industrial education and in building roads that the remote farmers desperately needed but which local governments could ill afford to finance.

In the 61st Congress (1909-1910), the agrarian Democrats made themselves available for insurgent Republican initiatives, and offered their own amendments in tandem with the gutsy western and midwestern rebels.[3] This agrarian-based coalition, powerful enough to dethrone Speaker Cannon, had limited success in shaping public policy (Hechler, 1940; Holt, 1967; Sarasohn, 1989). It managed to establish, in the Mann-Elkins and Valuation Acts, a basis for effective public control of railroad rates, pooling, and

Table 10.1 The Agrarian Statist Agenda: Progressive Era Fruits

Transportation		*Commodity Grading, Storage, Trading*		*Corporate Concentration (Monopolistic Practices)*	
1910	Mann-Elkins Act	1914	Cotton Futures Act	1914	Clayton Antitrust Act
1912	Panama Canal Act (railroad, shipping prohibitions)	1916	Warehouse Act		
		1916	Grain Standards Act		
1913	Valuation Act				
1916	Shipping Act				
Banking and Credit		*Trade*		*Taxation*	
1913	Federal Reserve Act (structure, public control, credit provisions)	1913	Underwood Tariff	1913	Income Tax
				1916	Revenue Act
1916	Federal Farm Loan Act				
Infrastructure: Social and Physical					
1914	Smith-Lever (Agricultural Extension) Act				
1916	Bankhead-Shackleford Federal Highways Act				
1917	Smith-Hughes Vocational Education Act				

discrimination based on geography and customer size, as well as to bring telephone and telegraph companies under ICC jurisdiction. But domination of Congress and the White House by the party of core industrial and financial capital meant—insurgency to the contrary—that such victories could only be partial. The loyalty of western Republicans from tariff-dependent (e.g., wool, hides, and sugar beet) regions and aversion to the "extremist" program of the southern Democrats minimized desertion from majority party ranks. In addition, President Taft stood willing to wield his patronage, bureaucratic, and veto powers to ward off change. The result was a tariff policy that made (in 1909) only a symbolic gestures to reform; a postal saving system that favored bondholders and northeastern banks more than farmers and immigrants; railroad legislation that sabotaged rate control with a new Commerce Court sympathetic to the railroads; and tax legislation that postponed the assault on great incomes. In these early legislative efforts, the small band of progressive Republicans were bold and persistent in their attempts to push their hide-bound party to the left, toward a powerful regulatory state; but their troops were furnished by the agrarian (largely southern) Democrats.[4]

When the Democrats took over the House in 1911, leadership was reversed. Giving the agrarian program a trial run, the periphery Democrats, (who now held 61% of the party's seats and controlled the speakership, caucus, and committee system) churned out tariff, railroad, income tax, shipping, and labor bills; passed a direct election amendment for the U.S. Senate; and conducted a mammoth investigation of the "Money Trust." Most of their initiatives were lost to Senate inaction or presidential vetoes (Sarasohn, 1989). In 1913, however, Democratic control of the White House and both chambers of Congress, and the party loyalty of a new contingent of northern Democrats cleared the way for enactment of the periphery's long-standing agenda for state expansion. While it is undoubtedly true that some business spokesmen could be found voicing their support for at least some version of each of the programs for state intervention listed in Table 10.1, it simply is not the case that a business elite, cohesive or not, championed this program and saw it to fruition. Rather, if one examines the legislative histories of these bills—and most had been around for a decade or more—one finds that the manufacturing belt Republicans who were the obvious spokesmen (and often the paid retainers) of the economic elite were fiercely opposed. Such representatives might (as in the case of the 1887 Interstate Commerce Act) be found backing a regulatory commission in preference to a punitive and "self-enforcing" statute, and might dream dreams of obsequious commissioners providing government sanction for their pools and cartels, but what they wanted was most assuredly not what they got (Sanders, 1986a). In railroad legislation, what they got were statutes that progressively, by 1913 (when Taft's Commerce Court was jettisoned by the agrarian coalition), tightened the regulatory noose by firmly establishing maximum rate control (with higher rates suspended while the ICC deliberated); banned pooling, long-short haul, and other discriminations; and prohibited carrying products they produced or had an interest in, or owning ships in the coastwise trade using the Panama Canal. In no sense can this be described as a "railroad agenda," and if other business interests in the great industrial cities supported stringent regulation, they somehow failed to communicate that support to their political representatives.[5]

Likewise, while regulation of commodity futures markets is a plausible candidate for Kolko's "rationalization" thesis, the 1914 law is much more accurately described as the product of years of agrarian agitation to overcome the information monopoly and manipulative speculation associated with the great commodity exchanges. While some cotton manufacturers had originally backed some form of public regulation, the importance of such business support was largely confined to the South, where it merely reinforced the impetus of cotton growers against the New York Cotton Exchange. There is no doubt that the great exchanges themselves adamantly opposed government regulation.[6] The 1914 Cotton Futures Act (CFA) was opposed by 7 to 1 among voting core Republicans, but passed with united Democratic support. Among representatives of 11 Massachusetts textile districts, three voted nay, two aye, and eight did not vote—hardly an indication of business endorsement.[7] The CFA, which established USDA control of the content of cotton futures contracts (including federally promulgated grades) and levied a prohibitive tax on nonconforming contracts, was greeted by an alarmist *New York Times* (June 30, 1914) as a law designed to destroy the New York Cotton Exchange "by taxing it out of existence."

Also opposed by northeastern Republicans was the 1916 Warehouse Act. A descendent of the radical "subtreasury" demand of 19th-century populists, it inaugurated federal licensing, inspection, and grading of stored products. It standardized warehouse operations and receipts so that the latter could be used as collateral for bank loans, and the resulting notes discounted by the new Federal Reserve banks. The Grain Standards Act, a companion piece to the 1916 Warehouse Act, instituted federal licensing of grain inspectors; prohibited their financial ties to grain elevators, warehouses or merchants; and applied criminal penalties to those convicted of misgrading (about which farmers had long and bitter complaints).

The Underwood Tariff Act of 1913 was the first item on the New Freedom Congress's agenda and represented the historical policy stance of the southern-dominated Democratic party. Even advocates of the business-dominance school find it hard to attribute this policy to the pervasive influence of the corporate elite.[8] Republicans, who had responded to business pleas for seven decades, cast only four (of their 129) votes for the Underwood Bill in the House.[9] Even if the largest industrial and financial enterprises could now view tariff cuts with less alarm than before, they abhorred, as did the business and professional class generally, the attachment to the tariff bill of the nation's first income tax. Designed to replace the lost tariff revenue and fund new federal programs in a redistributive, rather than regressive way, the tax bill was extremely popular with periphery Democrats, and insurgent farm state Republicans as well (Link, 1956, pp. 191-194). Because of the concentration of wealth in the industrial core, the tax had a sharply sectional impact. At the original 1913 rates, it extracted more revenue from the city of Chicago than from the 11 southern states combined; four states—New York, Pennsylvania, Massachusetts, and Illinois—supplied almost 60% of the combined income and corporation taxes established by the Act.[10] In 1916, agrarian congressmen cast aside Wilson's regressive proposals for raising the revenues necessary for his preparedness program, and instead passed an inheritance tax, a tax on the munitions industry, and a more steeply progressive income tax. If the core elite wanted war, the agrarian Democrats and insurgent Republicans argued, they should be prepared to pay for it (Link, 1954, pp. 192-196).

The same agrarian momentum drove antitrust policy. The Clayton bill was drafted by the Alabama congressman who chaired the House Judiciary Committee, and its principles—strengthening the Sherman Act by outlawing the specific corporate and individual activities that led to monopoly—were those of Bryan and the 1912 Democratic platform. After an agrarian-labor compromise that grafted labor union guarantees onto a set of stringent antitrust prohibitions, the Clayton bill sailed through the House with near-unanimous Democratic support and a majority of periphery and diverse-area Republicans (core Republicans opposed it by over 3 to 1). President Wilson's contribution was largely to support a subsequent weakening of the bill's criminal penalties and to foist a companion Federal Trade Commission bill on the reluctant agrarians. However, after years of touting the idea of a trade commission as an alternative to the Sherman Act, big business was not fooled by this Wilsonian invention of the same name. Core Republicans, the stout defenders of business privilege and autonomy, overwhelmingly opposed successful Senate moves to strengthen the commission's powers, as well as both the FTC and Clayton bills on final passage. When arch-conservative Senator Henry F. Lippitt of Rhode Island offered an amendment designed to transform the FTC into the kind of trade commission envisioned by the enlightened capitalists of the National Civic Federation—one that would approve business trade agreements and thus exempt them from antitrust prosecution—he secured the backing of only 14 senators, all Republicans concentrated in the core industrial states (Sanders, 1986a).

It seems clear that agrarians and the business elite had very different political agendas in the early 20th century and that, on balance, the state expansion that occurred in the progressive era reflected agrarian interests to a far greater extent than business demands. Even the 1914-1916 labor legislation that completed the major legislative program of the Wilson years represented the agrarian Democrats' payoff to their northern urban co-partisans and was, in that sense, a long-standing part of the agrarian agenda. The labor guarantees contained in the Clayton Act were, along with its antitrust prohibitions, anathema to substantial businessmen; they deluged Congress and President Wilson with demands that the Clayton bill be scrapped (particularly as the 1914 recession deepened and the threat of impending war in Europe further unsettled business conditions). In these extraordinary times, it was the agrarian drive to complete the main outlines of the Democratic program before the difficult 1914 elections that saw the new antitrust program through to enactment—at what was probably the last possible political moment.

The Corporate Agenda for the National State

Can big business and finance be said to have had a positive regulatory program, aside from reactive strategies in the face of radical agrarian demands, and creative efforts to evade the potential force of the Sherman Act? Kolko, Weinstein, Wiebe, Urofsky and other historians have argued, principally on the basis of elite correspondence and trade association records, that there was such an agenda. Its earmarks, they argue, were a drive for rationalization of market processes, elimination of internecine competition, protection from obnoxious and incoherent regulation by the individual states, and a centralized capacity in the national state that would serve business and financial needs as well as control labor and other potentially disruptive forces. Unfortunately for capitalists and the corporate liberalism interpretation, Congress in the progressive era was not a sympathetic forum for these wishes in their specific policy incarnations.

Perhaps the best case for elite dominance is the creation, in 1913, of a new federal banking system—an institution that had not existed since the Jacksonians allowed it to die in 1834. The principal extant proposal for meeting the widely shared consensus that the nation needed a national banking system had been developed by Nelson Aldrich and the National Monetary Commission (NMC) and reflected the preferences of large northeastern bankers (Livingston, 1986). The Aldrich Plan embodied national centralization of reserves and private control. Its board of directors was to be comprised mainly of bankers and businessmen, with a handful of presidential appointees subject to removal by the member banks. Its currency was to be issued only on the basis of gold and short-term commercial paper. The more politically astute among the bankers and academic economists active in banking reform circles realized that a national central bank based on the European model had little chance of passage in the U.S. Congress. These reformers thus developed modified versions of the NMC plan which combined a decentralized reserve system with central coordination of note issue. Economist H. Parker Willis drafted such a plan for the conservative Virginian who chaired the House Banking Committee, Carter Glass (himself a sharp critic of the Aldrich scheme) (Link, 1956, pp. 199-240; Stephenson, 1971; West, 1977). Without an alternative of their own in the works, the more radical agrarians of the House and Senate, with the aid of Bryan in the Cabinet, now maneuvered to attack the Glass plan's obnoxious features and to graft on to it the essential elements of a periphery-molded bank reform. They broadened its definition of "assets" to include agricultural paper, provided for national bank loans based on farm property, lowered the gold backing for currency and—most significantly—imposed on the plan public control via a presidentially appointed board, and made the new federal reserve notes obligations of the national government rather than the individual banks. The agrarians were dissuaded from persistent attempts to incorporate a distinct farm credit system and a ban on interlocking bank directorates by an administration pledge to support such legislation later (the Clayton Act and the Federal Farm Loan Act of 1916 redeemed this pledge).

The agrarian revisions, together with the Glass bill's division of the new reserve system into 12 independent regional banks with pitifully low capitalization requirements made the congressional Democrats' reserve system extremely loathsome to the northeastern banking fraternity. The Federal Reserve Act was greeted, in 1913, with outraged abuse. *The New York Sun* blasted the revised bill as "the preposterous offspring of ignorance and unreason . . . covered all over with the slime of Bryanism,"[11] and core Republicans responded to it in the same vein (Link, 1956, p. 216). On final passage of the conference bill, core Republicans opposed it 4 to 1, while the majority of periphery Republicans broke away to join the Democrats in support. Whatever the function of the Federal Reserve System in later years, the Agrarians viewed it as a great triumph in 1913. It established public control over private finance, gathered up some of the enormous reserves "piled up in the city of New York and used to aid stock speculation" and distributed them "back to the different parts of the country from whence they came"; provided a new, government-backed, and elastic currency to meet the farm region's needs "during the seasons of the year when crops are moved"; and established the foundation for a great expansion of farm credit.[12]

Public Over Private Power

The Federal Reserve Act exemplifies a key trait of the progressive era agrarian agenda: their willingness to expand public power to an unprecedented degree in order to control the powerful forces of industrial capitalism to their own benefit—in short, to use their political power to compensate for economic weakness. Southern representatives, traditionally stereotyped as proponents of states' rights and limited national power, were actually in the forefront of agrarian-led state expansion. In debate over warehouse regulation, for example, southern Democrats like Representative A. F. Lever of South Carolina impatiently pushed aside Republican states' rights arguments with "general welfare" justifications. Lever professed, "when there is a great general good to be accomplished by legislation, I am not so squeamish about the Constitution" (Cong. Rec. 63-3, 475). When confronted by entrenched private monopoly in critical sectors of the economy, the agrarians did not hesitate to endorse public enterprise. Thus, during the shipping crisis inaugurated by the outbreak of European war, they supported not just rate and service regulation for maritime shipping, but also the creation of a government shipping corporation to build, charter, and operate an ocean fleet (the 1916 Shipping Act).

Latter-day populists like Senators Benjamin R. Tillman of South Carolina and Henry F. Ashurst of Arizona, along with North Carolinian Josephus Daniels in Wilson's Cabinet, led the fight for a government armor plate factory in order to deny the "steel trust" monopoly profits on Navy ships. After the armor plate manufacturers (Carnegie, Midvale, and Bethlehem) threatened to raise the plate price to an even more exorbitant level, public outrage speeded passage of the bill over powerful business opposition (Cronon, 1963, p. 126n; Link, 1964, pp. 335-336; Simkins, 1944, pp. 512-513; Urofsky, 1989, pp. 117-151).

Similarly, the agrarians secured passage of a provision creating a federal nitrate plant (ultimately sited in the Muscle Shoals area of northwest Alabama). Representative William C. Houston of Tennessee spoke for a large number of representatives when he argued that the bill:

> while safeguarding the water power of America from the grasp of monopoly, will provide such development of that power as will enable us to cheaply manufacture nitrate [for explosives]. . . . And it is not the less gratifying to me that in thus making provision for a great national military need we may at the same time . . . provide a larger and cheaper supply of fertilizer for the benefit of the farmers of our country. (Cong. Rec. 64-1, 7598)

In the face of such benefits, the agrarians were not daunted by cries of "socialism!" As Senator Robert L. Owen of Oklahoma reminded his colleagues, Congress had recently established an agricultural extension service, authorized government-owned railroads in Panama and Alaska, and spent millions on public works; besides, the government owned the post office. The term "socialism" could be applied to these and many other beneficial activities, Owen argued,

> They are all socialistic in one sense—they involve the use of the combined powers
> of the people for the common benefit of all the people. . . . and I want to say that,
> in my judgment, [this] is good, solid Democratic doctrine. (Cong. Rec. 64-1, 6031)

The opposition of core Republicans and almost half the core Democrats
defeated the nitrate bill in the House, but Owen and his fellow agrarians
restored the provision in the Senate, adding it to an army appropriations bill.
A New York Republican noted bitterly that the same people who had backed
the nitrate plant had opposed the raising of a continental army (Cong. Rec.
64-1, 7612), leaving the suspicion that they were far more interested in cheap
fertilizer and regional development than in munitions.[13] Indeed, it was the
periphery that furnished most of the opposition, in both parties, to Wilson's
preparedness efforts, for in one momentous sense, the agrarians were not
statists: far more than other sectors, they opposed war, standing armies, and
imperialism.[14]

The Channeling and
Containing of Agrarian Radicalism

To argue that the momentum for progressive era state expansion originated
with the farmers of the hinterland does not imply that the force of agrarian
grievances flowed unchecked into new legislation. Rather, that force was
blunted, channeled, and interpreted by powerful alternative agendas held by
congressional conservatives, diverse area progressives, the public service
intelligentsia, and President Wilson himself.

In Congress, conservative opposition emanated mainly from core Republicans, to a lesser extent from their tariff-dependent western allies and—
depending on the issue—from northern urban Democrats and a scattering of
southern Democrats from budding piedmont industrial regions. The legislative fruits of core elite statism—if core industrialists and financiers can be
said to have had a cohesive "statist vision"—were rather modest in the
progressive era. One might include here: (1) the highly consensual Pure Food
and Drug and Meat Inspection Acts of 1906, which limited "competition"
from small and unscrupulous food and drug firms, but also protected the
public (Wood, 1986, pp. 65-136); (2) the Federal Child Labor Acts favored
by manufacturers in northern states (who feared competition from the southern textile industry); (3) elements of the 1903-1906 railroad legislation that
outlawed rebates (an increasingly expensive practice); (4) legislation like the
1913 Newlands Act, also favored by labor, that created mechanisms for

voluntary mediation of railway labor disputes; and (5) support for foreign trade through commercial attachés and information services in the State and Commerce Departments (Becker, 1981). However, in the years following the remarkable 1897-1903 merger movement, the great corporations had little need for government services in rationalizing markets, limiting competition, improving exports, or repressing labor. What they wanted most from national government was negative—to be let alone to enjoy the power their remarkable market strength gave them. In this respect, big business realized its vision of the state with the aid of the courts, not Congress.

Pacific and midwestern progressives presented a very different problem for the agrarians. As representatives of diverse industrial/farm economies, they often took an intermediate position on regulatory issues between the opposing poles of core Republicans and periphery Democrats. They found the southern Democratic tariff policy, for example, far too crude and potentially destructive for the nation's industrial fabric. Yet they acknowledged that the rates demanded by core Republicans were too high. The solution was a "scientific tariff," constructed by a board of experts who would determine differential costs of production and set an ideal duty for each product traded. Core Republicans, faced with the sharp legislative reductions of the Wilson years, embraced the tariff commission idea and Wilson, looking for a moderate way to mitigate business hostility in an election year, endorsed a weak version in 1916.

A similar process took place on antitrust policy, as western and midwestern progressives, unhappy with the simple prohibitions and criminal penalties of the Clayton Act, championed the creation of an expert commission with discretionary power to discourage "unfair competition." Here, too, the progressives found an ally in the president who, as business conditions worsened, sought a more moderate antitrust policy. Farther back in regulatory history, midwestern Senate Republicans had promoted commission regulation of railroads, as against the southern-plains agrarian preference (dominant in the Democratic House in 1886) for specific prohibitions coupled with criminal penalties. The 1887 Interstate Commerce Act, like the 1914 antitrust policy, was a composite of the two approaches (Sanders, 1986a). The diverse regions produced advocates of autonomous commission regulation for a variety of reasons rooted in political economy. These areas of the upper midwest and Pacific coast contained significant farm populations agitated by the behavior of railroad, banking, and industrial monopolies. And yet, because their agricultural production found markets almost entirely within the continental U.S.—as did the products of their industries—voters and politicians here found their fate very much linked to that of domestic industry. Hence, they opposed free trade, divestiture of large enterprise, and overly punitive railroad legislation; and when such policies were proposed by periphery representatives, they sought compromises that would limit the worst abuses of industrial and financial capital without threatening its survival. Commission regulation was the ideal compromise. Further, the principles embodied in "strong commission" regulation (as distinct from weak, "business-government partnership" regulation) found much favor in the midwest and Pacific states. With large middle classes, strong state universities, and long-standing support for scientific agriculture, expertise was highly valued there. For political reasons, too, the insurgent Republicans from these regions could back institutions of neutral administrative competence, independent—as they themselves aspired to be—of control by capital, labor, or political party.

Finally, the progressive Republicans were nationalists, for reasons both of regional economics and political history. The tariff, the Panama Canal, the Alaska Railroad, benevolent control of the backward colonies wrested from Spain,[15] and a strong positive state to spur internal development and reconcile class and regional conflicts, were all aspects of the nationalist ideology proudly embraced by the insurgent progressives. The nonimperialist internationalism of the cotton and wheat regions, along with those regions' abhorrence for bureaucracy and dubious nationalism thus made any coalition of New Nationalist and New Freedom progressives a risky proposition. These regional divergences underlay Wilson's decision to govern on the traditional basis of party caucus rather than attempt to construct a bipartisan coalition of progressives. They also explain the rapid embitterment of the insurgents with the agrarian program of 1913-1914, and their willingness to join the Republican chorus that blamed that program for the business depression of 1914 and Wilson's "weak" response to international crisis in 1914-1916 (Holt, 1967, pp. 81-119; Leuchtenburg, 1952; Margulies, 1977, pp. 158-162).

The Farmer and the Bureaucratic State

The regulatory method preferred by the periphery was a legislatively determined set of specific prohibitions, accompanied by criminal penalties (as represented, for example, by the 1886 House-passed Interstate Commerce Act and the House version of the 1914 Clayton Act). Thus, it seems paradoxical that, given this antagonism to administrative discretion, bureaucracy itself was a powerful force blunting the radical edge of the agrarian interventionist program.

The Department of Agriculture presents a telling example of the role that well-positioned actors—even in a minimal state—could play, channeling extreme demands into the moderate, discretion-laden programs of an expanding bureaucratic state. Given the importance of agriculture in the U.S. economy and the historic militance of farmers, it is not surprising that the Department of Agriculture should be the most dynamic portion of the national state in the early 20th century. From an agency that had first endeared itself to the rural public by dispensing free seeds and animal husbandry tips, the Department encompassed, by the beginning of the progressive era, a reserve of expertise and administrative capability that put it in a position to harvest the fruits of the farmers' discontent as well as to respond to new middle-class concerns.[16]

The USDA's bureaucratic entrepreneurship was already clearly in evidence in the first decade of the 20th century when its officials lobbied for, and got, new regulatory responsibilities for forest conservation (1905), pure food and drugs (1906), meat inspection (1906), and additional export inspection and certification functions (1908) (Faulkner, 1951, pp. 350-351; Gaus & Wolcott, 1940, pp. 24-25). Before 1901, the Department (which had only obtained cabinet status in 1889) had only two bureaus. Between 1900 and 1906 it acquired the Forest Service from the Department of the Interior, created six new bureaus (including a Bureau of Statistics), and doubled its expenditures (from $2.9 to $5.8 million). By 1915, expenditures were $19 million (Wiest, 1923, pp. 34-35). By comparison, total federal outlays rose 43% in those 15 years; the USDA budget, 558%. In number of Washington employees, the USDA was, in 1917, the second largest department (after the Treasury) (U.S. Dept. of Commerce, 1975, p. 1224; U.S. Civil Service Commission, 1917, p. 213; Wiest, 1923, p. 35).

Wilson's Secretary of Agriculture, David F. Houston, played a pivotal role in charting new progressive missions for the Department. A Harvard-trained economist and former university president, Houston brought to the job the prototypical outlook of the progressive era intellectual: faith in the application of expert intelligence to social problems, and a thoroughgoing contempt for "Bryanism." When it appeared that cotton futures might be taxed out of existence in 1913, Houston quickly developed a proposal to regulate these transactions instead. Similarly, old populist schemes for a currency based on warehouse receipts were transformed into the moderate provisions of the Federal Reserve and Warehouse Acts. Additional farm credit legislation was initially opposed by the Secretary, but once it appeared inevitable (in the form of the Federal Farm Loan Act), he shrewdly offered to assist in its administration (Houston, 1926, pp. 37-38; Link, 1956, pp. 137-139). Over the opposition of the land-grant colleges, the Secretary intervened in 1914 to secure a large role for the USDA in planning and supervising the new extension work of the state land-grant colleges, and began the effective conversion of farm education services from a distributive adjunct of the state universities to a network of information and control for the federal government (Grantham, 1958, pp. 256-260; Houston, 1926, p. 302). The USDA also won jurisdiction over the Federal Highways Act and secured a role in the implementation of the Smith-Hughes vocational education act.

After Houston's departure, the Department he had reorganized and redirected continued to urge the agrarian impulse into more moderate regulatory channels. Thus, for example, congressional proposals for government acquisition and operation of stockyards were superseded by the regulatory approach of the Packers and Stockyards Act, and bills to abolish all speculation in grain futures were sidetracked by the Futures Trading and Grain Futures Acts.

The bureaucratization of periphery-generated regulatory initiatives made them less threatening to the core elite and won positive approval among the urban intelligentsia. Economists, who generally scorned any proposals for state intervention, finding economic concentration natural and business self-regulation adequate, were less resistant to USDA jurisdiction than, for example, to proposals for simply abolishing futures trading. (Cowing, 1965, pp. 47-58, 108) The agrarian representatives themselves, faced with overwhelming opposition to their schemes—and charges from academic experts that the old populist solutions would lay waste the modern marketing system on which the farmer's prosperity depended—yielded, without too much opposition, to the bureaucratic turn. The Department of Agriculture had been around for a long time, and had generally pleased the farmers. It was, at least, *their* bureaucracy (in a way the ICC, FTC, and Tariff Commission could never be).

The political force that ultimately persuaded the agrarian Democrats to accept these elements of the "New Nationalist" regulatory program was their party leader and president, Woodrow Wilson. In the first, critical year of the New Freedom, Wilson had put his incomparable prime-ministerial skills behind a program that was much more the making of the agrarian Democratic party than his own. He had served the party nobly on the Underwood Tariff, yielded to Bryan and the agrarians on the Federal Reserve Act, and, despite his own very weak record on labor and antitrust policy, seen them through to the enactment of the Clayton antitrust and labor rights program. However, as the recession took hold in 1914 and virulent business criticism poured in, the president "worked incessantly . . . to make it clear that he would tolerate no reckless assaults on business." (Link, 1956, pp. 34-36, 446-448). In this guise, the president signaled his unwillingness to support securities regulation (Link, 1956, p. 426n) and backed the weakening of the Clayton Act and its subordination to Federal Trade Commission.

The new attitude was particularly revealed in Wilson's conservative appointments to the new and existing regulatory commissions, which provoked bitter confrontations with his own party and progressive Republicans (Link, 1956, pp. 449-457). The president made another momentous shift after 1914, however; that shift supports the characterizations of Link and contemporary observers who discerned a subsequent Wilsonian tilt toward the New Nationalist agenda of the 1912 Progressive party.

Despite Wilson's overtures to business, the Democrats suffered heavy losses in the 1914 elections. As the mass of northern progressives returned to the Republican party and the recession and business outcry took their toll, congressional Democrats fell before GOP "tidal waves" in the northeastern industrial states, signaling, according to the *New York Times,* that the "country no longer took delight in heckling the corporations" or traveling "along the road toward radicalism" (November 4, 1914). As his own reelection approached in 1916, Wilson and his advisors resolved to pursue "independent" progressive voters (middle class, farm, and labor), particularly in the West and Midwest; the corollary was, in effect, to write off the Northeast (Baker, 1937, 262-263; Link, 1965, pp. 39-48, 108-109; Roseboom, 1957, 383-387). This political agenda yielded a new surge of legislation in 1916. Some of it—particularly the Tariff Commission, woman suffrage, and the Child Labor Act—either represented clear departures from the traditional Democratic platform and/or evoked significant opposition from southern Democrats, but it would be inaccurate to characterize the agrarian bloc as opposing Wilson's shift toward an "advanced progressive" program, in defense of a narrowly "pro-competitive" or "laissez faire" agrarian stance. In fact, the Democrats' endorsement of the social welfare planks of the 1912 Progressive Party platform was a strategy first recommended by Bryan ally Robert Owen of Oklahoma (Link, 1965, pp. 39-40, 108-109) and (with the exception of textile-state opposition to the child labor law), agrarian Democrats enthusiastically backed the labor legislation of 1916;[17] further, as I have argued, the agrarian agenda was far from narrowly conceived and had a strong "positive" cast. With regard to the farm credit program, as well as the government nitrates, highway, and armor plate undertakings, the agrarian congressional wing was the leader, and Wilson the follower. Thus the relationship between Wilson and the agrarian Democrats, while not without its tensions, was still a strongly cooperative one. The agrarians grumbled but did not rebel when Wilson initiated his rapprochement with business in 1914 and pulled the nation much farther along the road to war than they (or the agrarian Republicans) were willing to go. They really had no alternative. Victorious through a fluke of three-party politics in 1912, they knew very well that they must broaden their coalition or relinquish power in 1916. For this purpose they willingly swallowed tariff and trade commissions and other "advanced progressive" flourishes. At some points, the disparate goals of the president and congressional agrarians were simply fused in a single legislative package. Wilson grafted his plan for an expanded merchant marine onto an agrarian bill to regulate shipping in the 1916 Shipping Act; his Tariff Commission was fused with the radical agrarian Revenue Act of the same year; the FTC was made a companion measure to the Clayton Act; the nitrate and armor plate provisions were made components of the administration's military appropriation bills, and so on. Without the president's cooperation, the agrarians would have had scant hope of achieving their aims, and his reelection depended, above all, on the rural progressives of the South, West, and Plains.

That much was clear in the results of the 1916 elections. The Democrats narrowly hung on to control of Congress and the White House by holding the South and improving their margins in the Midwest and West. Despite the Democrats' strongest-ever delivery for labor, the Republicans scored a landslide in the great industrial cities and in the manufacturing belt generally (Link, 1965, pp. 156-164; Roseboom, 1957, pp. 387-388; also *New York Times,* November 8 and 10, 1916). The GOP won the core in the old-fashioned way: it scourged the Democrats for their position on the tariff, their "capitulation" to labor, their antibusiness stance, and their inadequate defense of the national interest. The great "outback" of the South, West, and Plains, rallied to the Democrats' progressive, pacifist statism in what was less a victory for new nationalism than the last hurrah of old populism.

Conclusion

For most historians, as for the insurgent Republicans themselves, the preeminent reformers and statists of the early 20th century were the urban intellectuals and midwestern diverse area Republicans who championed new discretionary bureaucracies to investigate, disseminate information on, and regulate vital aspects of the new industrial economy, from labor relations and industrial structure to food and drug purity. Against this grain, and in contradistinction to most variants of state theory, I have argued that the most numerous, cohesive and dynamic forces for political reform and state expansion emanated from the "Great Outback" of the United States: the South, Plains, and Rocky Mountain regions. Even after the defeat of populism and the southern agony of racist reaction and disfranchisement, the political economy of the periphery, combined with the exaggerated influence conferred on rural states by the American electoral system, continued to support a movement for expanded public power to deal with the complex socioeconomic disturbances of a maturing industrial economy.

Had urban labor been able to augment the agrarian forces with a cohesive voting bloc organized around a positive program of social reform, the American state would look very different today. The agrarians seized the opportunity provided by the disruption within Republican ranks in 1910-1916 to put through a large and varied program of benefit to the farmers of the periphery. They were quite willing, in seizing this moment, to give labor almost everything it wanted. The problem was that organized labor wanted so little from the state, and brought so little sustenance to the electoral coalition of reform forces. By the time (decades later) that labor finally found a commitment to the positive state and an ability to mobilize labor votes, creeping industrialization was submerging populism in the old agrarian regions. As the periphery began to undergo significant industrialization and capital accumulation, the old anticapitalist momentum faded (Sanders, 1986b).[18]

In the 1940s, the resurgence of a race-focused politics in the South further subdued the impetus to economic democracy in that region. The old states' rights doctrines were dusted off for new purposes and the hostility to distant and discretionary bureaucracy that had always marked the periphery took on new life. In the 1970s as well, national regulatory bureaucracy and expanded labor law would be seen as plainly hostile to periphery industrialization; in the 1980s an anti-statist momentum would yoke the old periphery and new capital in support for Reaganism. However, these recent developments should not obscure our understanding of the past. In the populist and progressive eras, the periphery was against bureaucracy, but certainly not anti-statist (except in its antimilitarist manifestation). The program often mislabeled as Reaganite "populism" today bears very little resemblance to the original.

Notes

1. Two recent works that highlight the role of the statist intelligentsia in American political development, although without explicit connections between class interests and state expansion,

are Skowronek (1982) and Tomlins (1985, especially pp. 148-243). See also Sanders (1982, 1986a).

2. Two other political developments should be mentioned here for their influence on agrarian reform politics. One was the development of the party primary election which, despite its instrumentality for maintaining white supremacy and one-party dominance, did permit poor white Southerners an enhanced influence within Democratic Party ranks. (See, e.g., Kirwan, 1951, Chap. 11.) A second development was the agrarian drive, successful by 1913, to amend the Constitution so that senators were elected by direct popular vote rather than by (as had been the case in earlier decades) business-bribed and dominated state legislators.

3. Of the 33 insurgent House Republicans ("insurgency" indicated by position in the "Cannon Revolt" of 1909-1910), only six represented districts in the industrial heartland, and these were not "policy" insurgents, but, as the evidence suggests, merely momentary rebels against Cannon's autocratic habits. The policy-oriented insurgents (as measured by their stands on railroad, tariff, labor, and antitrust policies) came overwhelmingly from the corn and wheat sections of the midwest.

4. Roll call tables have been omitted in the interests of brevity. More complete empirical support for the reported party and regional patterns will be provided in Sanders, forthcoming.

5. Consider the House vote, in 1910, to concur in Senate strengthening amendments to the Mann-Elkins Bill (*Congressional Record,* 61-2, 7577). Core representatives (of whom 80% were Republicans) voted 18 yea to 81 nay (periphery representatives, 112-39). On the 1913 House vote to abolish the Commerce Court (*Congressional Record,* 63-1, 4620), core Republicans abstained in large numbers, acknowledging inevitability. Those who voted opposed abolition by more than 6 to 1, while periphery representatives (of both parties) supported abolition by a 3 to 1 margin.

6. On the history of the anti-speculation movement and its sectional underpinnings, see Cowing (1965). Something of the agrarian animus against the New York Cotton Exchange can be gleaned from the charge made by a Farmer's Union spokesman that the NYCE has "dictated the price of cotton for almost 40 years . . . and held the South in political slavery, and will not, if possible, permit the Southern farmer anything more than a bare living" (quoted in Saloutos, 1960, p. 200).

7. *Congressional Record,* 63-2, 12581. The two ayes were Democrats supporting the agrarian-defined party position.

8. Wiebe (1962, pp. 128-129) argues that "the usual mass of special pleaders" descended upon Washington to fight reductions. Disappointed in their efforts, "the dissatisfied industrialists exploded, yet the opposition lacked depth."

9. It must also be remembered that the tariff was the linchpin in the Republican coalition, linking western wool and sugar producers to the dominant manufacturing centers. To oppose protection would risk breaking those bonds and facilitating prolonged dominance of the national polity by a party perceived as dangerously radical. Further, as Hilferding (1981, pp. 311-314) has argued, protection of domestic markets yields extraordinary profits for large corporations, enhances control of competition, and subsidizes export penetration abroad.

10. From tables inserted in the *Congressional Record,* 64-1, 10742-43, by Representative Mann of Illinois. On the politics of the income tax in the populist and progressive eras, see King (1983).

11. See also the criticism of Vanderlip, Aldrich, and Hill in the *New York Times,* Oct. 31, 1913, p. 1. Wiebe, while acknowledging the intransigent opposition of Wall Street, nevertheless contends in *Businessmen and Reform,* pp. 123-137, that a majority of businessmen must have been "conciliationists." However, the enthusiasm he finds for the Democratic reserve bill

appears to have been largely confined to country bankers and small businessmen in the South and Midwest. Link (1956, p. 224) argues that "a minority of bankers, mainly in the South and Middle West, favored the Federal Reserve bill either outright or with minor amendments."

12. From remarks by insurgent Representative Lenroot of Wisconsin, *Congressional Record*, 63-2, 1442. Contrast the angry charge of Senator Root of New York that "this bill presents the financial heresy twice repudiated by the people of the United States. . . ." *Ibid.*, 835; this, despite Kolko's implication (1963, p. 244) that Root supported the Democratic bill. The New York senator consistently opposed the Federal Reserve Act, both in debate and on roll calls.

13. The combination of the weak Army bill and the government nitrate plant left leaders of the preparedness movement—mostly Republicans—"sick at heart," notes Link (1964, pp. 329-332).

14. For sectional divisions on imperialism, see Bensel (1984, pp. 88-103). On opposition to World War I, and support for Philippine independence, see Link (1964, Chapters 2-7, 11) and Bensel (1984, pp. 105-208). The periphery-backed Clarke Amendment for Philippine independence was ultimately defeated by the opposition of Wilson, the Catholic Church, and congressional Republicans; a more limited Philippine autonomy bill was passed in 1916.

15. On support for imperialism among progressive Republicans, see Leuchtenburg (1952).

16. On the significance of this capacity for the New Deal, see Theda Skocpol and Kenneth Finegold (1982).

17. The periphery provided the bulk of support for the Adamson Act of 1916 (limiting working hours of railroad labor) as well as for the Clayton, Seamen's, and Child Labor Acts and for ending Justice Department prosecutions of labor under the Sherman Act. At the end of the 64th Congress a union man sat in the cabinet as Secretary of Labor and the AFL credited the New Freedom congresses with 37 pro-labor bills (Karson, 1965, p. 85).

18. The decisive southern break with the agrarian tradition did not come until the 1940s. Most southern representatives were loyal New Dealers in the 1930s, and the periphery regions pushed the administration to the left (toward more radical state intervention) in several policy areas (Sanders, 1982).

11

The Relative Decline of Relative Autonomy

Global Capitalism and the Political Economy of State Change

ROBERT J. S. ROSS

The social relations of capitalism are in transition from monopoly capitalism to a new variant, global capitalism (Ross & Trachte, 1990). This transformation can be discerned in the three strategic relations within capitalism: those between capital and labor, between competing capitals, and in the relation between capital and the state.

The emergence of the global variant of modern capitalism underlies the common threads of political change in North America and Western Europe over the last 15 years. Among the political changes this analysis seeks to explain are the "conservative" trend, restraints on the social wage, and the renewed dependence on market initiatives in these nations. This transition produces changes in state policy in the older industrial states, and these express a decline in the relative autonomy of the state.

Strategic Relations of Capitalism in Monopoly and Global Capitalism

The transformations of capitalism are presented here as they are manifested in the three strategic social relations of capitalism.

Capital-to-Labor

The conflict (latent or manifest) between workers and their employers is the central engine which drives capitalist societies through history. The most *direct* dimension of this relationship is the wage relation, which is the easiest to quantify but not the only dimension of this conflict.

Employers engage laborers in order to make use of their ability to work—their "labor power." The problem for the employer is to make maximum use of this ability, and usually, to pay the least for it. This imperative leads employers to craft strategies for controlling and disciplining labor.

The forms of class conflict, the sites of class struggle, and the nature of class organization vary in the course of capitalist development (Wright, 1978). The forms of class struggle are a crucible which tests a given variant of capitalism in comparison to others. A form of capitalist organization which proves superior in managing class struggle will obtain critical advantages in competition with other forms of enterprise. As this form becomes dominant in a social formation, a new variant, or submode of capitalism can be identified.

In each variant of capitalism the structure of power rests on a distinctive leverage, *a lever of exploitation,* whereby capital is able to enforce its ability to extract surplus from workers.

Capital-to-Capital

The second relationship is that which obtains between separate firms, proprietors, and industrial or financial blocs each of which is subject to a unitary source of control. Firms and blocs compete for inputs (e.g., raw materials or credit), in extracting value (crudely, labor costs), and for markets. These are impersonal processes which take place between aggregates of capital. The signals which catalyze the competitive behavior of firms are profits measured in monetary terms.

Individuals of the capitalist class, especially at its commanding heights, may have personally cordial relations facilitated by all sorts of social institutions—clubs, balls, colloquia, and associations (Domhoff, 1967, 1970, 1974). Cartels or price-fixing conspiracies may come and go. Political coalitions may unite the interests of a variety of capitals in common cause. Yet, these are still the cautious dances of scorpions at the alert. Whatever the form, the fundamental relation of private aggregations of capital is competitive. As against labor there may be important elements of unity; in the marketplace, more usually, an impersonal competitive necessity drives the behavior of individual firms.

Capital-to-[the] State

The capitalist state regulates the conditions which reproduce capitalism and the ability of the capitalist class to maintain its dominant position. As that institution with a monopoly of legitimate violence, the state is the "final" expression of power relations within its territory and within the global structure of power. Amidst the particularities of nation-states at similar levels of capitalist development there are strong comparative similarities side by side with the endless variety of historical experience.

Across the history of capitalist development the relative ability of classes and class fractions to obtain state policies which implement their interests also varies. To say that the capitalist class is politically dominant in capitalist societies may be true, but it is not adequately specific. In this analysis "dominance" is highly relative.

From the perspective of the investor, the relative balance of class forces as expressed in public policies has a spatial dimension. Within nations and between them, jurisdictions appear as a mosaic of differential conditions, some more and others less propitious for a given type of activity. Policy profiles are an important dimension of this national and international mosaic.[1]

The Capital-to-Labor Relation
Under Global Capitalism

As new variants of capitalism emerge and become dominant the mechanisms of extraction available to capital in its struggles with workers change. In the competitive era the presence of a reserve army of labor provided the lever that capital needed to discipline labor. Under monopoly capitalism the principal lever of exploitation was the bifurcation of the working class into two relatively distinct segments: those engaged in the monopoly and competitive sectors. In turn, for the dominant monopoly firms this translated into two primary strategies for maximizing rates of capital accumulation: unequal exchange with competitive sector firms and monopoly pricing.

The social regime of monopoly capitalism included the unionization of labor in basic industries. Monopoly pricing power allowed employers to accept unions, despite resistance, and to accommodate their wage and benefit demands by passing on their costs to consumers and suppliers. A new stratum of consumers was created: "middle income" workers whose wage allowed them to purchase the output of mass production industry. This has been termed the regime of "intensive accumulation" or Fordism (Aglietta, 1979, p. 381; Lipietz, 1982).

The gains of labor in the well-organized, especially monopoly sector firms became problematic in two distinct ways. There is some evidence that compensation outdistanced productivity in the late 1960s (Aglietta, 1979; Arrighi, 1978; Mandel, 1978, 1980). This depressed average rates of profit in manufacturing, and was particularly evident in some sectors, such as steel and auto production. The stagflation of the 1970s was part of the result. Another result was the pursuit of locations for production which cut labor costs or pursued local policy advantages.

The successes of workers in the industrial nations, and within them, in their older industrial regions, also made their employers vulnerable to challengers who could bring the same (or more up-to-date) products to the market with less costly labor embodied in them.

Both these forces—internal stagnation and external challenge—evoked a new axis of competition in the 1970s, a spatial axis: labor from some areas was cheaper than that of others (Storper & Walker, 1983, 1984). The result is global competition which erodes monopoly pricing power. Now enterprises in globally competitive markets control cost factors with particular attention to direct labor costs.

The organization of production relations characteristic of monopoly sectors is not usually propitious for the control of direct labor costs. A new lever for reducing the bargaining power of labor is required. The use or threatened use of capital mobility becomes the primary lever of exploitation in sectors where the global variant emerges as dominant. Monopoly sector and other firms become global by locating parts of their production processes in regions where low-wage and/or politically repressed working classes are located. This lowers labor costs, and indirectly the *threat* of further relocations provides the leverage needed to extract concessions from the work force still employed at older production sites.

The increased bargaining power of employers reinforces existing tendencies to replace living labor with machines. Now the employer argues that "survival" of the firm, of *some* jobs, requires the sacrifice of others. Labor is forced to relinquish many of its prerogatives (e.g., work rules) and is forced to accede to technological change.

By altering the relative balance of power between capital and organized labor, global capital mobility undermines the ability of monopoly sector workers to defend the relative material well-being gained during the era of monopoly capitalism. At the workplace this takes such forms as job loss, decline of real wages, and a loss of control over work rules (Ross & Trachte, 1990). In the sphere of reproduction, deteriorating housing and health conditions are among the losses suffered by those workers most vulnerable to offshore competition (Ross & Trachte, 1983).

The Capital-to-Capital Relation
Under Global Capitalism

Compared to the competitive era of capitalism, monopoly capitalism saw the emergence of giant firms, the end of price competition in many industrial sectors, and the stabilization of market shares. Production was relatively concentrated within the space of national economies.

Under global capitalism giant firms of different national origins compete aggressively for shares of a global market in many different national markets. Price competition frequently returns and erodes monopoly pricing power. Market shares of older firms become vulnerable, some firms fail, mergers become numerous, and new strategies for accumulation are implemented.

A variety of factors account for the intensified competition of the global era. Some of these are conjunctural and others can be derived from the basic dynamics of the capitalism. The conjunctural factors include the reconstruction of European and Japanese economies after World War II; the development of new information technologies; the maturation of specific products and markets (making their production more routinized, thus exportable to formerly nonindustrial sites); and the emergence of more nationalist regimes in the Third World (Evans, 1979; Frobel, Heinrich, & Kreye, 1980; Rowthorn, 1971; Vernon, 1971, pp. 66-77). The more systemic processes will be discussed below.

The characteristic organization of global capitalism is the MNC—the multinational corporation—or the global firm. Often such firms are not only global, producing and selling in many nations, they are also conglomerates— they unite under a singular authority divisions and subsidiaries producing disparate commodities or services. The global conglomerate is a design for survival under the competitive conditions of the new era. Its ability to "scan" the globe for investment possibilities makes possible rational assignment of resources, and ruthless pursuit of the exact combination of local policies, labor conditions, transport considerations, and so forth, for production of any given commodity or part.

The global firm and the conglomerate are well-adapted to conditions of class struggle on a world scale. "Multisourcing" for example, allows a firm to avoid the consequences of labor difficulties at any one site. Conglomeration, for another example, prevents labor organized in a given industrial sector from jeopardizing the profit flow of a highly diversified corporate structure. The consequence of both is to insulate the employer from labor's power and organization, and to increase the employer's bargaining power.

The Capital-to-State Relation
Under Global Capitalism

During the monopoly era the state's regulatory role expanded. Elements of this role implied devoting increasing shares of the state budget to the assumption of the social (i.e., legitimation) costs of accumulation (O'Connor, 1973). Included among these were additions to the social wage. The expansion of these forms of state expenditure depended politically upon an uneasy accord between monopoly capital and monopoly labor.

Although monopoly capital exercised relative domination over the state, the expansion of government expenditures also reflected a relative increment in the capacity of monopoly sector labor to influence state policy. The price of social stability was the cost of legitimation expenses. With the global firm becoming dominant, however, the threat of capital mobility (i.e., job loss) provides capital with a more direct method of disciplining labor. Under the competitive pressures of global capitalism, capital, particularly its global fraction, finds state regulation less acceptable and social expenditures designed to maintain the social peace less necessary.

With enhanced ability to move production to regions where state policies may be more favorable to capital, global capital is in a position to demand changes in state policy. The ability of the state to accommodate the demands of labor declines as a consequence of the internationalization of production.

As global capital finds itself more able to discipline labor, such firms find the behavior of their competitors less disciplined. Faced with competition from global firms of different national origins, national fractions of capital prevail upon their home states to restrain regulations, cut taxes, and allocate more public funds toward subsidizing their production costs. The threat to relocate production to alternative investment sites is utilized as a lever to convince state officials to enact (or repeal) legislation (Goodman, 1979; Harrison & Kantor, 1978). In short, while under monopoly capitalism the state was relatively autonomous from the immediate enterprise-based interests and political power of capital, under global capitalism, this autonomy declines.

The Transition to Global Capitalism

The monopoly variant of capitalism was dominant through the 1960s, and throughout the advanced capitalist countries. But the constellation of forces were not static. Two kinds of forces disrupted the stability of this moment.

Inherent contradictions of capitalist accumulation appeared in new forms; and new entrants to world capitalism's competitive system forced change in the political behavior of the older oligopolists.

The crises of the 1970s and 1980s were not of the apocalyptic "breakdown" nature which Marxist theory long anticipated. Rather, the recent period has been one of "restructuring" (Frank, 1987). Just as the crises of the late 19th century witnessed the emergence of monopoly capitalism out of the shell of competitive capitalism, so this era is one in which global capitalism succeeds monopoly capitalism.

A Crisis of Restructuring

Marxist have proclaimed and conservatives have warned that the contradictions of capitalism will produce its ultimate breakdown. Three general types of crisis tendencies have been emphasized in political economy: "rising organic composition," "class struggle," and "realization crisis."

Evidently, however, the obstacles to capital accumulation, the manifestation of crisis tendencies, may result in changed relations *within* capitalism, that is, restructuring, rather than extinction. This essay does not "choose" which among the venerable tendencies is "fundamental" or "decisive" in the current restructuring process. Rather, it asserts that *any* one (or combination) of the proposed obstacles to accumulation could plausibly produce a "global" solution in the medium run.

The Organic Composition of Capital and the Tendency of the Rate of Profit to Fall

Most simply, the organic composition of capital can be thought of as the ratio of the value of machines to human labor in the economic unit, the ratio of dead labor (constant capital, c) to living labor (variable capital—wages—plus surplus value, v and s) in production.[2] A rise in the organic composition of capital then means an increase in the ratio ($c/v + s$).

Graham, and Gibson and colleagues, have performed a number of technical studies which indicate that on a sector-by-sector basis, since 1958, the U.S. industries most likely to internationalize were those in which the rise in organic composition of capital was appearing to drive falling rates of profit. (Gibson, Graham, Horvath, & Shakow, 1986; J. Graham, 1983). The link from this finding to the transition to global capitalism is as follows:

(1) $s/c + v$ (the rate of profit) tends to decline because c (constant capital) increases relative to v.

(2) Increases in s/v (the rate of surplus value, or the "rate of exploitation") can compensate for this decline by depressing v—wages.

(3) This strategy has but limited use in the older regions where labor retains some bargaining resources, some political influence, and where the historical level of reproduction of labor power (i.e., the material conditions of workers) is high.

(4) By performing substantial fractions of the production process in low or "lower" wage sites of production—where the rate of exploitation is higher—the rate of surplus value is buffered. Thus, production capital flows from the older core to the newly industrializing countries, and to the "semiperiphery" of the core itself (e.g., Ireland, Greece, Spain).

(5) The threat and reality of the above strategy erodes the very bargaining power of the labor it was meant to evade. The rate of wage gains in the older regions erodes.

Class Struggle and the Rate of Profit

Class struggle theories of capitalist crisis are those which emphasize the obstacles to accumulation caused by workers' ability to raise their share of national income. Such success would similarly produce a flow of capital away from political economic jurisdictions where labor is strong, towards those in which it was weak, or in which the combination of discipline and state policy kept its costs low (e.g., those socialist and former socialist countries courting foreign investment for export production). This flow depends on the uneven development across political space of working class organization and class struggle. While the rising organic composition theory and class struggle are often depicted as mutually exclusive, elements of the "class struggle" analysis are behaviorally and conceptually compatible with organic composition theories, as follows:

Capitalists in the older industrial regions replace living labor with dead labor. This occurs because living labor has become more costly or less disciplined, from the perspective of the firm, than the alternative machine. Despite this tendency the economic bargaining power of monopoly sector workers in the older industrial regions remains relatively high. Their political influence in some states and regions supplements this bargaining power through increases in the social wage and other regulations which favor working-class interests. Faced with this *relative* balance of class power, monopoly sector firms seek out means for employing alternative, lower cost, less powerful reserves of labor. The relative shift in the balance of class forces characteristic of monopoly capitalism in the older regions then creates a dynamic that also propels the restructuring of capitalist *production* on a *global* basis.

Realization Failure: Overproduction/Underconsumption

The last of the crisis tendencies which could plausibly lead to global transition is that of realization failure—insufficient demand in the mature economies, leading to a dearth of acceptably profitable investment opportunities. This is linked to the historic tendency for capital to become more concentrated. Firms within industrial sectors of a given national economy in the older regions become fewer in number and larger in size. Their immense capital plants afford them economies of scale; but that same size requires very large production runs to reach a break-even point. Thus, concentration of capital *permits,* and surplus productive capacities *compels* firms to penetrate one another's markets. They embark upon a course of fierce competition for markets located in newer regions. This competition impels each capital to search for cost advantages over their rivals. Labor costs are obvious candidates.

The immense reserve of low-wage workers in less industrialized areas offers itself as an attractive source of competitive advantage. At the same time it offers new investment opportunities, markets, for capital goods. When one firm brings to the world market a commodity produced with contemporary technology and with a substantial fraction of low-wage labor in it, the others are forced to follow. The concentration of capital, a dynamic inherent to the capitalist mode of production, thus produces global diffusion of manufacturing facilities.

In sum, the transition to global capitalism is the plausible result of each of the proposed crisis tendencies of capitalism.

The Historical Basis of Relative Autonomy of the State

The emergence of global capitalism restructures the relationship of relative antonomy which characterized the state in the era of monopoly capitalism.

State autonomy had material and ideological sources. One source was the need for capitalists to compose their differences—at least enough to face the political efforts of labor successfully, and to guide state activity toward acceptable ends. This produced state activity which was, in a general sense "pro-business," but which was justified in terms of its "consensual," "public interest" nature.

Another source of relative independence of state policy under monopoly capitalism was the ability of labor and consumers and other democratic forces to win legislative benefits and small bridgeheads of bureaucratic influence (e.g., Labor Departments which, in practice, were the voice of organized labor in both conservative and liberal administrations).

Yet another source of state autonomy was the need to cloak the actions of state policy in terms which reflected its alleged democratic nature. The democratic form of the political process does, indeed, make possible the benefits that labor and other noncapitalist forces are able to obtain. In the monopoly era, state expenditures for the poor and regulations and programs for the working class served to justify those other aspects of state policy which made capital accumulation possible.

The particularities of state-society relations which were depicted by structuralism as producing a "relatively autonomous" state in the 1950s and 1960s were the result of the strategic situation characteristic of "monopoly capitalism." The regime of monopoly capitalism required management of the tensions inherent in a system in which actual dominance was exercised by monopolistic firms and the class fractions which controlled them, within a social formation in which "individual, free enterprise" and entrepreneurial character was lionized. These tensions, with but few exceptions, have been a neglected feature of discussions of legitimation in the advanced capitalist countries.[3] Yet they have been central to the 20th-century history of the political right in every country of the West. The "autonomy" of state managers to impose sometimes unpopular policies on the capitalist class has rested on either the ability of large-scale capital to prevail over competitive capital (Kolko, 1963), or the ability of finance capital (e.g., through central banks) to impose its regulatory preferences over all others.

The upheaval of the 1930s and the Second World War produced pressures on large-scale capital which impelled its concessions to the Welfare State. Leading these pressures was the de facto enfranchisement of labor. Indeed, the ideological legitimation of the Western system became much more complex in the post-Popular Front/New Deal era: both small-scale capital *and* labor had to be governed. By midcentury, to take but one indicator, the most politically sensitive economic indicator in the West was the unemployment rate.

New variants of capitalism will have uneven effects on the political power of classes and class fractions. While the transition from competitive to monopoly capitalism yielded the economic enfranchisement of organized labor, concentrated in the monopoly sector, a stratified or "segmented" labor force yielded a far from privileged secondary labor market and its concomitant—a marginal proletariat sometimes characterized as "underclass" (Gordon, Edwards, & Reich, 1982). Within the capitalist class, large firms with concentrated market power were usually able to mold state policy to their advantage.

So the transition to monopoly capitalism entailed, in the long run, an increase in the political influence of organized labor in the advanced industrial nations, and a relative decrease in the influence of small-scale and competitive capital. Competitive sector capital, and especially small firms, did not acquiesce to this regime. In a price-competitive environment, without the ability of larger firms to pass on the costs of labor legislation, taxation, or regulatory burdens, competitive industries and small firms opposed the social policies and regulatory environment of monopoly capitalism. But the trend was toward concentration of capital, and the apparent marginalization of the national political influence of such forces.

Thus, under monopoly capitalism, the state was relatively autonomous from the momentary interests and direct political intervention of particular fractions of capital.

But autonomy from the more "conservative" preferences of competitive capital was a function, in large part, of the relative dominance of monopoly capital within the capitalist class, and the relative ability, in turn, of monopoly capital to make concessions to labor. Labor's enfranchisement was both the predicate and the motivation for these concessions.

It should be recalled that the concept of "the relative autonomy of the state" denoted relative autonomy of state behavior from:

(1)   the transient will of fractions of the capitalist class; and
(2)   the direct intervention or influence of incumbency by capitalist class personnel
       (Kasinitz, 1983; Miliband, 1973; Poulantzas, 1973, 1975).

As Ralph Miliband put it "while the state does act . . . *on behalf* of the 'ruling class,' it does not for the most part act *at its behest*" (emphasis in original; Miliband, 1977, p. 74). "Autonomy" implied discretion for decision makers. The zone of discretion produced state policy which, under the conditions of monopoly capitalism appeared to be "imposed" on various fractions of capital.

The "test" of the first of these assertions were those instances where "enlightened" capitalist class leadership implemented or tolerated policies rejected by that class's numerical majority: for example, many "progressive era" and New Deal reforms in America, and a variety of social and industrial policies in Western Europe.

The test of the second assertion—the independence of state policy from the biographies of official incumbents—has been the relative continuity of state policies when governments have been formed by social democratic and labor parties, while Cabinets have been recruited from outside the ranks of corporate leadership.

In addition to these two widely accepted aspects of relative autonomy, this analysis includes a third:

(3) relative autonomy also entailed discretionary power of state managers to accommodate some of the needs/demands of labor in the political system.

Global Capitalism and Change in the Capitalist State

The assertion that we now live in an era of transition to a new variant of capitalism is manifest in the following propositions:

(1) American and European economic hegemony is in retreat.
(2) Price competition appears on a global scale, including a vital component in which differential labor costs in different geopolitical regions is central to world market competition.
(3) Working-class levels of living in the formerly rich countries are stagnant or declining.
(4) Rather than a segmented labor force and monopolisitic pricing as the chief lever of surplus extraction, the threat and reality of capital mobility on a global scale is the major lever by which capital extracts favorable labor and political terms.

None of these observations/propositions is consistent with the older model derived from the theory of monopoly capitalism.

From the perspective of the global firm the regions of the world form a mosaic of differentiated sites of potential investment to which the policy output of national states or subnational bodies of government are important contributors. Part of this political environment is state policy in regard to industrial relations, policies, and laws which mediate the capital-to-labor relation. No longer held hostage to unique local agglomerations of infrastructure and labor, global capital can now threaten to withdraw investment from localities or nation-states whose governments adopt policies relatively favorable to labor. Global capital and its local allies are in a strategic position which allows them to demand the repeal or rollback of programs adopted during the monopoly era but which global capital no longer regards as necessary.

With vastly expanded choice for investment sites, capital's need to propitiate labor politically, and to cloak its actions ideologically has declined: *the fear of want pacifies discontent where the charade of compassion once sufficed.*

What is changed under global capitalism are political goals and mechanisms: equality drops away and markets are elevated as preferred agencies for achieving "public interests."

This view of contemporary capitalism results in a thesis distinguished from both recent extensions of structuralism, and from the "orthodox" criticism of that work (Berberoglu, 1981; Block, 1977, 1980; Poulantzas, 1975). In particular, we reject the proposition that relative autonomy *declined* under monopoly capitalism. Rather, this analysis asserts, it does decline under global capitalism. The emergence of global capitalism shifts the balance of class forces toward capital, and the result is decline in the relative autonomy of the state from transient capitalist class will and ideology.

Scientific study of the state entails a response to the fundamental questions of "why, how, and with what effect states change." The concept of "relative autonomy" implies that if autonomy is not absolute, it may vary. Variation implies a historical dimension. The question of autonomy is historically specific (Mills, 1959, p. 149).

At the most general level, the implication of this analysis is that important changes in the state will occur when underlying class relations are transformed.[4]

In theoretical terms, therefore, among the sources of change in states is structural transformation of a mode of production from one characteristic and dominant *variant* to another. The analysis of state change "descends" to a level more specific than the mode of production in general (e.g., "capitalism") and examines change among its historical variants.

Within capitalism, state change will eventually result from obstacles to accumulation, through the medium of restructuring. Though "crisis" theory has come in and out of respectability in both Marxist and non-Marxist theory,[5] it has focused, as previously noted, on a "breakdown" problematic (i.e., the analysis of those dynamics within capitalism which will or might produce its historical termination as a mode of production).

But capitalism has survived its crises through structural change which preserves its general characteristics. These have been "restructuring" crises which are the midwives of transition to new variants of capitalism. State policy and political processes become responsive to newly dominant class fractions—or new bases of unity among them.

Under global capitalism political structures rest upon a new dimension of political unity within the capitalist class. This political unity, not so paradoxically, is formed in the face of a new dimension of competition—price competition based on a global search for appropriate, but low-wage labor.

The global scale of this competition grants and compels new strategic resources in capital's demands on state policy. The threat and practice of *global mobility of capital* disciplines both labor and state decision makers, who lose discretionary power over some major matters—taxation, social policy, entitlements—lest investment decline within their areas of jurisdiction. Capital prevails over labor more frequently and more nakedly in the political realm.

The political stability of monopoly capitalism depended in part on state activity which meliorated the condition of the poor. The expenses of these activities both facilitated accumulation (by buffering aggregate demand) and legitimated the system by promoting social peace through welfarist policy and ideology (O'Connor, 1973, pp. 1-12). These programs also bolstered the bargaining power and potential militancy of workers in general, for the consequences of striking or changing one's employment were buffered by the variety of income maintenance and social transfer programs (Piven & Cloward, 1982).

As monopoly capitalism gives way to global capitalism, all sectors of labor decline in bargaining power, in social potency, and political influence. Social expenditures give way to market coercion as the mode of enforcing discipline. The threat of penury rather than the promise of social justice maintains order.

Workers (and others) support market-oriented regimes through a blend of motives. Without relinquishing their preferences for welfarist policies, they nevertheless are persuaded in some degree and previously unusual numbers, that conservative regimes can best attract the golden goose of investment which lays the egg of jobs (i.e., maintain a healthy "business climate").

The articulation of capitalist-class interests with the state also changes in the transition from one submode to another. At the turn of the century finance and monopoly capital began the construction of an institutional relation to state power which supplanted the personalistic advantages enjoyed by the entrepreneurial founders of family fortunes (Useem, 1984). The institutional order which prevailed by mid-century throughout the capitalist West afforded special access and favorable policy for the monopoly sector.

Now, spurred by competition in the search for low-wage labor, and constrained by access to finance, large-scale capital becomes global. Politically, however, the project of producing abroad has a domestic face of coalition with competitive sector conservatives in an assault on the social wage, and on the discretionary state expenditures of the state. Capitalist class unity is reforged around resistance to the organizational and policy demands of labor. Combined, these changes can be grossly summarized as:

(1) a relative increase in the power of investors and employers in relation to labor; and

(2) the increasingly transparent shift from legitimation activities to those state activities which attempt to facilitate capital accumulation.

With labor in decline, and capital struggling to cope with changes in its competitive environment, state managers have less "space" to take actions which meet either the long-term needs of the social formation, or the demands of labor. The autonomy of the state declines in relation to the period in which national oligopolies were the dominant form of enterprise.

The Theoretical Basis of the Theory of Global Capitalism and State Change

Does the theory of the transition from monopoly to global capitalism denote a theory of state change dependent on the simple equation of apparently crude Marxism: change in base = change in superstructure? The answer is *not* quite as simple as the question.

(1) Yes: when fundamental aspects of the strategic relations of capitalism change, class-to-state relations change also.

(2) However, these are not the *only* sources of state change.

National revolutions, and war which has often preceded revolution, are entwined with the interstate system. The particularities of national transformations embody complex determinations and specific political histories. That is, there are *other* sources of state change as well.

(3) The state is both actor in, and recipient of, the changes which produce global capitalism. State policy is a vital component of the determinants of capital mobility on an international scale. The relative attractiveness of different jurisdictions, from the perspective of production capital, is quite important to investment and therefore growth. In this sense, state policy, "superstructure,"

contributes to the determination of other production relations. This contribution is not unidimensional (i.e., favorable or unfavorable to labor). For example, state policy may encourage industry and labor to locate advantageous market niches, or technological strategies, which allow a locality to preserve levels of living, or augment them, without draconian policies toward labor. This depends on endowments of human and social resource, the strength and creativity of labor in the political realm, the relative position of a formation's level of reproduction of labor in the world system, and so forth.

(4) Returning to the most general level, and the first point, the transition from monopoly to global capitalism is not merely conjunctural. The systemic properties of capitalism lead to barriers to accumulation. State policy either facilitates or obstructs accumulation, or some combination, but the determinant process is capital accumulation. In this particular sense the theory of global capitalism is a return to orthodoxy. Whether this relation is specific to this moment in capitalist development remains to be seen; when all the world's labor has been absorbed into the capitalist process, when there is nowhere left to hide from organized labor and the state environment it helps to mold, then the dynamics of change may indeed be different.

Relative Autonomy: An Alternative View

The decline of relative autonomy is not a consensual inference from the facts of the current era. In his essay on the politics of economic decline in the U.S. and the U.K., for example, Krieger (1986, Chap. 7) reaches the *opposite* conclusion. Krieger claims that the "management" of decline in both the U.S. and the U.K., seen here as an aspect of restructuring on a world scale, resulted in *dirigiste* regimes in both nations. But his theoretical reflection on the *increase* of relative autonomy rests on his focus on macroeconomic pain rather than microeconomic lust.

Krieger notes that at various moments financial or industrial elites in both the U.K. and the U.S. articulated clear opposition to Reagan and Thatcher policies (J. Krieger, 1986, pp. 33, 162-167). His conclusion is that both regimes developed unusually high degrees of autonomy from capitalist-class interventions. This conclusion rests upon a misunderstanding of the concept of relative autonomy, and the nature of the changes in the current global system.

Consider the American case. Krieger reports the financial community's early and articulate concerns about the massive deficits caused by Reaganomics. He argues that the Reagan Administration's ability to continue its reckless fiscal course indicates its "autonomy" from capitalist-class intervention.

Krieger's analysis of autonomy neglects the distinction between the financial community's interest in macroeconomic aggregates, and the capitalist class's interest in prevalence over labor. However "voodoo" the Reagan Administration's fiscal policies—it's gutting of the NLRB, of OSHA, the erosion of the social wage, the massive redistribution to upper-income groups through the Tax Act of 1981—these policies, and others, were what Krieger calls "policy plums" which "justifiably delighted" business elites who received "administration favors" to a "wide set of capitalist interests" (J. Krieger, 1986, pp. 161, 162). This indicates exactly the decline of autonomy from a "transient" will of the capitalist class (which welcomed these policies). The idea of relative autonomy was, centrally, autonomy of the state to act, in Miliband's words, on behalf of the capitalist class, rather than at its behest. What the Reagan administration did in its first term was to act at the behest of the common program of anti-labor small-scale capital and the internationally pressured large-scale capital. This program of rollback of social democratic tendencies has been called an attack on the social wage (Bluestone & Harrison, 1982; Piven & Cloward, 1982).

Krieger may be right that the Reagan program was not in some putative long-run interest of the capitalist class, in the sense that it sows the seeds of future instability, inflation, and so forth. But the idea of relative autonomy is one in which just such long-range interests may be imposed on the temporary will of a class whose political problem is often the contradiction between firms and individuals, on one hand, and long-term class interests. Despite the apparently irresponsible fiscal impact of Reagan policy, the consensus of business support for him contrasts sharply with the desertion among large-scale elites that Goldwater faced in 1964.[6] The difference is not to be found in the policies advocated by the two political figures: it was, rather, the structural imperatives, experienced at the level of the firm, 20 years later. In this sense, then, Krieger's comments about elites' concern over the Reagan program are the exception that proves (i.e., tests) the proposition about the decline of relative autonomy. The Reagan government was more sensitive to the transient microeconomic needs of capital in the global era, than it was to the macroeconomic views of financial managers. The reason, from the point of view of our theory is clear: macroeconomic wisdom is abstract; but political unity in the Republican party was forged around the common program long held by small-scale capital, but newly held by global capital: the concessions to big labor, in the global context were no longer desirable or necessary.

Conclusion and Reprise

Global capitalism is succeeding monopoly capitalism as the dominant form of modern capitalism on a world scale. This change underlies the conservative swing in the democracies of the older industrial nations, and in theoretical terms, brings about a change in the relation of state to society. The relative autonomy of the state from the transient will of the capitalist class declines, and other classes experience a decline in their political influence. Not discussed, but still an open question, are the implications of this transformation for the men and women who sell their labor, and hope to raise their children in a world of decency and civility.

Notes

1. It should be noted that the label "capital-to-state," because it always implies a relation of relative, not pure, dominance, is *simultaneously* a substantive discussion of a "labor-to-state" relation as well.

2. This expression is adopted from Wright (1978, p. 126). As he notes this is not the traditional definition of the organic composition of capital, which has been to express it as the ratio of constant capital to variable capital. This change in definition reflects the view of a number of recent authors that the ratio c/v is not an adequate measure of capital intensity; they have substituted the ratio $c/v + s$.

3. A major exception is Edward Greer's (1979) study of Gary, Indiana—once a major location of the U.S. Steel Corporation. Greer found that the corporation and the local petite bourgeoisie were in historic alliance, and from the founding of the city, the junior partner's interests were a matter of both planning and compromise by the corporation.

4. There are two caveats: first, while such underlying changes are *sufficient,* they may not be *necessary*. There are other sources of state change. Second, changes in the form, process, and policy outputs of states clearly *lag* changes in underlying class relations.

5. Theories of capitalism's "breakdown" tendencies are hardly restricted to Marxism. Schumpeter's classic *Capitalism, Socialism, and Democracy* (1976) is an obvious example.

6. In 1964, Henry Ford III led a corporate fund-raising effort for Lyndon Johnson in the campaign against Goldwater.

References

Abbott, G. (1935). Mothers' Aid. *Social Work Yearbook 1935* (pp. 282-285).

Abbott, G. (1937). Mothers' Aid. *Social Work Yearbook 1937* (pp. 284-288).

Abraham, D. (1981). *The collapse of the Weimar Republic: Political economy and crisis.* Princeton, NJ: Princeton University Press.

Aglietta, M. (1979). *A theory of capitalist regulation: The U.S. experience.* London: New Left Books.

Alford, R., & Friedland, R. (1985). *Powers of theory: Capitalism, the state, and democracy.* New York: Cambridge University Press.

Amsden, A. H. (1979). Taiwan's economic history: A case of etatism and a challenge to dependency theory. *Modern China, 5* 341-380.

Amsden, A. H. (1985). The state and Taiwan's economic development. In P. Evans, D. Rueschemeyer & T. Skocpol (Eds.), *Bringing the state back in* (pp. 78-106). New York: Cambridge University Press.

Anderson, L. (1987). The state in the Middle East and North Africa. *Comparative Politics, 20*(1), 1-18.

Anderson, P. (1974). *Lineages of the absolute state.* London: New Left Books.

Anene, J. C. (1966). *Southern Nigeria in transition: 1885-1906.* Cambridge, UK: Cambridge University Press.

Arrighi, G. (1978). Towards a theory of capitalist crisis. *New Left Review, 3,* 3-24.

Aubin, H. (1966). Medieval agrarian society in its prime: The lands east of the Elbe and German colonization eastwards. In M. M. Postan (Ed.), *Cambridge economic history of Europe, 1: Agrarian life of the Middle Ages* (2nd ed.). Cambridge, UK: Cambridge University Press.

Azarya, V., & Chazan, N. (1987). Disengagement from the state in Africa: Reflections on the experience of Ghana and Guinea. *Comparative Studies in Society and History, 29*(1), 106-131.

Badie, B., & Birnbaum, P. (1983). *The sociology of the state.* Chicago: University of Chicago Press.

Badie, B., Ulderstate, P., & Brown, M. K. (1981). *Working the streets.* New York: Russell Sage Foundation.

Baker, R. S. (1937). *Woodrow Wilson VI: Facing war 1915-1917.* Garden City, NY: Doubleday, Doran.

Balbus, I. (1971). The concept of interest in pluralist and Marxist analysis. *Politics and Society, 1*(2).

Baldwin, R., & Kinsey, R. (1982). *Police powers and politics.* London: Quartet Books.

Baran, P. A. (1957). *The political economy of growth*. New York: Monthly Review Press.

Baran P., & Sweezy, P. (1966). *Monopoly capital*. New York: Monthly Review Press.

Barrett, R. E., & Whyte, M. K. (1982). Dependency theory and Taiwan: Analysis of a deviant case. *American Journal of Sociology, 87,* 1064-1089.

Bates, R. H. (1982). *Markets and states in tropical Africa*. Berkeley: University of California Press.

Bayley, D. H. (1979). Police function, structure and control in Western Europe and North America: Comparative and historical studies. In N. Morris & M. Tonry (Eds.), *Crime and justice* (vol. 1, pp. 109-143). Chicago: University of Chicago Press.

Bayley, D. H. (1985a). *Patterns of policing: A comparative international analysis*. New Brunswick, NJ: Rutgers University Press.

Bayley, D. H. (1985b). *Social control and poltical change* (Research Monograph No. 49). Center for International Studies, Woodrow Wilson School of Public and International Affairs. Princeton, NJ: Princeton University.

Becker, W. H. (1982). *The dynamics of business-government relations: Industry and exports 1893-1921*. Chicago: University of Chicago Press.

Behrens, B. (1977). Government and society. In E. E. Rich & C. H. Wilson (Eds.), *Cambridge economic history of Europe, 5: The economic organization of early modern Europe*. Cambridge, UK: Cambridge University Press.

Beirne, P. (1979). Empiricism and the critique of Marxism on law. *Social Problems, 26,* 375-385.

Bell, D. (1973). *The coming of post-industrial society*. New York: Basic Books.

Benjamin, R., & Duvall, R. (1985). The capitalist state in context. In R. Benjamin & S. Elkin (Eds.), *The democratic state*. Lawrence: University of Kansas Press.

Bennett, D. C., & Sharpe, K. (1985). *Transnational corporations versus the state*. Princeton, NJ: Princeton University Press.

Bensel, R. (1984). *Sectionalism and American political development*. Madison: University of Wisconsin Press.

Bentley, A. (1935). *The process of government*. Evanston, IL: Principia Press.

Berberoglu, B. (1981). The capitalist state: Its "relative autonomy" reexamined. *New Political Science, 2,* 135-140.

Berger, S. D. (Ed.). (1981). *Organizing interests in Western Europe*. Cambridge, UK: Cambridge University Press.

Bittner, E. (1980). *The functions of the police in modern society*. Cambridge, UK: Oegleschlater, Gunn & Hain.

Black, D. (1971). The social organization of arrest. *Stanford Law Review, 23,* 1087-1111.

Blackbourn, D., & Eley, G. (1984). *The peculiarities of German history: Bourgeois society and politics in nineteenth-century Germany*. Oxford, UK: Oxford University Press.

Blau, P. (1987). Contrasting theoretical perspectives. In J. C. Alexander et al. (Eds.), *The micro-macro link* (p. 83). Berkeley: University of California Press.

Bloch, M. (1961). *Feudal society* (2 vols). Chicago: University of Chicago Press.

Bloch, M. (1966a). *French rural history: An essay on its basic characteristics*. Berkeley: University of California Press.

Bloch, M. (1966b). The rise of dependent cultivation and seigniorial institutions. In M. M. Postan (Ed.), *Cambridge economic history of Europe, 1: Agrarian life of the Middle Ages*. Cambridge, UK: Cambridge University Press.

Block, F. (1977). The ruling class does not rule: Notes on the Marxist theory of the state. *Socialist Review, 33*(May-June), 6-28.

Block, F. (1980). Beyond relative autonomy: State managers as historical subjects. *Socialist Register*, 227-243.

Block, F. (1987). *Revising state theory*. Philadelphia: Temple University Press.

Bluestone, B., & Harrison, B. (1982). *The deindustrialization of America*. New York: Basic Books.

Blum, J. (1957). The rise of serfdom in Eastern Europe. *American Historical Review, 62*, 4.

Bowles, S., & Gintis, H. (1986). *Democracy and capitalism: Property, community, and the contradictions of modern social thought*. New York: Basic Books.

Bracher, K. D. (1970). *The German dictatorship: The origins, structure and effects of national socialism*. New York: Praeger.

Brenner, R. (1976). Agrarian class structure and economic development in pre-industrial Europe. *Past and Present, 70*.

Bright, C., & Harding, S. (1984). Processes of statemaking and popular protest. In C. Bright & S. Harding (Eds.), *Statemaking and social movements* (pp. 1-15). Ann Arbor: University of Michigan Press.

Brodeur, J. (1983). High policing and low policing: Remarks about the policing of political activities. *Social Problems, 30*(5), 507-520.

Brogden, M. (1982). *The police: Autonomy and consent*. New York: Academic Press.

Brown, J. C. (1940). *Public relief, 1919-1939*. New York: Henry Holt.

Brown, M. K. (1981). *Working the streets*. New York: Russell Sage Foundation.

Buchanan, J., & Tullock, G. (1962). *The calculus of consent*. Ann Arbor: University of Michigan Press.

Buck, S. J. (1913). *The granger movement*. Cambridge, MA: Harvard University Press.

Buenker, J. (1978). *Urban liberalism and progressive reform*. New York: Norton.

Bunyan, T. (1976). *The political police in Britain*. New York: St. Martin's.

Bureau of Public Assistance. (1941). *Aid to Dependent Children: A study in six states* (Public Assistance Report No. 2). Division of Administrative Surveys, U.S. Bureau of Public Assistance, Social Security Board, Federal Security Agency.

Burton, A. (1966). Treasury control and colonial policy in the late nineteenth century. *Public Administration, 44*.

Callaghy, T. M. (1984). *The state society struggle: Zaire in comparative perspective*. New York: Columbia University Press.

Caplan, J. (1977). Theories of fascism: Nicos Poulantzas as historian. *History Workshop, 3*(Spring), 83-100.

Carnoy, M. (1984). *The state and political theory*. Princeton, NJ: Princeton University Press.

Carsten, F. L. (1954). *Origins of Prussia*. Oxford, UK: Clarendon.

Carter, H. M., & Marenin, O. (1981). Law enforcement and political change in post civil war Nigeria. *Journal of Criminal Justice, 9*(2), 125-149.

Cash, W. J. (1941). *The mind of the South*. Garden City, NY: Doubleday, Anchor.

Chan, S. (1987). Growth with equity: A test of Olson's theory for the Asian Pacific-Rim countries. *Journal of Peace Research, 24*, 133-149.

Chan, S. (1988). Developing strength from weakness: The state in Taiwan. *Journal of Developing Societies, 4*, 38-51.

Charney, C. (1987). Political power and social class in the neo-colonial African state. *Review of African Political Economy, 38*, 48-65.

Chazan, N. (1988). Patterns of state-society incorporation in the neo-colonial African state. In D. Rothchild & N. Chazan (Eds.), *The precarious balance: State and society in Africa* (pp. 121-148). Boulder, CO: Westview.

Chazan, N. (1988). *Politics and society in contemporary Africa.* Boulder, CO: Lynne Rienner.

Chilcote, R. H. (1981). *Theories of comparative politics.* Boulder, CO: Westview.

Choucri, N. & North, R. C. (1975). *Nations in conflict: National growth and international conflict.* San Francisco: Freeman.

Clapham, C. (1985). *Third world politics.* Madison: University of Wisconsin Press.

Clark, C. (1987). The Taiwan exception: Implications for contending political economy paradigms. *International Studies Quarterly, 31,* 327-356.

Clark, G. L., & Dear, M. (1984). *State apparatus.* Boston: Allen & Unwin.

Clark, W. W. (1943). *An appraisal of ADC in Illinois.* Springfield, IL: State Department of Public Welfare.

Clarke, S. (1985). State, class struggle and the reproduction of capital. *Kapitalistate, 10-11,* 113-130.

Cohen, G. A. (1978). *Karl Marx's theory of history: A defense.* Princeton, NJ: Princeton University Press.

Coleman, D. C. (1956). Labour in the English economy of the seventeenth century. *Economic History Review,* [2nd series] *8,* 3. In E. M. Carus-Wilson (Ed.), *Essays in economic history* (Vol. 2). (1962). London: Edward Arnold.

Coleman, D. C. (1977). *The economy of England, 1450-1750.* Oxford, UK: Oxford University Press.

Coleman J. S. (1960). *Nigeria: Backgrond to nationalism.* Berkeley: University of California Press.

Committee on Economic Security. (1937). *Social security in America: The factual background of the Social Security Act as summarized from staff reports to the Committee on Economic Security.* Social Security Board. Washington, DC: Government Printing Office.

Connolly, W. (1983). *The terms of political discourse* (2nd ed.). Princeton, NJ: Princeton University Press.

Conway, J. (Trans.). (1966). *The path to dictatorship: 1918-1933.* New York: Anchor.

Cordner, G., & Girvan, R. (1988). *Police administration in popular culture.* Paper presented at the meeting of the Academy of Criminal Justice Sciences Conference, San Francisco.

Council for Economic Planning and Development. (1987). *Taiwan statistical data book.* Taipei: Author.

Cowing, C. B. (1965). *Populists, plungers and progressives: A social history of stock and commidity speculation 1890-1936.* Princeton, NJ: Princeton University Press.

Crane, G. T. (1982). The Taiwanese ascent: System, state, and movement in the world economy. In E. Friedman (Ed.), *Ascent and decline in the world system* (pp. 93-113). Beverly Hills, CA: Sage.

Cronon, E. D. (Ed.). (1963). *The cabinet diaries of Josephus Daniels.* Lincoln: University of Nebraska Press.

Cumings, B. (1984). The origins and development of the Northeast Asian political economy: Industrial sectors, product cycles, and political consequences. *International Organization, 38,* 1-40.

Dahl, R. (1956). *A preface to democratic theory.* Ann Arbor: University of Michigan Press.

Dahl, R. (1961). *Who governs?* New Haven, CT: Yale University Press.

Dahl, R. (1985). *A preface to economic democracy.* Berkeley: University of California Press.

Dahl, R. A., & Lindblom, C. (1953). *Politics, economics, and welfare.* New York: Harper & Row.

Dahrendorf, R. (1959). *Class and class conflict in industrial society.* Stanford, CA: Stanford University Press.

Dahrendorf, R. (1979). *Society and democracy in Germany.* New York: Norton.

Dancey, M. H. (1939). Mothers' pensions and the Aid to Dependent Children program in Michigan. *Social Service Review, 3*(4), 634-651.

Danns, G. K. (1982). *Domination and power in Guyana.* New Brunswick, NJ: Transaction Books.

Davis, D. S. (1984). The production of crime policies. *Crime and Social Justice, 20,* 121-137.

Davis, R. (1966). The rise of protection in England, 1689-1786. *Economic History Review, 19,* 2 (2nd series).

Deist, W. (1981). *The Wehrmacht and German rearmament.* London: Macmillan.

Derthick, M. (1970). *The influence of federal grants: Public assistance in Massachusetts.* Cambridge, MA: Harvard University Press.

Dike, K. O. (1956). *Trade and politics in the Niger Delta: 1830-1885.* London: Oxford University Press.

Dobb, M. (1946). *Studies in the development of capitalism.* London: Routledge & Kegan Paul.

Dobb, M. (1963). *Studies in the development of capitalism.* New York: International Publishers.

Domhoff, G. W. (1974). *The bohemian grove and other retreats.* New York: Harper & Row.

Domhoff, G. W. (1970). *The higher circles.* New York: Random House.

Domhoff, G. W. (1967). *Who rules America?* Englewood Cliffs, NJ: Prentice-Hall.

Douglas, M., & Isherwood, B. (1979). *The world of goods.* New York: Norton.

Downs, A. (1957). *An economic theory of democracy.* New York: Harper & Row.

Dresang, D. L. (1975). *The Zambia civil service: Entrepreneurialism and development administration.* Nairobi: East African Publishing House.

Duby, G. (1968). *Rural economy and country life in the medieval west.* London: Edward Arnold.

Duby, G. (1974). *The early growth of the European economy.* Ithaca, NY: Cornell University Press.

Duvall, R. D., & Freeman, J. R. (1983). The techno-bureaucratic elite and the entrepreneurial state in dependent development. *American Political Science Review, 77,* 569-587.

Duvall, R. D., & Freeman, J. R. (1981). The state and dependent capitalism. *International Studies Quarterly, 25,* 99-118.

Easton, D., & Dennis, J. (1969). *Children in the political system: The origins of legitimacy.* New York: McGraw-Hill.

Eckstein, D. (1979). On the "science" of the state. In S. R. Graubard (Ed.), *The state* (pp. 1-20). New York: Norton.

Ehrenberg, R. (1922). *Das Zeitalter der Fugger: Geldkapital und Creditverkehr im 16. Jahrhundert* (3rd ed.). Jena: Gustav Fischer.

Eley, G. (1983). What produces fascism: Preindustrial traditions or a crisis of a capitalist state? *Politics and Society, 12*(1)

Engels, F. (1884). The origin of the family, private property and the state. In K. Marx & F. Engels, *Selected works in one volume.* New York: International Publishers.

Engels, F. (1888). Ludwig Feuerbach and the end of classical German philosophy. In Engels, F. (1890a). Letter to Joseph Bloch, September 21-22. In K. Marx & F. Engels, *Selected correspondence.* Moscow: Progress Publishers.

Engels, F. (1890b). Letter to Conrad Schmidt, October 27. In K. Marx & F. Engels, *Selected correspondence.* Moscow: Progress Publishers.

Engels, F. (1962). Uber den Verfall des Feudalismus und das Aufkommen der Bourgeoisie. In K. Marx & F. Engels, *Werke* (Vol. 21). Berlin: Dietz.

Engels, F. (1972). *The origin of the family, private property, and the state.* New York: International Publishers.

Ergas, Zaki (Ed.). (1987). *The African state in transition*. New York: St. Martin's.

Ericson, R. V. (1982). *Reproducing order: A study of police patrol work*. Toronto: University of Toronto Press.

Esping-Andersen, G. (1985). *Politics against markets*. Princeton, NJ: Princeton University Press.

Evans, P. B. (1979). *Dependent development: The alliance of multinational, state, and local capital in Brazil*. Princeton, NJ: Princeton University Press.

Evans, P., Rueschemeyer, D., & Skocpol, T. (Eds.). (1985). *Bringing the state back in*. Cambridge, UK: Cambridge University Press.

Faulkner, H. U. (1951). *The decline of laissez-faire 1897-1917*. White Plains, NY: Sharpe.

Ferrero, G. (1944). *Macht*. Berne: Verlag A. Francke A. G.

Final report of the WPA program, 1935-1943. (1946). Washington, DC: Government Printing Office.

Fiorina, M. P. (1981). *Retrospective voting in american national elections*. New Haven, CT: Yale University Press.

Fisher, F. J. (1940). Commercial trends and policy in sixteenth-century England. *Economic History Review, 10*(2). In E. M. Carus-Wilson (Ed.), *Essays in economic history* (Vol. 1). London: Edward Arnold, 1954.

Flint, J. E. (1960). *Sir George Goldie and the making of modern Nigeria*. London: Oxford University Press.

Flint, J. E. (1974). *Cecil Rhodes*. Boston: Little, Brown.

Fogelson, R. M. (1977). *Big city police*. Cambridge, MA: Harvard University Press.

Foucault, M. (1979). *Discipline and punish*. New York: Vintage.

Frank, A. G. (1987). Global crisis and transformation. In R. Peet (Ed.), *International capitalism and industrial restructuring: A critical analysis* (pp. 293-312). Boston: Allen & Unwin.

Frobel, F., Heinrich, J., & Kreye, O. (1980). *The new international division of labor: Structural unemployment in industrialized countries and industrialization in developing countries*. Cambridge, UK: Cambridge University Press.

Galenson, W. (Ed.). (1979). *Economic growth and structural change in Taiwan: The postwar experience of the Republic of China*. Ithaca, NY: Cornell University Press.

Gallagher, J., & Robinson, R. (1953). The imperialism of free trade. *Economic History Review* [2nd series], *6*, 1.

Gann, L. H. (1964). *A history of Northern Rhodesia: Early days to 1953*. London: Chatto & Windus.

Ganshof, F. L., & Verhulst, A. (1966). Medieval agrarian society in its prime: France, the low countries, and Western Germany. In M. M. Postan (Ed.), *Cambridge economic history of Europe, 1: Agrarian life of the Middle Ages* (2nd ed.). Cambridge, UK: Cambridge University Press.

Gaus, J. M., & Wolcott, L. O. (1940). *Public administration and the United States Department of Agriculture*. Chicago: Public Administration Service.

Gerschenkron, A. (1943). *Bread and democracy in Germany*. Berkeley: University of California Press.

Gerth, H., & Mills, C. W. (Eds.). (1946). *From Max Weber*. New York: Oxford University Press.

Geyer, M. (1987). The Nazi state reconsidered. In Richard Bessel (Ed.), *Life in the Third Reich*. New York: Oxford University Press.

Gibson, K. D., Graham, J., Horvath, R., & Skakow, D. (1986). *Toward a Marxist empirics*. Unpublished manuscript.

Gibson, K., Graham, J., Shakow, D., & Ross, R. (1984). A theoretical approach to capital and labor restructuring. In Phil O'Keefe (Ed.), *Regional restructuring under advanced capitalism*. London: Croom Helm.

Giddens, A. (1971). *Capitalism and modern social theory*. Cambridge, UK: Cambridge University Press.

Giddens, A. (1984). *The construction of society: Outline of the theory of structuration*. Berkeley: University of California Press.

Giddens, A., & Gaventa, J. (1980). *Power and powerlessness: Quiescence and rebellion in an Appalachian Valley*. Urbana: University of Illinois Press.

Glamann, K. (1974). European trade 1500-1750. In C. M. Cipolla (Ed.), *The Fontana economic history of Europe, 2: The sixteenth and seventeenth centuries*. London: Collins/Fontana.

Gleizal, J. J. (1981). Police, law, and security in France: Questions of method and political strategy. *International Journal of the Sociology of Law, 9*, 361-382.

Glick, F. A. (1940). *The Illinois Emergency Relief Commission: A study of administrative and financial aspects of emergency relief* (Social Service Monograph No. 45). Chicago: University of Chicago Press.

Gold, D. A., Lo, C. Y., & Wright, E. O. (1975). Recent developments in Marxist theories of the capitalist state. *Monthly Review, 27*(5), 29-43.

Gold, T. B. (1986). *State and society in the Taiwan miracle*. Armonk, NY: Sharpe.

Goldstein, H. (1977). *Policing a free society*. Cambridge, MA: Ballinger.

Goodman, R. (1979). *The last entrepreneurs*. New York: Simon & Schuster.

Goodwyn, L. (1978). *The populist moment*. Oxford, UK: Oxford University Press.

Gordon, D., Edwards, R., & Reich, M. (1982). *Segmented work, divided workers*. New York: Cambridge University Press.

Gordon, S. (1984). *Hitler, Germans, and the "Jewish question."* Princeton, NJ: Princeton University Press.

Gottdiener, M. (1987). *The decline of urban politics: Political theory and the crisis of the local state*. Newbury Park, CA: Sage.

Gottdiener, M., & Feagin, J. (1988). The paradigm shift in urban sociology. *Urban Affairs Quarterly, 24*(2), 163-187.

Gottdiener, M., & Komninos, N. (Eds.). (1989). *Crisis theory and capitalist development: Accumulation, regulation and spatial restructuring*. London: Macmillan.

Goubert, P. (1956). The French peasantry of the seventeenth century: A regional example. *Past and Present, 10*.

Gourevitch, P. (1986). *Politics in hard times*. Ithaca, NY: Cornell University Press.

Graham, J. (1983). *Economic restructuring in the United States, 1958-1980: Theory, method and identification*. Unpublished doctoral dissertation, Clark University, Worcester, MA.

Graham, L. (1980). Centralization and decentralization dilemmas in the administration of public services. *International Review of Administrative Sciences, 3*.

Gramsci, A. (1957). *The modern prince and other writings*. New York: International Publishers.

Gramsci, A. (1971). *Selections from the prison notebooks* (Q. Hoare & G. N. Smith, Eds. & Trans.). New York: International Publishers.

Grantham, D. (1958). *Hoke Smith*. Baton Rouge: Louisiana University Press.

Greenberg, E. S. (1985). *Capitalism and the American political ideal*. Armonk, NY.: Sharpe.

Greenberg, E. S. (1986). *The political effects of workplace democracy*. Ithaca, NY: Cornell University Press.

Greenberg, E., & Page, B. (1988, May). *Why the state does what it does: A nested model*. Paper presented at the conference on state change, University of Colorado, Boulder.

Greer, E. (1979). *Big steel: Black politics and corporate power in Gary, Indiana*. New York: Monthly Review Press.

Gulalp, H. (1987). Capital accumulation, classes and the relative autonomy of the state. *Science and Society, 51*(3), 287-313.

Habermas, J. (1975). *Legitimation crisis*. Boston: Beacon.

Hackney, S. (1969). *Populism to progressiveism in Alabama*. Princeton, NJ: Princeton University Press.

Haggard, S., & Moon, C. I. (1983). The South Korean state in the international economy: Liberal, dependent, or mercantile? In J. G. Ruggie (Ed.), *The antinomies of interdependence: National welfare and the international division of labor* (pp. 131-189). New York: Columbia University Press.

Hamilton, C. (1983). Capitalist industrialisation in East Asia's four little tigers. *Journal of Contemporary Asia, 1,* 35-73.

Hamilton, N. (1982). *The limits of state autonomy: Post-revolutionary Mexico.*

Hamilton, R. (1982). *Who voted for Hitler*. Princeton, NJ: Princeton University Press.

Hargreaves, J. D. (1963). *Prelude to the partition of West Africa*. London: Macmillan.

Hargreaves, J. D. (1974). *West Africa partitioned. Vol. I: The loaded pause, 1885-1889*. London: Macmillan.

Hargreaves, J. D. (1985). *West Africa partitioned. Vol. II: The elephant and the grass*. London: Macmillan.

Harring, S. (1977). Class conflict and the enforcement of the Tramp Act in Buffalo during the depression of 1893-1894. *Law and Society Review, 11,* 873-911.

Harring, S. (1981). The Taylorization of police work: Prospects for the 1980s. *Insurgent Sociologist, 10,* 4; *11,* 1, 25-32.

Harring, S. (1983). *Policing a class society: the experience of American cities*. New Brunswick, NJ: Rutgers University Press.

Harrington, T. (1983). Explaining state policy making: A critique of some recent dualist models. *International Journal of Urban and Regional Research, 7*(2), 202-217.

Harrison, B., & Kantor, S. (1978). The political economy of states' job-creation business incentives. *Journal of the American Institute of Planners, 44*(October), 424-435.

Heaton, H. (1937). Heckscher on mercantilism. *Journal of Political Economy, 45*(3).

Hechler, K. W. (1940). *Insurgency: Personalities and politics of the Taft era*. New York: Columbia University Press.

Heckscher, E. F. (1955). *Mercantilism* (2nd ed.; E. F. Soderlund, Ed.). London: Allen & Unwin.

Heclo, H. (1974). *Modern social politics in Britain and Sweden*. New Haven, CT: Yale University Press.

Heclo, H. (1978). Issue networks and the executive establishment. In A. King (Ed.), *The new American political system*. Washington, DC: American Enterprise Institute.

Helgerson, J. L. (1971). *Institutional adaptation to rapid political change: A study of the legislature in Zambia from 1959 to 1969*. Doctoral dissertation, Duke University.

Heussler, R. (1968). *The British in Northern Nigeria*. London: Oxford University Press.

Hilferding, R. (1981). *Finance capital*. London: Routledge & Kegan Paul.

Hill, C. (1961). *The century of revolution, 1603-1714*. New York: Norton.

Hilton, R. (1978). A crisis of feudalism. *Past and Present, 80.*

Hinich, M. J. (1984). *The spatial theory of voting*. New York: Cambridge University Press.

Hirsch, J. (1973). Elemente einer materialistischen Staatstheorie. In C. von Braunmuhl et al., *Probleme einer materialistischen Staatstheorie*. Frankfurt am Main: Suhrkamp.

Hirsch, J. (1974). *Staatsapparat und Reproduktion des Kapitals*. Frankfurt am Main: Suhrkamp.

Ho, P. T. (1962). *The ladder to success in Imperial China: Aspects of social mobility, 1368-1911*. New York: Columbia University Press.

Ho, S. P. S. (1978). *Economic development in Taiwan, 1860-1970*. New Haven, CT: Yale University Press.

Hobsbawm, E. J. (1954). The general crisis of the European economy in the 17th century. *Past and Present, 5,* 6.

Hochstedler, E. (1981). Testing types: A review and test of police types. *Journal of Criminal Justice, 9,* 451-466.

Hoey, J. (1937). Some administrative problems in state assistance programs. *Public Welfare News, 10,* 2-5.

Holloway, J., & Picciotto, S. (Eds.). (1979). *State and capital*. Austin: University of Texas Press.

Holt, J. (1967). *Congressional insurgents and the party system*. Cambridge, MA: Harvard University Press.

Holt, R. T., & Turner, J. E. (1966). *The political basis of economic development: An explanation in comparative political analysis*. Princeton, NJ: Van Nostrand.

Hoogenboom, A., & Hoogenboom, O. (1976). *A history of the ICC*. New York: Norton.

Höpfner, H. (1983). *Deutsche Sudosteuropapolitik in der Weinarer Republik*. Frankfurt am Main: Bern.

Horvat, B. (1982). *The political economy of socialism: A Marxist social theory*. Armonk, NY: Sharpe.

Houston, D. F. (1926). *Eight years with Wilson's cabinet* (Vol. 1). Garden City, NY: Doubleday.

Hsiung, J. E. (Ed.). (1981). *Contemporary Republic of China: The Taiwan experience, 1950-1980*. New York: Praeger.

Huang, C. (1989). The state and foreign investment: The case of Taiwan and Singapore. *Comparative Political Studies, 22,* 93-121.

Humphries, D., & Greenberg, D. (1981). The dialectics of crime control. In D. Greenberg (Ed.), *Crime and capitalism* (pp. 209-254). Palo Alto, CA: Mayfield.

Jacoby, N. H. (1966). *U.S. aid to Taiwan: A study of foreign aid, self-help, and development*. New York: Praeger.

Jakubs, D. L. (1977). Police violence in times of political tension: The case of Brazil, 1968-1971. In D. H. Bayley (Ed.), *Police and society*. Beverly Hills, CA: Sage.

Jessop, B. (1978). Capitalism and democracy: The best possible shell? In G. Littlejohn et al. (Eds.), *Power and the state*. London: Croom Helm.

Jessop, B. (1982). *The Capitalist state: Marxist theories and methods*. New York: New York University Press.

Johnson, C. (1981). Introduction—The Taiwan model. In J. C. Hsiung (Ed.), *Contemporary Republic of China: The Taiwan experience, 1950-1980* (pp. 9-18). New York: Praeger.

Jones, L. E. (1972). "The dying middle": Weimar Germany and the fragmentation of bourgeois policies. *Central European History, 5*(1).

Kalecki, M. (1971). *Selected essays on the dynamics of the capitalist economy: 1933-1970*. Cambridge, UK: Cambridge University Press.

Kamen, H. (1971). *The iron century: Social change in Europe, 1550-1660*. New York: Praeger.

Karson, M. (1965). *Labor unions and politics*. Boston: Beacon.

Kasinitz, P. (1983). Neo-Marxist views of the state. *Dissent, 30*(Summer), 337-346.

Katzenstein, P. (1978). Introduction: Domestic and international forces and strategies of foreign economic policy. In P. Katzenstein (Ed.), *Between power and plenty*. Madison: University of Winconsin Press.

Katznelson, I. (1985). Working class formation and the state. In P. Evans, C. Rueschemeyer, & T. Skocpol (Eds.), *Bringing the state back in*. Cambridge, UK: Cambridge University Press.

Kautsky, K. (1966). *die Agrarfrage: Eine Uebersicht uber die Tendenzen der modernen Landwirtschaft und die Agrarpolitik der Sozialdemokratie*. Hanover: J. H. W. Dietz Nachf.

Keohane, R. O. (1983). Associative American development, 1776-1860: Economic growth and political disintegration. In J. G. Ruggie (Ed.), *The antinomies of interdependence: National welfare and the international division of labor* (pp. 43-90). New York: Columbia University Press.

Key, V. O., Jr. (1937). *The administration of federal grants to states*. Chicago: Public Administration Service.

Kieve, R. A. (1983). The Hegelian inversion: On the possibility of a Marxist dialectic. *Science and Society, 47*, 1.

Kieve, R. A. (1986). From necessary illusion to rational choice? A critique of neo-Marxist rational-choice theory. *Theory and Society, 15*, 4.

Kieve, R. A. (1987). *States of crisis: Studies in the development of the state in Sweden and the Netherlands*. Doctoral dissertation, University of California, Los Angeles.

King, R. (1983). From redistributive to hegemonic logic: The transformation of American tax politics, 1894-1963. *Politics and Society, 12*, 8-20.

Kirby, J. T. (1972). *Darkness at the dawning*. Philadelphia: J. B. Lippincott.

Kirwan, A. D. (1951). *Revolt of the rednecks*. Lexington: University of Kentucky Press.

Kolko, G. (1963). *The triumph of conservatism: A reinterpretation of American history, 1900-1916*. New York: Free Press.

Kolko, G. N. (1967). *The triumph of conservatism*. Chicago: Quadrangle Books.

Korpi, W. (1983). *The democratic class struggle*. London: Routledge & Kegan Paul.

Kossman, E. H. (1960). Symposium on the general crisis of the seventeenth century. *Past and Present, 18*.

Kousser, J. M. (1974). *The shaping of southern politics*. New Haven, CT: Yale University Press.

Krasner, S. (1978). *Defending the national interest*. Princeton, NJ: Princeton University Press.

Krasner, S. D. (1983). United States commercial and monetary policy: Unravelling the paradox of external strength and internal weakness. In P. J. Katzenstein (Ed.), *Between power and plenty: Foreign economic policies of advanced industrial states* (pp. 51-87). Madison: University of Wisconsin Press.

Krasner, S. D. (1984). Approaches to the state. *Comparative Politics*, 223-246.

Krasner, S. D. (1988). Sovereignty: An institutional perspective. *Comparative Political Studies, 21*, 1.

Krieger, J. (1986). *Reagan, Thatcher and the politics of decline*. New York: Oxford University Press.

Krieger, L. (1957). *The German idea of freedom*. Boston: Beacon.

Kuhn, T. S. (1970). *The structure of scientific revolutions*. Chicago: University of Chicago Press.

Kuznets, S. (1955). Economic growth and income inequality. *American Economic Review*, 1-28.

Lange, O. (1963). *Political economy, Vol. I*. New York: Pergamon.

Lászlóecker-r, L. (1936a). The state sales tax as a source of relief revenue. *Monthly Report of the Federal Emergency Relief Administration, October 1 through December 31, 1935*, pp. 121-132.

Lászlóecker-r, L. (1936b). Sources of local emergency relief funds. *Monthly Report of the Federal Emergency Relief Administration, December 1 through December 31, 1935*, pp. 121-132.

Lee, J. M., & Petter, M. (1982). *The colonial office war and development policy*. London: Maurice Temple Smith.

Lemmon, S. M. (1954). The ideology of Eugene Talmadge. *Georgia Historical Quarterly, 38*(3), 226-248.

Lenin, V. I. (1964). *The development of capitalism in Russia* (2nd rev. ed.). Moscow: Progress Publishers.

Lenroot, K., & Field, E. (1937). See *Social Security in America*.

Leuchtenburg, W. E. (1952). Progressivism and imperialism: The progressive movement and American foreign policy, 1898-1916. *Mississippi Valley Historical Review, 39*, 483-504.

Levi, M. (1981). The predatory theory of rule. *Politics and Society, 10*(4), 431-465.

Levine, A., Sober, E., & Wright, E. O. (1987). Marxism and methodological individualism. *New Left Review, 162*, 67-84.

Levine, D. (1988a). *Needs, rights and the market*. Boulder, CO: Lynne Rienner.

Levine, D. (1988b). The myth of expertise: A comment. *Social Concept, 4*(2).

Levy, M. J., Jr. (1953-1954). Contrasting factors in the modernization of China and Japan. *Economic Development and Cultural Change, 2*, 161-197.

Lindblom, C. (1977). *Politics and markets*. New York: Basic Books.

Link, A. S. (1947). *Wilson 1: The road to the White House*. Princeton, NJ: Princeton University Press.

Link, A. S. (1954). *Woodrow Wilson and the Progressive Era*. New York: Harper & Row.

Link, A. S. (1956). *Wilson, 2: The new freedom*. Princeton, NJ: Princeton University Press.

Link, A. S. (1964). *Wilson 4: Confusions and crises*. Princeton, NJ: Princeton University Press.

Link, A. S. (1965). *Wilson 5: Campaigns for progressivism and peace*. Princeton, NJ: Princeton University Press.

Lipietz, A. (1982). Towards global Fordism. *New Left Review, 132*(March-April), 33-47.

Lipset, S. M. (1963). *Political man*. Garden City, NY: Doubleday.

Lipset, S. M. (1968). *Agrarian socialism*. Garden City, NY: Doubleday.

Lipsky, M. (1980). *Street level bureaucracy*. New York: Russell Sage Foundation.

Livingston, J. (1986). *Origins of the Federal Reserve system*. Ithaca, NY: Cornell University Press.

Lockwood, W. W. (Ed.). (1965), *The state and economic enterprise in Japan*. Princeton, NJ: Princeton University Press.

Lowi, T. J. (1969). *The end of liberalism*. New York: Norton.

Lublinskaya, A. D. (1968). *French absolutism: The crucial phase, 1620-1629*. Cambridge, UK: Cambridge University Press.

Lukacs, G. (1971). *History and class consciousness*. Cambridge: MIT Press.

Lukes, S. (1974). *Power: A radical view*. London: Macmillan.

MacIver, R. (1969). *The modern state*. New York: Oxford University Press.

MacKinnon, C. A. (1983). Feminism, Marxism, method and the state: Toward feminist jurisprudence. *Signs, 8*(4), 635-658.

Macpherson, F. (1981). *Anatomy of a conquest: The British occupation of Zambia, 1884-1924*. New York: Longman.

Madison, J. *Federalist No. 10*.

Malowist, M. (1959). The economic and social development of the Baltic countries from the fifteenth to the seventeenth centuries. *Economic History Review*, [2nd series] *12*, 2.

Mandel, E. (1975). *Late capitalism*. London: New Left Books.

Mandel, E. (1978). *The second slump* (J. Rothschild, Trans.). London: NLB.

Mandel, E. (1980). *Long waves of capitalist development*. Cambridge, UK: Cambridge University Press.

Manley, J. (1983). Neo-Pluralism: A class analysis of pluralism I and pluralism II. *The American Political Science Review, 77*(2), 368-383.

Manning, P. K. (1979). *Police work*. Cambridge: MIT Press.

Marenin, O. (1982). Parking tickets and class repression: The concept of policing in critical theories of criminal justice. *Contemporary Crises, 6,* 241-266.

Marenin, O. (1985). Policing Nigeria: Control and autonomy in the exercise of coercion. *African Studies Review, 28*(1), 73-93.

Marenin, O. (1987). The managerial state in Africa: A conflict coalition perspective. In Z. Eras (Ed.), *The African State in Transition* (pp. 61-85). New York: St. Martin's.

Marenin, O. (1988). The Nigerian state as process and manager: A conceptualization. *Comparative Politics, 20*(2), 215-232.

Marglin, S. A. (1984). *Growth, distribution, and prices*. Cambridge, MA: Harvard University Press.

Margulies, H. F. (1977). *Senator Lenroot of Wisconsin*. Columbia: University of Missouri Press.

Marx, K. (1847). The poverty of philosophy. In K. Marx & J. Engels, *Collected works* (Vol. 6, 1976). New York: International Publishers.

Marx, K. (1849). Wage labour and capital. In K. Marx & F. Engels, *Selected works in one volume* (1975). New York: International Publishers.

Marx, K. (1852). The eighteenth brumaire of Louis Bonaparte. In K. Marx & F. Engels, *Collected works* (Vol. 6, 1976). New York: International Publishers.

Marx, K. (1865). Wages, price and profit. In K. Marx and F. Engels, *Selected works in one volume* (1968). New York: International Publishers.

Marx, K. (1875). Critique of the Gotha Programme. In K. Marx & F. Engels, *Selected works in one volume* (1968). New York: International Publishers.

Marx, K. (1963-1971). *Theories of surplus-value* (3 vols.). Moscow: Progress Publishers.

Marx, K. (1967). *Capital* (3 vols.). New York: International Publishers.

Marx, K. (1970). *A contribution to the critique of political economy*. New York: International Publishers.

Marx, K. (1973). *Grundrisse*. New York: Random House.

Marx, K., & Engels, F. (1846). The German ideology. In K. Marx & F. Engels, *Collected Works* (Vol. 6, 1976). New York: International Publishers.

Marx, K., & Engels, F. (1848). The communist manifesto. In K. Marx & F. Engels, *Collected Works* (Vol. 6, 1976). New York: International Publishers.

Marx, K., & Engels, F. (1968). *Selected works in one volume*. New York: International Publishers.

Marx, K., & Engels, F. (1975). *Selected correspondence*. Moscow: Progress Publishers.

Marx, K., & Engels, F. (1976). *Collected works* (Vols. 5, 6, 11). New York: International Publishers.

Mason, T. W. (1977). *Sozialpolitik im Dritten Reich*. Opladen: Westdeutscher Verlag.

McDonald, T., & Ward, S. (Eds.). (1984). *The politics of urban fiscal policy*. Beverly Hills, CA: Sage.

Meade, H. N. (1981). Russell vs. Talmadge: Southern politics and the New Deal. *Georgia Historical Quarterly, 65*(1, Spring), 28-45.

Migdal, J. S. (1988). *Strong societies and weak states: State-society relations and state capabilities in the third world*. Princeton, NJ: Princeton University Press.

Miles, A. P. (1941). *Federal aid and public assistance in Illinois* (Social Service Monograph No. 49). Chicago: University of Chicago Press.

Miliband, R. (1969). *The state in capitalist society.* New York: Basic Books.

Miliband, R. (1973). Poulantzas and the capitalist state. *New Left Review, 82,* 83-92.

Miliband, R. (1977). *Marxism and politics.* New York: Oxford University Press.

Miliband, R. (1983). *Class power and state power.* London: Verso.

Miller, E. (1963). The economic policies of governments: France and England. In M. M. Postan & E. Miller (Eds.), *Cambridge economic history of Europe, 3: Economic organization and policies in the Middle Ages.* Cambridge, UK: Cambridge University Press.

Mills, C. W. (1959). *The sociological imagination.* New York: Oxford University Press.

Milward, A. S. (1965) *The German economy at war.* London: Athlone.

Monkonnen, E. H. (1981). *Police in urban America, 1860-1920.* Cambridge, MA: Harvard University Press.

Moore, B., Jr. (1966). *Social origins of dictatorship and democracy: Lord and peasant in the making of the modern world.* Boston: Beacon.

Moore, J. R. (1975). The New Deal in Louisiana. In J. Brakeman, R. H. Bremner, & D. Brody (Eds.), *The New Deal: The state and local levels* (pp. 137-165). Columbus: Ohio State University Press.

Mosle, G. L. (1964). *The crisis of German ideology: Intellectual origins of the Third Reich.* New York: Grosset & Dunlap.

Mosse, G. L. (1978). *Nazism: A historical and comparative analysis of national socialism.* Rutgers, NJ: Transaction Books.

Moulder, F. V. (1977). *Japan, China and the modern world economy: Toward a reinterpretation of East Asian development, ca. 1600 to ca. 1918.* London: Cambridge University Press.

Mowry, G. E. (1958). *The era of Theodore Roosevelt.* New York: Harper & Row.

Mozaffar, S. (1987). A research strategy for analyzing the colonial state in Africa. *Working papers in African studies* (No. 128). African Studies Center, Boston University.

Muir, W. K., Jr. (1977). *Police: Streetcorner politicians.* Chicago: University of Chicago Press.

Mulford, D. C. (1964). *The Northern Rhodesia general election 1962.* Nairobi: Oxford University Press.

Mullins, W. A. (1972). On the concept of ideology in political science. *American Political Science Review, 66,* 2.

Neumann, F. (1942). *Behemoth: The structure and practice of national socialism.* Toronto: Oxford University Press.

Nettl, J. P. (1968). The state as a conceptual variable. *World Politics, 20*(4), 559-592.

Nicholson, I. F. (1969). *The administration of Nigeria: 1900-1960.* Oxford, UK: Clarendon.

Nie, N., Verba, S., & Petrocik, J. R. (1976). *The changing American voter.* Cambridge, MA: Harvard University Press.

Nordlinger, E. (1981). *On the autonomy of the democratic state.* Cambridge, MA: Harvard University Press.

Norman, E. H. (1940). *Japan's emergence as a modern state.* New York: Institute of Pacific Relations.

North, D. C. (1979). A framework for analyzing the state in economic history. *Explorations in Economic History, 16.*

North, D. (1981). *Structure and change in economic history.* New York: Norton.

North, D. C., Thomas, R. P. (1973). *The rise of the western world: A new economic history.* Cambridge, UK: Cambridge University Press.

O'Connor, J. (1973). *The fiscal crisis of the state.* New York: St. Martin's.

O'Donnell, G. (1979). Tensions in the bureaucratic-authoritarian state and the question of democracy. In D. Collier (Ed.), *The new authoritarianism in Latin America* (pp. 285-318). Princeton, NJ: Princeton University Press.

Offe, C. (1975). The theory of the capitalist state. In L. Lindberg et al. (Eds.), *Stress and contradiction in modern capitalism.* Lexington, MA: Lexington Books.

Offe, C. (1984a). European socialism and the role of the state. In C. Offe (Ed.), *Contradictions of the Welfare State* (pp. 239-251). Cambridge: MIT Press.

Offe, C. (1984b). Competitive party democracy and the Keynesian welfare state. In T. Ferguson & J. Robers (Eds.), *The political economy* (pp. 349-368). Armonk, NY: Sharpe.

Olson, M. (1965). *The logic of collective action.* Cambridge, MA: Harvard University Press.

Olson, M., Jr. (1963). Rapid growth as a destabilizing force. *Journal of Economic History, 23,* 529-552.

Olson, M., Jr. (1982). *The rise and decline of nations: Economic growth, stagflation and social rigidities.* New Haven, CT: Yale University Press.

Pal, L. A. (1986). Relative autonomy revisited: The origins of Canadian unemployment insurance. *Canadian Journal of Political Science, 19*(1), 71-92.

Palmer, I. (1985). State theory and statutory authorities: Points of convergence. *Sociology, 19*(4), 523-540.

Parker, D. (1971). The social foundation of French absolutism 1610-1630. *Past and Present, 53.*

Parker, D. (1983). *The making of French absolutism.* London: Edward Arnold.

Parker, G. (1979). *Europe in crisis, 1598-1648.* Ithaca, NY: Cornell University Press.

Pashukanis, E. (1978). *Law and Marxism: A general theory.* London: Ink Links.

Patenaude, L. (1983). *Texans, politics and the New Deal.* New York: Garland.

Patterson, J. T. (1969). *The New Deal and the states: Federalism in transition.* Princeton, NJ: Princeton University Press.

Peterson, P. (1981). *City limits.* Chicago: University of Chicago Press.

Pickvance, C. G. (1984). The structuralist critique in urban studies. In M. Smith (Ed.), *Cities in transformation.* Beverly Hills, CA: Sage.

Pierson, C. (1983). New theories of state and civil society: Recent developments in post-Marxist analysis of the state. *Sociology, 18*(4), 561-571.

Pirenne, H. (1937). *Economic and social history of medieval Europe.* New York: Harcourt Brace Jovanovich.

Piven, F., & Cloward, R. (1982). *The new class war.* New York: Pantheon.

Pois, R. A. (1986). *National socialism and the religion of nature.* New York: St. Martin's.

Pomper, G. (1968). *Elections in America: Control and influence in democratic politics.* New York: Dodd, Mead.

Pomper, G. (1975). *Voters choice.* New York: Dodd, Mead.

Postan, M. M. (1972). *The medieval economy: An economic history of Britain, 1100-1500.* Berkeley: University of California Press.

Poulantzas, N. (1973). *Political power and social classes.* London: New Left Books.

Poulantzas, N. (1974). *Fascism and dictatorship.* London: New Left Books.

Poulantzas, N. (1975). The capitalist state: A reply to Miliband and Laclau. *New Left Review, 95.*

Poulantzas, N. (1977). *Classes in contemporary capitalism.* London: New Left Books.

Przeworski, A. (1980). Material interests, class compromise, and the transition to socialism. *Politics and Society, 10*(1), 125-153.

Przeworski, A. (1985). *Capitalism and social democracy.* Cambridge, UK: Cambridge University Press.

Przeworski, A., & Wallerstein, M. (1988). Structural dependence of the state on capital. *American Political Science Review, 82,* 11-29.

Quinney, R. (1980). *Class, state and crime.* New York: Longman.

Rabinbach, A. (1974). Towards a Marxist theory of fascism and national socialism: A report on developments in West Germany. *New German Critique, 1*(3).

Rabinbach, A. (1976). The aesthetics of production in the Third Reich. *Journal of Contemporary History, 11*(4).

Rasler, K. A., & Thompson, W. (1985). War-making and state-making: Governmental expenditures, tax revenues, and global wars. *American Political Science Review, 79,* 491-507.

Rauschning, H. (1939). *Hitler speaks: A series of political conversations with Adolph Hitler on his real aims.* London: Heinemann.

Rawls, J. (1971). *A theory of justice.* Cambridge, MA: Harvard University Press.

Rehmus, C. M., & McLaughlin, D. B. (Eds.). *Labor and American politics.* Ann Arbor: University of Michigan Press.

Reich, R. (Ed.). (1988). *The power of public ideas.* Cambridge, MA: Ballinger.

Reiner, R. (1978). *The blue-coated worker.* Cambridge, UK: Cambridge University Press.

Reiner, R. (1980). Review of policing freedom. *International Journal of the Sociology of Law, 8,* 449-454.

Reiner, R. (1986). Policing, order and legitimacy in Britain. *Research in Deviance, Law and Social Control* (Vol. 8, pp. 174-196). Greenwich, CT: JAI Press.

Reiner, R. (1988). British criminology and the state. *British Journal of Criminology, 28*(2), 138-158.

Reuss-Ianni, E. (1983). *Two cultures of policing: Street cops and management cops.* New Brunswick, NJ: Transaction Books.

Rex, J., & Moore, R. (1967). *Race, community and conflict.* London: Oxford University Press.

Rhodes, J. M. (1980). *The Hitler movement: A modern millenarian revolution.* Stanford, CA: Stanford University Press.

Ripley, R. B. (1976). *Congress, the bureaucracy, and public policy.* Homewood, IL: Dorsey.

Robinson, C. D. (1978). The deradicalization of the policeman: A historical analysis. *Crime and Delinquency, 24,* 129-151.

Robinson, R., & Gallagher, J. (1961). *Africa and the Victorians.* London: Macmillan.

Rock, P. (1983). Law, order and power in late seventeenth- and early eighteenth-century England. In S. Cohen & A. Scull (Eds.), *Social control and the state* (pp. 191-221). New York: St. Martin's.

Rogers, D. T. (1982). In search of progressivism. *Reviews in American History, 10,* 112-132.

Roseboom, E. H. (1957). *A history of presidential elections.* New York: Macmillan.

Rosenberg, H. (1958). *Bureaucracy, aristocracy, autocracy: The Prussian experience, 1660-1815.* Boston: Beacon.

Ross, R., & Trachte, K. (1983). Global cities and global classes: The peripheralization of labor in New York City. *Review, 6*(3), 393-431.

Ross, R., & Trachte, K. (in press). *Global capitalism: The new Leviathan.* Albany, New York: State University of New York Press.

Rostow, W. W. (1960). *The stages of economic growth: A non-communist manifesto.* London: Cambridge University Press.

Rothchild, D. (1970). African federations and the diplomacy of decolonization. *The Journal of Developing Areas, 4.*

Rothchild, D., & Chazan, N. (Eds.). (1988). *The precarious balance: State and society in Africa.* Boulder, CO: Westview.

Rowthorn, B. (1971). Imperialism in the seventies—Unity or rivalry? *New Left Review, 69,* 31-51.

Rude, G. (1980). *Ideology and popular protest.* New York: Pantheon.

Rueschemeyer, D., & Evans, P. (1985). The state and economic transformation: Toward an analysis of the conditions underlying effective intervention. In P. Evans, D. Rueschemeyer, & T. Skocpol (Eds.), *Bringing the state back in* (pp. 44-77). Cambridge, UK: Cambridge University Press.

Rupp, L. (1978). *Mobilizing women for war: German and American propaganda, 1939-1945.* Princeton, NJ: Princeton University Press.

Saloutos, T. (1960). *Farmer movements in the South, 1865-1933.* Berkeley: University of California Press.

Sandel, M. (1988). The political theory of the procedural republic. In R. Reich (Ed.), *The power of public ideas.* Cambridge, MA: Ballinger.

Sanders, E. (1982). Business, bureaucracy and the bourgeoisie. In A. Stone & E. Harpham (Eds.), *The political economy of public policy* (p. 240). Beverly Hills, CA: Sage.

Sanders, E. (1986a). Industrial concentration, sectional competition and antitrust politics in America. *Studies in American Political Development, 1,* 142-214.

Sanders, E. (1986b). The regulatory surge of the 1970s in historical perspective. In E. Bailey (Ed.), *Public regulation* (pp. 117-150). Boston: MIT Press.

Sanders, E. (in press). *Farmers, workers and the state, 1890-1916.* Chicago: University of Chicago Press.

Sarasohn, D. (1989). *The party of reform.* Jackson: University of Mississippi Press.

Sassower, R. (1988). The myth of expertise. *Social Concept, 4,* 2.

Saunders, P. (1983). On the shoulders of which giant? In P. Williams (Ed.), *Social process and the city.* Sydney: Allen & Unwin.

Scarritt, J. R. (1986). The explanation of African politics and society: Toward a synthesis of approaches. *Journal of African Studies, 13,* 3.

Schattsneider, E. E. (1960). *The semi-sovereign people.* New York: Holt, Rinehart & Winston.

Schmoller, G. (1895). *The mercantile system and its historical significance.* New York: Macmillan.

Schoenbaum, D. (1968). *Hitler's social revolution: Class and status in Nazi Germany 1933-1939.* New York: Anchor.

Schumpeter, J. (1976). *Capitalism, socialism, and democracy* (5th ed.). London: Allen & Unwin.

Schwartz, M. (1976). *Radical protest and social structure.* New York: Academic Press.

Shawe, E. K. (1937). An analysis of the legal limitations on the borrowing power of the state governments. *Monthly report of the Federal Emergency Relief Administration, June 1 through June 30, 1935,* pp. 121-132.

Sherman, L. (1980). Causes of police behavior. The current state of quantitative research. *Journal of Research in Crime and Delinquency, 17*(1), 69-100.

Silver, A. (1967). Demand for order in civil society: A review of some themes in the history of urban crime, police and riot. In D. J. Bordua (Ed.), *The police* (pp. 1-24). New York: John Wiley.

Simkins, F. B. (1944). *Pitchfork Ben Tillman.* Baton Rouge: Louisiana State University Press.

Sironneau, J. (1982). *Secularisation et religions politiques.* The Hague, Paris, and New York: Mouton.

Sklar, M. (1988). *The corporate reconstruction of American capitalism.* Cambridge, UK: Cambridge University Press.

Skocpol, T. (1979). *States and social revolutions.* Cambridge, UK: Cambridge University Press.

Skocpol, T. (1985). Bringing the state back in: Strategies of analysis in current research. In P. Evans, D. Rueschemeyer, & T. Skocpol (Eds.), *Bringing the state back in* (pp. 3-37). Cambridge, UK: Cambridge University Press.

Skocpol, T., & Finegold, K. (1982). State capacity and economic intervention in the early New Deal. *Political Science Quarterly, 97,* 255-278.

Skolnick, J. H., & Bayley, D. H. (1986). *The new blue line. Police innovation in six American cities.* New York: Free Press.

Skowronek, S. (1982). *Building a new American state.* New York: Cambridge University Press.

Skowronek, S. (1982). *Building a new American state: The expansion of national administrative capacities.* Cambridge, UK: Cambridge University Press.

Smelser, R. (1988). *Robert Ley: Hitler's labor front leader.* New York: Berg.

Social Security Yearbook, 1939. U.S. Social Security Administration.

Social Service Review (1941). The ABC of A.D.C. in Chicago. *XV*(4), 753-757.

Spielvogel, J. J. (1988). *Hitler and Nazi Germany: A history.* Englewood Cliffs, NJ: Prentice-Hall.

Spitzer, S. (1981). The political economy of policing. In D. F. Greenberg (Ed.), *Crime and capitalism* (pp. 314-340). Palo Alto, CA: Mayfield.

Steedman, C. (1984). *Policing the Victorian community: The formation of English provincial police forces, 1856-80.* London: Routledge & Kegan Paul.

Steindl, J. (1952). *Maturity and stagnation in American capitalism.* Oxford, UK: Blackwell.

Stepan, A. (1978). *The state and society: Peru in comparative perspective.* Princeton, NJ: Princeton University Press.

Stephens, J. D. (1979). *The transition from capitalism to socialism.* New York: Macmillan.

Stephenson, N. W. (1971). *Nelson W. Aldrich.* Port Washington, NY: Kennikat.

Stevenson, M. (1937). Public welfare reorganization. *Social Service Review, XI*(3), 349-359.

Stevenson, M. (1939). Trends in public welfared legislation. *Social Service Review, XIII*(3), 450-459.

Stone, L. (1965). *The crisis of the aristocracy 1558-1641.* Oxford, UK: Oxford University Press.

Storper, M., & Walker, R. (1983). The theory of labor and the theory of location. *The International Journal of Urban and Regional Research, 7*(1), 1-41.

Storper, M., & Walker, R. (1984). The spatial division of labor: Labor and the location of industries. In L. Sawers & W. K. Tabb (Eds.), *Sunbelt/snowbelt: Urban development and regional restructuring.* New York: Oxford University Press.

Stoye, J. (1969). *Europe unfolding, 1648-1688.* New York: Harper & Row.

Sundquist, J. L. (1973). *Dynamics of the party system: Alignment and realignment of political parties in the United States.* Washington, DC: Brookings.

Sweezy, P. M. (1976). A critique. In Rodney Hilton et al., *The transition from feudalism to capitalism.* London: New Left Books.

Takagi, P. (1983) *The iron fist and the velvet glove.* Berkeley, CA: Crime and Social Justice.

Talmon, J. L. (1961). *The origins of totalitarian democracy.* New York: Praeger.

Tawney, R. H. (1961). *The agrarian problem in the sixteenth century.* New York: Burt Franklin.

Taylor, I. (1986). Martyrdom and surveillance: Ideological and social practices of police in Canada in the 1980s. *Crime and Social Justice, 26,* 60-78.

Therborn, G. (1978). *What does the ruling class do when it rules?* London: New Left Books.

Therborn, G. (1986). Neo-Marxist, pluralist, corporatist, statist theories and the welfare state. In A. Kazancigil (Ed.), *The state in global perspective* (pp. 204-231). Paris: Gower/UNESCO.

Thompson, E. P. (1978). *The poverty of theory and other essays.* New York: Monthly Review Press.

Thorelli, H. J. (1955). *The federal antitrust policy.* Baltimore, MD: Johns Hopkins Press.

Tilly, C. (1975). Reflections on the history of state making. In C. Tilly (Ed.), *The foundation of national states in Europe* (pp. 3-83). Princeton, NJ: Princeton University Press.

Tilly, C. (1985). War making and state making as organized-crime. In P. Evans, D. Rueschemeyer, & T. Skocpol (Eds.), *Bringing the state back in* (pp. 169-191). New York: Cambridge University Press.

Tindall, G. B. (Ed.). (1966). *A populist reader.* New York: Harper Torchbooks.

Tomlins, C. L. (1985). *The state and the unions.* Cambridge, UK: Cambridge University Press.

Topolski, J. (1974). Economic decline in Poland from the sixteenth to the eighteenth centuries. In P. Earle (Ed.), *Essays in European economic history 1500-1800.* Oxford, UK: Clarendon.

Trevor-Roper, H. R. (1959). The general crisis of the 17th century. *Past and Present, 16.*

Trimberger, E. K. (1978). *Revolution from above: Military bureaucrats and development in Japan, Turkey, Egypt, and Peru.* New Brunswick: Transaction Books.

Truman, D. (1951). *The governmental process.* New York: Knopf.

Turk, A. (1982). *Political criminality.* Beverly Hills, CA: Sage.

U.S. Civil Service Commission. (1917). *34th Annual Report.* Washington, DC: U.S. Government Printing Office.

U.S. Department of Commerce, Bureau of the Census. (1975). *Historical statistics of the United States, colonial times to 1970.* Washington, DC: Government Printing Office.

Urofsky, M. (1969). *Big steel and the Wilson administration.* Columbus: Ohio State University Press.

Useem, M. (1984). *The inner circle: Large corporations and the rise of business political activity in the U.S. and U.K.* Oxford, UK: Oxford University Press.

Vernon, R. (1971). *Sovereignty at bay.* New York: Basic Books.

Viner, J. (1948). Power versus plenty as objectives of foreign policy in the seventeenth and eighteenth centuries. *World Politics, 1, 1.*

Vries, J. de. (1976) *The economy of Europe in an age of crisis, 1600-1750.* Cambridge, UK: Cambridge University Press.

Walker, S. (1983). *The police in America.* New York: McGraw-Hill.

Wallerstein, I. (1974). *The modern world-system: Capitalist agriculture and the origins of the European world-economy in the sixteenth century.* New York: Academic Press.

Walzer, M. (1970). *Obligations.* Cambridge, MA: Harvard University Press.

Weber, M. (1946). Capitalism and rural society in Germany. In H. H. Gerth & C. W. Mills (Eds.), *From Max Weber: Essays in sociology.* New York: Oxford University Press.

Weber, M. (1978). *Economy and society.* Berkeley: University of California Press.

Weinstein, F. (1980). *The dynamics of Nazism: Leadership, ideology, and the holocaust.* New York: Academic Press.

Weinstein, J. (1968). *The corporate ideal in the liberal state.* Boston: Beacon.

Weir, M., & Skocpol, T. (1985). State structures and possibilities for "Keynesian" responses to the Great Depression in Sweden, Britain, and the United States. In P. Evans, D. Rueschemeyer, & T. Skocpol (Eds.), *Bringing the state back in.* Cambridge, UK: Cambridge University Press.

West, R. C. (1977). *Banking reform and the Federal Reserve system 1863-1923.* Ithaca, NY: Cornell University Press.

Whiting, T. E. (1942). *Final statistical report of the Federal Emergency Relief Administration.* Works Project Administration. Washington, DC: Government Printing Office.

Wickens, J. F. (1975). Depression and the New Deal in Colorado. In J. Braeman, R. H. Bremmer, & D. Brods (Eds.), *The New Deal: The state and local levels* (pp. 269-310). Columbus: Ohio State University Press.

Wiebe, R. (1962). *Businessmen and reform.* Chicago: Quadrangle Books.

Wiebe, R. (1967). *The search for order.* New York: Hill & Wang.

Wiest, E. (1923). *Agricultural organization in the United States.* Lexington: University of Kentucky Press.

Wildavsky, A. (1974). *The politics of the budgetary process.* Boston: Little, Brown.

Williams, A. (1979). *The police of Paris, 1718-1789.* Baton Rouge: Louisiana State University Press.

Williams, E. A. (1939). *Federal aid for relief.* New York: AMS Press.

Wills, A. J. (1973). *An introduction to the history of central Africa* (3rd ed.). London: Oxford University Press.

Wilson, C. H. (1967). Trade, society and the state. In E. E. Rich & C. H. Wilson (Eds.), *Cambridge economic history of Europe, 4: The economy of expanding Europe in the sixteenth and seventeenth centuries.* Cambridge, UK: Cambridge University Press.

Wilson, J. Q. (1975). *Varieties of police behavior.* Cambridge, MA: Harvard University Press.

Witte, E. E. (1962). *The development of the Social Security Act.* Madison: University of Wisconsin Press.

Witte, E. F. (1936). Social security legislation in Nebraska. *Social Service Review, X*(1), 79-108.

Wittfogel, K. A. (1957). *Oriental despotism.* New Haven, CT: Yale University Press.

Wolf, E. R. (1982). *Europe and the people without history.* Berkeley: University of California Press.

Wolfe, A. (1977). *The limits of legitimacy.* New York: Free Press.

Wolfe, M. (1966). French views on wealth and taxes from the Middle Ages to the old regime. *Journal of Economic History, 26,* 4.

Wood, D. J. (1986). *Business and government in the progressive era.* Marshfield, MA: Pitman.

Woodward, C. V. (1971). *Origins of the New South.* Baton Rouge: Louisiana State University Press.

Wright, E. O. (1978). *Class, crisis, and the state.* London: New Left Books.

Young, C. (1984). Zaire: Is there a state? *Canadian Journal of African Studies, 18*(1), 80-82.

Young, C. (1988). The African colonial state and its political legacy. In D. Rothchild & N. Chazan (Eds.), *The precarious balance: State and society in Africa* (pp. 25-66). Boulder, CO: Westview.

Author Index

Subject Index

Accumulation, 149-152, 161
  intensive, 208
  obstacles to, 213, 218, 221
  priority given to, 154-156, 164
  sacrifice of, 149, 158
  structural tension between accumulation,
    legitimacy, and control, 149, 150, 164
  See also Capital, accumulation of
Administration
  of law, 105
  state, 110
Agency for International Development
  (AID), 142
Agrarian Radicalism, 185-193, 199, 205f
  containment of, 196-198
  Colored Farmers' Alliance, 186
  Farmers' Alliance, 186
Agrarian Society
  land reform, 139, 141
  traditional, 134
Agrarian Statism, 187, 194, 198
  legislative agenda, 189, 192
Aid to Dependent Children (ADC), 35,
  94-114
Allende, Salvador, 71f
American Revolution, 15, 178
Anti-semitism, 75, 84
Anti-statism, 203
Antitrust Policy, 188, 192, 197, 200
Antitrust Regulation, 190, 193
  Clayton Act, 192, 194, 197-202, 205f
  Interstate Commerce Act, 187, 197, 198
  Sherman Act, 187, 192, 205f

Assistance Programs
  categorical, 94
  centralized, 99, 112
  federal, 102
  noncentralized, 112
  safety-net programs, 97
  See also Public Assistance
Auschwitz, 89
Authoritarian Movement, 73
Authoritarian Organization, 115
Authoritarianism, 14, 21, 77
  bureaucratic, 142
Authority
  division of, 102
  patriarchal, 74
  political, 12, 14, 44
  traditional, 155, 156, 160, 161

Banking System
  Aldrich plan, 193
  Federal Reserve System, 194
  national, 193
Base and Superstructure, 43, 44, 220
Berlin Conference (1884-1885), 153, 154
Big Business, 78, 86, 183, 192, 193, 197.
  See also Capitalism, monopoly
Biological Mysticism, 84, 85
Bonapartism, 79
Bourgeoisie, 73, 78, 79
  national, 135
Bryan, William Jennings, 186, 187, 192,
  199, 201

248

About the Authors

Steve Chan is Professor of Political Science at the University of Colorado, Boulder. His current research interests are in the area of international political economy, especially with regard to the empirical relationships among defense security, economic growth, and social welfare. His recent work has appeared in a number of journals, including the *American Political Science Review, Comparative Political Studies, International Interactions, International Studies Quarterly, Journal of Conflict Resolution, Journal of Developing Societies, Journal of Peace Research,* and *Western Political Quarterly.*

Edward S. Greenberg is Professor of Political Science and Director of the Research Program on Political and Economic Change in the Institute of Behavioral Science at the University of Colorado, Boulder. He teaches and conducts research on American politics, the capitalist state, and workplace democracy. His research has been supported since 1976 by the National Science Foundation. He is the author of *The American Political System* (1989), *Capitalism and the American Political Ideal* (1985), and *Workplace Democracy* (1986), as well as numerous articles in specialized research journals. He recently served as department chairperson.

M. Gottdiener is Chair of the Program in Urban Studies and Professor of Sociology at the University of California, Riverside. He is the author or editor of six books including: *The Social Production of Urban Space* (1985), and *Crisis Theory and Capitalist Development* (1989). Gottdiener's main interests are in the new urban sociology, theories of the state and politics, semiotics and culture, and empirical analyses of current socio-spatial restructuring.

Russell L. Hanson is Associate Professor of Political Science at Indiana University, Bloomington. He is coeditor of *Political Innovation and Conceptual Change* (1989), and author of *The Democratic Imagination in America: Conversations with Our Past*. Hanson has also written articles and chapters on American state politics, and is currently investigating the evolution of federal welfare policy in the United States (from which the chapter in this volume is taken).

David Levine is Professor of Economics in the Graduate School of International Studies at the University of Denver. His current research centers on the theoretical underpinnings of political economy. His most recent book is *Needs, Rights and the Market* (1988).

Otwin Marenin is currently Associate Professor in the Department of Political Science/Justice at the University of Alaska, Fairbanks. Before coming to Alaska, he taught for four years in the Criminal Justice Department at Washington State University and four years in the Political Science Department at Ahmadu Bello University in Nigeria. He also spent one year in Nigeria as a Senior Fulbright Research Fellow. He has conducted research on the police, on ethnic relations, and on state behavior in the United States and in Nigeria. His research and writings focus on the impact of police behavior on the state's legitimacy and its capacity for policy-making and implementation.

Thomas F. Mayer is a member of the Department of Sociology and the Institute of Behavioral Science at the University of Colorado, Boulder. His main intellectual interests lie in the areas of political economy, class analysis, and social conflict. Currently he is applying the ideas of game theory to Marxist concepts for the purpose of analyzing class conflict in corporate capitalist and state socialist societies.

Tracy L. Mott is a member of the Program on Political and Economic Change in the Institute of Behavioral Science, and an Assistant Professor in the Department of Economics of the University of Colorado, Boulder. His research is concerned with extending the ideas of Michal Kalecki and John Maynard Keynes on the relation of financial considerations to economic activity and on philosophical and doctrine-historical aspects of Kaleckian and Keynesian economics. His recent publications include "The Money Supply Process Under Alternative Federal Reserve Operating Procedures: An Empirical Examination," with Hamid Baghestani, *Southern Economic*

Journal (October, 1988); and "A Post Keynesian Perspective on a 'Cashless Competitive Payments System,' " *Journal of Post Keynesian Economics* (Spring, 1989).

Shaheen Mozaffar is an Associate Professor of Political Science at Bridgewater State College and a Research Fellow in the African Studies Center at Boston University. His research interests include theories of the state, state-society relations, state-ethnic relations, state formation, and public policy in Africa. He is currently working on a book-length study of the colonial state and social transformation in Nigeria.

Robert A. Pois is a Professor in the Department of History at the University of Colorado, Boulder. His main areas of interest are modern German history with an emphasis on the Weimar Republic and National Socialism. His other concerns include historiography with emphasis on psycho-history, and German expressionism in the plastic arts. Professor Pois has written widely on these subjects: his most recent book is *National Socialism and the Religion of Nature* (1986).

Robert J. S. Ross is Professor and former Chair of the Department of Sociology at Clark University. He has taught at the University of Michigan, MIT, and Harvard. His articles on global capitalism have been published in *The International Journal of Urban and Regional Research, Policy Sciences, Economic Geography,* and *Review.* His latest book (with Kent Trachte) is *Global Capitalism: The New Leviathan* (1990). Ross was a founder of Students for A Democratic Society and is a policy consultant and speech writer. He has completed one novel about dope, murder, and presidential politics, and is writing another about the downfall of a decent political operative caught in an ethics scandal.

Elizabeth Sanders is a Professor of Political Science at the New School for Social Research. She is the author of *The Regulation of Natural Gas: 1938-1978* and articles on regulation, the presidency, bureaucracy, and voting. She currently is completing a book titled *Farmers, Workers, and the State, 1880-1916.*

James R. Scarritt is a Professor of Political Science and Faculty Research Associate in the Institute of Behavioral Science at the University of Colorado, Boulder. His research interests include theories and techniques for the study of sociopolitical change and comparative change in African politics, focusing on the politics of ethnicity and class and policies for the increased protection of human rights. He is coauthor and editor of *Analyzing Political Change in Africa* (1980), coeditor of *Global Human Rights* (1981), author of numerous articles in professional journals, and is completing a book on sociopolitical change in Zambia since 1973.